ROGER ZELAZNY

MODERN MASTERS OF SCIENCE FICTION

Edited by Gary K. Wolfe

Science fiction often anticipates the consequences of scientific discoveries. The immense strides made by science since World War II have been matched step by step by writers who gave equal attention to scientific principles, human imagination, and the craft of fiction. The respect for science fiction won by Jules Verne and H. G. Wells was further increased by Isaac Asimov, Arthur C. Clarke, Robert Heinlein, Ursula K. Le Guin, Joanna Russ, and Ray Bradbury. Modern Masters of Science Fiction is devoted to books that survey the work of individual authors who continue to inspire and advance science fiction.

A list of books in the series appears at the end of this book.

ROGER ZELAZNY

F. Brett Cox

UNIVERSITY OF
ILLINOIS PRESS
Urbana, Chicago, and Springfield

Library of Congress Cataloging-in-Publication Data
Names: Cox, F. Brett, 1958– author.
Title: Roger Zelazny / F. Brett Cox.
Description: Urbana : University of Illinois Press, [2021] | Series: Modern masters
    of science fiction | Includes bibliographical references and index.
Identifiers: LCCN 2020053123 (print) | LCCN 2020053124 (ebook) | ISBN 9780252043765
    (cloth ; acid-free paper) | ISBN 9780252085758 (paperback ; acid-free paper) |
    ISBN 9780252052668 (ebook)
Subjects: LCSH: Zelazny, Roger--Criticism and interpretation. | Fantasy fiction,
    American—History and criticism. | Science fiction, American--History and criticism.
Classification: LCC PS3576.E43 Z64 2021 (print) | LCC PS3576.E43 (ebook) | DDC 813/.54--dc23
LC record available at https://lccn.loc.gov/2020053123
LC ebook record available at https://lccn.loc.gov/2020053124

contents

ACKNOWLEDGMENTS

All books owe their existence to many people other than the author, and this one is no exception. My heartfelt thanks to my editors at University of Illinois Press, William Regier, Marika Christofides, James Englehardt, and series editor Gary K. Wolfe, for their unqualified support and saintly patience.

I thank the Norwich University College of Liberal Arts, Department of English and Communications, Office of Academic Research, and Faculty Development Office, which have supported my work through release time, travel grants, and continual encouragement. Particular thanks to Dr. Karen Hinkle, Dr. David Westerman, and Dr. Lea Williams, whose leadership of the Academic Research and Faculty Development offices during the research and writing of this book ensured that I had both time and money to do my work.

I am grateful as well to the staff of the Syracuse University Libraries Special Collections Research Center and the Albin O. Kuhn Library and Gallery of the University of Maryland, Baltimore County, who provided invaluable assistance before, during, and after my visits to their collections of Zelazny's papers.

Jeffrey D. Smith kindly gave permission to reprint the interview with Roger Zelazny.

The numerous writers and editors who have shared with me memories of, responses to, and information concerning Roger Zelazny deserve gratitude. In particular, Fred Lerner, Max Gladstone, Elizabeth Bear, Laird Barron, Michael Cassutt, and especially Walter Jon Williams provided informative and insightful replies to my presumptuous emails. Special thanks to Zelazny's most enduring and thoughtful champion, Samuel R. Delany, who, in brief but crucial conversations, kindly took the time to share some of his memories.

Thank you to my predecessors in Zelazny scholarship, especially Carl Yoke, Theodore Krulik, Jane Lindskold, and Christopher S. Kovacs. In Zelazny's *Collected Stories*, Kovacs and the other editors and researchers of the New England Science Fiction Association have provided a resource for which *invaluable* is too weak a term.

I am especially grateful to my wife, Jeanne Beckwith, whose support and patience exceed even that of my editors.

My brother, James C. Cox Jr., provided me with my first copy of *Lord of Light* and took me to my first science fiction convention, the 1974 Worldcon, because Roger Zelazny was the guest of honor. This all started there.

ROGER ZELAZNY

When Roger Zelazny's death from cancer was announced in June 1995, the response of the science fiction and fantasy community was heartfelt and acute. In an appreciation in *Locus: The Newspaper of the Science Fiction Field*, Robert Silverberg spoke for many when he wrote: "[Zelazny] wrote a lot of magnificent, unforgettable science fiction, sure, but so did my late and still lamented friends X, Y, and Z, and yet their deaths didn't have the kick-in-the-belly impact of Roger's." The agonized response to Zelazny's death, as expressed in Silverberg's and others' tributes, was rooted in several causes, not the least of which was shock. Not only did he die at the insupportably early age of fifty-eight, but also there had been almost no public indication of how ill he really was. Zelazny's *Locus* obituary began by asserting that he was "one of the most popular and admired writers of the post-Campbell/Astounding period," a writer whose meteoric rise to fame in the 1960s captivated readers as well as an entire generation of writers. In tributes that appeared alongside Silverberg's, Michael Bishop noted that his own "enthusiasm for SF kindled significantly because of the gorgeous fuel that Roger supplied all us admiring wannabes," Norman Spinrad proclaimed Zelazny "one of the handful of mature prose stylists that the field has produced," and George R. R. Martin and Walter Jon Williams recalled how Zelazny's best-known standalone novel, *Lord of Light* (1967), permanently altered their sense of the possibilities of science fiction literature.[1]

Zelazny was popular and admired personally, as well. The tributes printed in *Locus* are unanimous in their portrait of Zelazny as a quiet, even a shy, man; in an editorial accompanying the obituary, Charles N. Brown, the magazine's editor and publisher, remembered Zelazny as enjoying social gatherings but preferring to "sit, listen, and comment instead of being the center of the scene." Yet Zelazny's many friends and colleagues also remembered him as strikingly erudite, articulate, and—perhaps more important in a field with its share of disputatious personalities—unfailingly kind and gracious. Silverberg affirmed, "I never heard him utter an unkind word about anyone. (Nor did I ever hear anybody utter an unkind word about *him*.)" And Martin, making the first announcement of Zelazny's death on behalf of the family, declared him "the kindest, gentlest, sweetest man I have ever been fortunate enough to know." Little wonder, then, that those who knew Zelazny reacted to his death with, as Edward Bryant's tribute put it, "a wrenching shock of loss."[2]

If such expressions of unconditional affection are among the most prominent features of the *Locus* tributes, equally notable is the almost complete absence of any mention of Zelazny's later work. The lone exception is Brown's editorial, in which he admits he found many of the novels that followed Zelazny's miracle decade of the 1960s, such as *Doorways in the Sand* (1976) and *Eye of Cat* (1982), "frustratingly incomplete."[3] Happily, the quarter-century since has yielded no reappraisals of Zelazny the man.[4] But the narrative implicit in the 1995 tributes (and briefly on full display in Brown's editorial) has become not merely explicit but dominant: Zelazny's breakthrough stories and novels were among the best and most important in the history of science fiction, but little, if any, of his later work displayed the same level of ambition, innovation, or sheer audacity. In the 2012 survey by *Locus* ranking readers' choices of the greatest science fiction and fantasy works of the twentieth century, only Robert A. Heinlein and Isaac Asimov have more titles listed than does Roger Zelazny. Of the nine Zelazny works included, however, seven were published between 1963 and 1970.[5]

This narrative is reinforced by the intensity of Zelazny's rise to fame. Although science fiction has produced several prodigies and "overnight sensations"—Asimov and Samuel R. Delany began publishing fiction professionally as teens, within two years of his first professional sale Heinlein was widely regarded as the leading American sf writer, and William Gibson and Paolo Bacigalupi, after publishing a handful of short stories, won both the Hugo and the Nebula Awards for their first novels—Zelazny's rise to prominence in the 1960s remains one of the most dramatic in the history of the sf field. His first professional appearance in a science fiction magazine, the short story "Passion Play," appeared in *Amazing Stories* in 1962, when the author was twenty-five. A year later, the novelette "A Rose for Ecclesiastes" appeared in the *Magazine of Fantasy and Science Fiction* (hereafter *F&SF*) and was a finalist for the Hugo Award. In the inaugural year of the Science Fiction Writers of America's Nebula Awards, Zelazny won in two of the four categories for the best fiction of 1965 for the novella "He Who Shapes" (in a tie with "The Saliva Tree" by Brian W. Aldiss) and the novelette "The Doors of His Face, the Lamps of His Mouth." In the same year he won the Hugo Award for Best Novel for . . . *And Call Me Conrad* (published in book form as *This Immortal*), in a tie with Frank Herbert's *Dune*; two years later he won the Best Novel Hugo again for *Lord of Light*. By 1968, at the age of thirty-one, Zelazny had won both of science fiction's most prestigious awards twice and was, with Delany, the American face of the genre's New Wave of writers who were moving toward more literarily ambitious work. Zelazny's fiction—equally shaped by the grandeur of classical mythology (Western and Eastern) and the hipster vibe of the musician and the noir detective, written in prose of unflagging energy and extraordinary poetic resonance—was unlike anything else in sf at that time. As Robert Silverberg later wrote, "He came out of nowhere."[6]

Cynics might expect such a meteoric rise inevitably to be followed by an equally meteoric fall. What actually happened was more complicated. While Delany and likeminded contemporaries such as Le Guin, Thomas M. Disch, Michael Moorcock, and J. G. Ballard continued to erase genre boundaries and established literary reputations outside science fiction and fantasy, Zelazny doubled down on his status as a genre writer. His short fiction of the late 1960s continued to display the conceptual and formal ambition that had marked his earlier work, but the two novels that followed *Lord of Light*, *Creatures of Light and Darkness* and *Damnation Alley* (both 1969), were not as well received as were their predecessors. With the 1970 publication of his novel *Nine Princes in Amber*, Zelazny began exploring more traditional fantasy landscapes within more conventional narrative frameworks, a path he would follow, with notable detours, for the rest of his career. He never lost the breezy energy and stylistic confidence that had helped make his reputation—a Zelazny story remained recognizable as such—and many of his nonseries science fiction novels continued to experiment with narrative structure. Yet there was a general consensus that little of his later work had the impact or achievement of his earlier work. In his obituary for Zelazny, sf editor, critic, and historian David Pringle bluntly expressed this consensus: "Zelazny once seemed the most promising writer in his field. Despite a wide readership and continued awards . . . he seemed never to have quite fulfilled that promise, settling instead into a steady career as a producer of stylish entertainments."[7]

This is not to say that Zelazny fell into obscurity after 1970. Far from it. The series that began with *Nine Princes in Amber* and continued through ten novels over the course of two decades became his greatest popular success and a landmark of contemporary fantasy. For the remainder of his career he wrote and published novels, short fiction, anthologies, and collaborations (including novels written with Philip K. Dick, Robert Sheckley, and, posthumously, Alfred Bester) prolifically. Although none of his later novels ever received the critical acclaim of the books of the 1960s, Zelazny continued to be honored for his short fiction, winning both the Hugo and the Nebula for his 1976 novella "Home is the Hangman" and receiving three more short fiction Hugos in the 1980s. For his entire career he remained a widely popular, influential, and even beloved figure within the sf community.

But from the 1970s on there was in some quarters disappointment in the direction that his later work took, a sense that his popular and commercial success came at the expense of his art and that it was no accident that his move away from the more adventurous work of the 1960s coincided with his decision to retire from his job with the Social Security Administration and write full-time. As early as 1973 Ursula K. Le Guin, responding to the Amber series, publicly complained that Zelazny did not take the materials of fantasy seriously;[8] a year later, in his review of Zelazny's 1973 novel *To Die in Italbar*, Sidney Coleman mourned, "We once had something unique and wonderful, and it is gone, and what we have in its place is only a superior writer of preposterous adventures."[9] By 1977 the narrative of Zelazny's decline was firmly in place. Also commenting on *To Die in Italbar*, the sf novelist writing as Richard Cowper (John Middleton Murry Jr.) declared the novel "wholly unworthy of the author of 'A Rose for Ecclesiastes' . . . the early promise remains unfulfilled."[10]

Cowper's essay, which appeared in the academic journal *Foundation*, also looks forward to the issue of Zelazny's long-term academic reputation. Zelazny's work, with its deep roots in mythology and unapologetic literary sensibility, lent itself well to the rise of science fiction scholarship in the 1960s and 1970s; in his 1986 book *Roger Zelazny*, Theodore Krulik declared, "Zelazny is a literary scholar's dream come true."[11] Yet the only book-length study of Zelazny to appear since Krulik's is a 1993 volume in Twayne Publishers' United States Authors series written by Jane M. Lindskold. The *Locus* obituary's prediction that these volumes would be followed by "many more" has not come to pass.[12] And though the indefatigable bibliophiles of the New England Science Fiction Association published in 2009 a six-volume edition of Zelazny's collected short fiction that includes "Literary Life of Roger Zelazny" by co-editor Christopher S. Kovacs, there are signs that twenty-first-century scholars and anthologists have begun to omit Zelazny altogether. For instance, a 2005 critical overview of science fiction literature, Roger Luckhurst's *Science Fiction*, does not even mention him, and two of the most comprehensive anthologies of the second decade of the twenty-first century—*The Wesleyan Anthology of Science Fiction*, edited by Arthur B. Evans et al. (2010), and Ann Vandermeer and Jeff Vandermeer's *Big Book of Science Fiction* (2016)—contain work by Delany, Le Guin, and Ballard but not Zelazny.

The arc of Zelazny's career outlined above is well documented and not in dispute. But is it fair? Do those early works remain the artistic triumphs they were considered to be at the time, and are the works written after 1970 in fact inferior to the early stories and novels that made his reputation? I believe that such a bifurcated evaluation of Zelazny's fiction is an oversimplification that does not address either the complexities or the consistencies of his career. More useful is to consider his work in terms of different impulses, always in tension with one another. In the following chapters I argue that across his entire career, Zelazny's fiction is in continual tension between his ambitions as a literary artist and literary professional and demonstrates a preoccupation with the autonomy of the individual—frequently explored in terms of political violence—that is just as noteworthy as his explorations of mythology and immortality. More significant this preoccupation evolves as the isolated and alienated protagonists of the early work give way to protagonists who recognize themselves as individuals within communities. To fully understand the energy and power of Zelazny's best work requires the reader to move beyond the well-analyzed issues of myth, immortality, and the hard-boiled hero and consider also the steady movement within those works from maintaining individual autonomy via terroristic violence to existing within a larger community, from blowing the system up to living within it.

Zelazny was an ambitious literary artist and the holder of a graduate degree in comparative literature. He spent his early twenties trying and ultimately failing to establish himself as a poet. When he returned to writing fiction, however, his prose displayed a fundamentally poetic impulse. The stories were allusive, figurative. They did not make conventional narrative connections as much as they followed what Hart Crane—the twentieth-century American poet whose "word magic," Zelazny later wrote, "probably had the most influence on whatever poetic style I may have"[13]—called the "logic of metaphor . . . the so-called illogical impingements of the connotations of words on the consciousness . . . [rather] than . . . the preservation of their logically rigid significations."[14] Crane's "logic" aptly described much of Zelazny's early fiction, and science fiction magazines had never seen anything like it.

But Zelazny was an equally ambitious professional, a writer who referred to his own writing as "copy"[15] and who worried that his intoxication with the English language might work against his desire to master narrative. As early as 1965 he wrote to Damon Knight, "I . . . go back over my old tales and wince at the over-writing and just plain verbal garbage. . . . I think I have now passed the fork in the trail where I stood hesitating for a time—that place where I asked myself whether I wanted to do pretty writing or story-telling—and decided that the subject was not just a thing to heap up words upon."[16] When Zelazny wrote this, he was at work on *Lord of Light*; two years later, he not only had published what became his most famous novel but also had finished writing the novel that for many signaled a permanent turn toward more conventional narrative, *Nine Princes in Amber*.

It is, however, difficult to mark clear borders. While moving from the lush far-future mythologizing of *Lord of Light* to the hardboiled sword and sorcery of the first Amber novel, Zelazny also produced *Creatures of Light and Darkness*, his most radically experimental novel, excerpted in that most radically experimental of magazines, Michael Moorcock's *New Worlds*. And though the standalone novels that followed through the 1970s and early 1980s—*Today We Choose Faces* (1973), *Bridge of Ashes* (1976), *Doorways in the Sand* (1976), *Roadmarks* (1979), and *Eye of Cat* (1982)—may have seemed "frustratingly incomplete" to readers such as Charles N. Brown, they all experiment to one degree or another with narrative. His final novel, *A Night in the Lonesome October* (1993), is an intricately woven, endlessly allusive horror fantasy whose central conceit (the story is narrated by Jack the Ripper's dog) is the very definition of high concept. Whether these later novels lacked achievement is debatable; it is difficult to argue that they lacked ambition.

Beyond questions of language and form is the matter of character. The typical Zelazny protagonist, as described by several critics, is in some ways strikingly consistent. Krulik identifies the "literary persona" that "cuts across all Zelazny's writings . . . a complex personality with special abilities, intelligent, cultured, experienced in many areas, but who is fallible, needing emotional maturity, and who candidly reflects upon the losses in his life."[17] Brian W. Aldiss, discussing Zelazny's first novel, singles out Conrad as "one of many such [narrators] in Zelazny's work—a man skilled in the martial arts, blessed with cunning insight, and a poetic tongue."[18] And Delany has noted Zelazny's propensity for writing about "men who are poets rather than adventurers, adventurers who are deeply unsure of themselves, or men who are deeply deceived in what sureness they possess."[19] To list key terms from these assessments is to list almost contradictory sets of qualities: intelligent, cultured, skilled, adventurous, and poetic, but also fallible, emotionally immature, unsure, and deceived.

Similarly, although much of the critical discussion of Zelazny's work has understandably centered on his frequent focus on mythology and immortality, his preoccupation with both is matched by his simultaneous fascination with and suspicion of larger systems. Beyond possessing the conflicted qualities listed above, the typical Zelazny protagonist is also, more often than not, radically alienated and standing apart from society as much from temperament as from circumstance. The near immortality of such characters as Conrad Nomikos or of Francis Sandow in *Isle of the Dead* (1969) may separate them from the world, but they also refuse to be subsumed within the larger frameworks of that world—as do, less cosmically, Fred Cassidy, the perpetual student of *Doorways in the Sand*, and the anonymous narrator of *My Name Is Legion* (1976). And, of course, the first Amber series is propelled by the various efforts of a family of obstreperous individualists to master a pattern in order to understand and control a system and is narrated by a dissenter who, once he does both, decides he wants no part of either.

Indeed, the refusal of many of Zelazny's characters to be coopted often takes the form of acts of political violence. Early on, Conrad was not merely a brooding immortal but a violent insurgent; Sam, the title character of *Lord of Light* who seeks to overthrow the ruling elite to which he once belonged, is described as a bomb-throwing anarchist; a key point of both plot and character in *My Name Is Legion* is the narrator's participation in an act of sabotage that he knows will result in fatalities. Political terrorism is also a plot point in one of Zelazny's best-known stories, "The Keys to December" (1966), as well as in the later novels *To Die In Italbar* and *Bridge of Ashes*.

Zelazny himself displayed a lifelong determination to go his own way no matter what, even admitting to "a somewhat paranoid element in my makeup when it comes to anyone or anything capable of exercising power over me."[20] Thus the young man who disdained team sports excelled in judo and took varsity letters in fencing three years running; the adult who avoided overt political commentary in his work claimed to lean toward liberalism in times of prevailing conservatism and vice versa. The ambitious literary professional was, at least initially, reluctant to involve his agent fully in his affairs; the novelist preoccupied with questions of structure and form hated writing outlines; the poet in love with language never took a university creative writing class. And the man with an extraordinarily deep knowledge of and love for the high canon of world literature was also a child of the pulps and utterly at home in the playful, punning world of science fiction fandom.[21]

And then there is what may be the most significant contradiction within Zelazny's career: the gap between what many of his readers expected of him and what he wanted to do. In the tribute to Zelazny that opens volume 6 of the NESFA *Collected Stories*, Jane Lindskold addresses objections to the more straightforward fantasy adventure narratives of Zelazny's later career by asserting that he wrote such fiction, at least in part, because that is what he had loved as a young reader and still loved. "Such works," she writes, "were what had hooked Roger on the field as a child. . . . He returned to sword and sorcery characters like Shadowjack and Dilvish the Damned. . . . He loved those 'lighter works' as much as he loved [the works that] brought him more critical acclaim. They were all part of him."[22]

To say that serious writers do not like to repeat themselves approaches cliché, as does the observation that readers often want more of what attracted them to the writer in the first place. To hit it big with a specific kind of writing and then write something different—William Gibson producing novel after novel that is not *Neuromancer*, Paolo Bacigalupi going from *The Windup Girl* to young adult fiction—is always a calculated risk. Sometimes it pays off. Gibson remains on the bestseller lists, and Bacigalupi's writing for younger readers has been nominated for a National Book Award. And sometimes it doesn't. When, for instance, Zelazny's contemporary, the British sf writer John Brunner, attempted to move into the mainstream with the historical fiction *The Great Steamboat Race* (1983), the novel failed both commercially and critically, and his career never recovered.[23]

In the long run, Zelazny's writing certainly paid off in material terms. The high anxiety he felt about quitting his day job and becoming a full-time writer in 1969 proved unfounded; by the time he relocated to Santa Fe in 1975, he was supporting himself and his family with his writing, and his subsequent life in New Mexico was prosperous. There is no denying the commercial impulses that steered Zelazny's career, especially in its later years. But there is also no question that, even as in those later years he hurriedly fulfilled one contract so that he could move on to the next, he never lost interest in developing his craft and never failed to give himself a chance, at least once in a while, to try something different and, ideally, learn something new.

Roger Zelazny was one of the most extraordinary figures in the history of science fiction and fantasy literature. Few sf writers have arrived more spectacularly, risen to the top more quickly, influenced the field more profoundly, seen their long-term critical standing rise and fall more problematically, or retained the loyalty of their readers and the affection of their peers more completely. In keeping with the legacy of a writer whose achievements were built on a network of contradictions, I hope the following chapters will serve as both a reconsideration and celebration of Zelazny's remarkable career.

CHAPTER 1

OUT OF NOWHERE
Beginnings—1963

The details of Roger Zelazny's early life, though largely unremarkable, trace a clear path toward his eventual career. He was born in Euclid, Ohio, near Cleveland and Lake Erie, on May 13, 1937, to Josephine Flora Sweet and Joseph Frank Zelazny. His mother was of Irish descent; his father was born in Poland. Although Euclid was (and remains) a major suburb of a major American city, in Zelazny's youth it retained a rural feel; his childhood home "was set on an acre of land on a dirt road surrounded by fields and woods."[1] Zelazny's recollections of growing up in Euclid model an almost stereotypical small-town American childhood of the middle third of the twentieth century: a childhood spent, when not in school or doing chores, at the lakefront amusement park, the movie theater, or the local drugstore that sold milkshakes for a quarter.[2]

Within this idyllic setting Zelazny grew up an only child, "solitary by circumstance and nature,"[3] who "never knew [he] needed a friend"[4] until, while a student at Noble Elementary School, he met Carl Yoke. Bonding over their mutual love of reading, the two became best friends and remained so for life, with Yoke eventually writing the first book-length scholarly examination of Zelazny's work.

Zelazny later claimed that he had decided by age six to be a writer. He read widely, with a special interest in mythology and fairy tales, and taught himself to type at age eleven after his father bought him a typewriter. At about the same time, he discovered science fiction via John Keir Cross's novel *The Angry Planet* (1946) and began not only writing stories but also learning how to prepare manuscripts and submit them for publication. Such precocity apparently did not include active market research, because he sent his first professional submission, a story in imitation of Ray Bradbury, to *Astounding Stories*, edited by the legendary John W. Campbell Jr.—who had seldom published Bradbury and was not interested in Zelazny's efforts. Undaunted, Zelazny kept writing stories and submitting them to magazines, and by age fifteen he had collected more than 150 rejection slips.[5]

As he aspired to professional status, Zelazny also developed his craft through student activities. He collaborated with Yoke on a series of humorous stories about two monsters named Zlaz and Yok, was active in the Euclid Senior High School Creative Writing Club, and in senior year served as editor-in-chief of the school newspaper, *The Survey*. By the time he graduated in 1955 he had published two poems and three short stories in the school literary magazine, *Eucuyo*. He had also, perhaps inevitably, discovered science fiction fandom, publishing in fanzines and co-editing his own fanzine, *Thurban*, with Warren Dennis. One of the stories that appeared in *Eucuyo*, "Mr. Fuller's Revolt," became his first professional fiction sale when it appeared in the October 1954 issue of *Literary Cavalcade*.[6]

In 1955 Zelazny entered Western Reserve University (now Case Western Reserve) in Cleveland, declaring a psychology major but switching to English in his junior year, in part because of the psychology program's emphasis on experimental psychology. Running rats through mazes did not interest Zelazny as much as did studying Jung and Freud. Convinced that the best academic support for becoming a writer was to accumulate as broad a base of knowledge as possible, he audited a large number of courses ranging from accounting to a seminar that introduced him to James Frazer's *Golden Bough*. After graduating in 1959 with a BA in English and minors in psychology and comparative literature, Zelazny entered the graduate program in English at Columbia University in New York, where he studied Elizabethan and Jacobean drama.[7]

Zelazny continued his creative work as an undergraduate and as a graduate student, but it took a different direction from that of his high school efforts. Despite a very promising start for a young writer, he weighed his single story sale against the accumulated mountain of rejections and came to a decision. From 1956 to 1961, Zelazny abandoned writing fiction and reading science fiction in favor of writing poetry. Although he later assessed his poetic efforts as "mostly bad, but improving somewhat as time went on,"[8] his student poetry demonstrated the same success and promise as had his student fiction: In addition to publishing in the Western Reserve student literary magazine *Skyline*, he won the university's Finley Foster Poetry Prize in 1957 for "Southern Cross" and in 1959 for "Decade Plus One of Roses."[9] The latter earned the praise of Cleveland poet Hazel Collister Hutchison, who forecast part of the critical response to Zelazny's future work when she noted the young author's "true ear for cadence and sensitiveness to deep, inner personal rhythms" and "natural sense of humor" while hoping that his "amusing ability" for cleverness would enable him to "finally escape from it."[10] While at Columbia he collected sixty of his poems under the title *Chisel in the Sky* and submitted the manuscript to the prestigious Yale Younger Poets competition. Its failure to win was, according to Christopher S. Kovacs, "a great disappointment" to Zelazny and strongly informed his decision to return to fiction writing.[11]

Zelazny completed his required coursework at Columbia, once again auditing many elective courses in a variety of subjects. In 1960 he submitted as his master's thesis, "Two Traditions and Cyril Tourneur: An Examination of Morality and Humor Comedy Conventions in 'The Revenger's Tragedy.'"[12] Zelazny's graduation was delayed, however, owing to his supervisor's refusal to submit the thesis—a circumstance that Carl Yoke attributed to "personality conflict."[13] While waiting for the situation to be resolved, and with his student status uncertain, Zelazny got ahead of the military draft for the Vietnam War by enlisting in the 137th Artillery Battalion of the Ohio National Guard. He trained at Fort Knox, Kentucky, and served a six-month tour of duty that included missile training in Fort Bliss, Texas. In 1961 Zelazny resubmitted the thesis, which was approved with honors; after passing comprehensive exams, he received his MA in English and comparative literature from Columbia in May 1962.[14]

Zelazny's time at Columbia was pivotal. Despite the setbacks with his thesis advisor, he clearly thrived in a graduate academic environment that allowed full immersion in the study of Elizabethan and Jacobean theater, an area well matched to his chief loves: the depth of myth, the energy of pulp adventure, the beauty of poetry, and the romance of all of it. As he later wrote, "I would be a very different sort of writer had it not been for early exposure to the 'bloody Elizabethans'."[15] Outside the classroom he pursued the interest in individual sports that had led to college varsity letters in fencing, now earning a green belt in judo.[16]

At the same time, he fell into the folk music and coffeehouse scene of Greenwich Village and became involved with folksinger Hedy West, whose song "500 Miles" became a national hit for the Kingston Trio and for Peter, Paul, and Mary.[17] They were engaged for six months, and Zelazny brought his fiancée home to Ohio to meet his family, only to have his mother disapprove on the ground that West was "too fast" for her son. By the fall of 1961 the couple had split up.[18] The breakup hit Zelazny hard, but it also provided the emotional core of his first major story.

Zelazny wrote "A Rose for Ecclesiastes" in October 1961 at the age of twenty-four. This story, which first thrust Zelazny into the spotlight, may have been fueled in part by a young man's heartbreak, but it also emerged from the combination of artistic ambition and commercial goals that marked Zelazny's entire career. His return to fiction was informed not only by his disappointment at losing the Yale competition but also by his doubts about making a living as a poet: "I realized that only Robert Frost and Carl Sandburg were making their livings writing poetry. . . . I wanted to be a full-time professional writer. I made my decision and wrote the story 'A Rose for Ecclesiastes' in October of 1961 and said good-bye to all that."[19]

And yet the science fiction story that resulted from this calculated decision to abandon poetry for fiction featured a protagonist who was a poet and an interplanetary setting that was far more poetic evocation than scientific extrapolation. The narrator of "A Rose for Ecclesiastes," Gallinger, is a linguistic prodigy, a world-famous poet, and a member of an expedition to Mars charged with learning about the planet's ancient humanoid inhabitants.

After being granted access to a religious temple, Gallinger, under the direction of the Martian matriarch M'Cwyie, begins a crash course in the ancient language of the Martian sacred texts. He falls in love and begins an affair with Braxa, a beautiful young Martian temple dancer; through her, he learns that the Martians are far older than previously thought, sterile as a result of an unspecified environmental catastrophe, and resigned to their imminent extinction. When Braxa disappears, Gallinger searches desperately for her in the desert. When he finds her, she reveals that she is carrying his child but that the pregnancy violates the long-ago decision of the Martian elders to accept the death of their race. Gallinger returns Braxa to the temple, where he reads to M'Cwyie and the assembled matriarchs from his own work and from his Martian translation of the Book of Ecclesiastes, whose pessimistic fatalism echoes the Martian Book of Locar. Thinking he has failed to convince them and has lost Braxa forever, Gallinger retreats, only to be informed by M'Cwyie that he has in fact fulfilled "the Promise of Locar . . . that a holy man would come from the Heavens to save us in our last hours" (1:62).[20] But he has still lost Braxa, who will remain on Mars to begin the renewal of the race—and who, according to M'Cwyie, never really loved him. The story concludes with Gallinger on the ship back to Earth after a failed suicide attempt.

Any reader who knows the events of Zelazny's life immediately before the story's composition will be hard pressed not to read the story biographically. Like Zelazny, Gallinger is a poet immersed in the literary and philosophical traditions of numerous cultures, a denizen of Greenwich Village, a practitioner of martial arts (in a story whose conflict is otherwise exclusively emotional and intellectual, Zelazny carefully details Gallinger's use of jiu-jitsu in a fight with a temple guard). He is also, like Zelazny in 1961, a young man with a broken heart whose rage at losing his love turns, at least in part, to self-hatred. Seven years after the story's composition, the author admitted as much, noting:

> I hated [Gallinger] because he was me. Once in my life I let a beautiful thing die, and now it can never be. . . . Life is full of these things, and one of them motivated this tale. I didn't want it to end that way, but it had to, because he was me. He was a better linguist than I, and a better poet. He was a very good, misunderstood man.[21]

Such a statement in the larger context of Zelazny's graduate student life in New York, his relationship with Hedy West, and his family's response to that relationship inevitably informs how we read this story of a brilliant young poet denied his true love by forces of authority led by a powerful matriarch. Such a reading depends, however, on relatively recent research and so cannot account for the degree to which "A Rose for Ecclesiastes" made Zelazny's initial reputation and has endured in the decades since its first publication. For that, we must turn to the story's formal achievements.

The operatic plot that unfolds on a scientifically obsolete version of Mars harks back skillfully and affectionately to the pulp masterpieces of Edgar Rice Burroughs and Leigh Brackett and the later reveries of Ray Bradbury. What distinguishes "A Rose for Ecclesiastes" from that earlier tradition is Zelazny's emphasis on character and style. *Argosy* and *Planet Stories* may have featured stories about Earth men falling in love with Martian women, but they were unlikely to feature stories about poets acting within sharply delineated family and workplace relationships. Gallinger's oration within the temple makes perfect sense coming from a character who, we are told early on, was raised by a fundamentalist Christian minister. Likewise, his strained relations with his fellow crew members stem not, as they might in a more conventional narrative, from the burdens of command (Gallinger is not the leader of the expedition) but from his own arrogant, abrasive, and distant personality. As one crew member notes, "I think he's spoken two dozen words to me since I met him" (1:42).

This relatively complex presentation of a protagonist who is not an alpha male hero breaks from earlier pulp tradition, but so did the groundbreaking 1950s work of authors such as Theodore Sturgeon and Alfred Bester. What was new was not what Zelazny was saying but how he was saying it. "A Rose for Ecclesiastes" is the first great expression of the energetically allusive style that set Zelazny apart from almost all of his contemporaries. The story is crammed with direct and indirect allusions to authors from Shakespeare and Dante to Jean-Paul Sartre and Havelock Ellis, and with a seemingly endless stream of metaphor. When Gallinger drives a jeep across the Martian desert, he observes, "Flames of sand, lousy with iron oxide, set fire to the buggy. . . . The Mountains of Tirellian shuffled their feet and moved toward me at a cockeyed angle. . . . I felt like Ulysses in Malebolge—with a terza-rima speech in one hand and an eye out for Dante" (1:30–31). As he advances both his study of Martian texts and his affair with Braxa, "the days [are] like Shelley's leaves: yellow, red, brown, whipped in bright gusts by the west wind" (1:49). And in the story's memorable final sentence, the narrator, staring out the spaceship's port window at a retreating Mars, tells us not that he is weeping. Rather, he states: "Blurred Mars hung like a swollen belly above me, until it dissolved, brimmed over, and streamed down my face" (1:63).

Shakespeare warned that a little more than a little is by much too much, and readers might understandably grow impatient with what seems showoff erudition, especially grating in an interplanetary romance. But Gallinger is a showoff—like the author who created him, he is a young man drunk on literature and language who, however exasperatingly, knows exactly what he's doing. Evoking classical Western mythology on Mars seems pretentious until we remember that "Ulysses in Malebolge" refers not to Homer but to Dante, who condemned the Greek hero to the eighth circle of hell for his part in the fall of Troy. The character who makes the reference is part of an expedition that, however well-intentioned its desire for knowledge, is nonetheless making a (presumably) uninvited incursion into an alien culture. The Shelley poem referenced, "Ode to the West Wind," is a cry to the cosmos for inspiration in the face of decay and death. Shelley concluded, "If Winter comes, can Spring be far behind?" but Gallinger realizes, "The wild west wind went by and something was not far behind. The last days were upon us" (1:50). And though comparing Mars to a swollen belly may be superficially grotesque, it is apt coming from a suicidal young man for whom leaving Mars means leaving his unborn child. "A Rose for Ecclesiastes" may be as lousy with allusion as the Martian sands are with iron oxide, but the allusions are precisely chosen, and the narration precisely matches the narrator.

The story also offers the first glimpse of other elements that became markers of Zelazny's fiction, such as setting off its conscious literariness with breezy, slang-filled dialogue and foregrounding non-Christian religious traditions. For instance, the first point of comparison that Gallinger offers for the Martian scriptures is the *Mahabharata*, and his first major book of poetry is titled *Pipes of Krishna*. Other aspects of the story have, perhaps, not worn as well for the twenty-first-century reader. Arguably, "A Rose for Ecclesiastes" offers a critique of some of the social underpinnings of the pulp tradition, as the team from Earth proceeds cautiously and respectfully in its examination of Martian culture and the team's leader allows Gallinger to go after the runaway Braxa because of his own memories of a relationship destroyed by racism—essentially, encouraging Gallinger to embrace the Other. But there is no denying the story's tacit acceptance of the colonialist assumption—an assumption firmly embedded, of course, in the pulp tales to which Zelazny was paying tribute—that not only can the problems of an alien race be fixed by human intervention but also that the race would embrace such intervention.

Another complicating factor is the story's presentation of women. Betty, the only human woman on stage, does seem to operate at parity with other members of the crew, but her main role is to sell out Gallinger by reporting, out of jealousy, his relationship with Braxa. The latter is presented solely in terms of erotic desire, often in infantilizing terms: "The little redheaded doll . . . looked up in wonder—as a child at some colorful flag on a high pole" (1:38). M'Cwyie, the Martian matriarch, employs her power, wisdom, and authority to save her race but also to rob Gallinger of what he wants most.

Some critics have suggested, however, that both Braxa and M'Cwyie possess far more agency than is usually the case with female characters within the pulp tradition, each knowing exactly what she wants and getting it on her own terms. Beverly Friend has argued that Braxa's rejection of Gallinger constitutes "a sharp slap at all the thick and heaving romanticizing of feminine sexual response which has characterized so much of the genre since its beginnings in the last century," an assertion echoed by John Huntington, who writes: "The emotional excess which can be generated by erotic involvement is identified with the man rather than the woman. . . . [Braxa] is motivated by a rational understanding of her duty to the continuation of Martian culture rather than by love."[22] Although later generations of readers and critics continued to critique Zelazny for unexamined colonialism and underdeveloped female characters, this story suggests that, from the beginning, Zelazny's work displayed at least some awareness of both issues.

Although "A Rose for Ecclesiastes" marked Zelazny's return to fiction writing in spectacular fashion, after completing the story he set it aside and did not submit it for publication until several months later. It is tempting to speculate that the young author required a cooling-off period after processing such intense emotion, but Zelazny's publicly stated reasons for the delay are more pragmatic: He recognized that the story was scientifically outdated.[23] With equal practicality, while writing the story Zelazny filed for unemployment and looked for a job.[24] In February 1962 he accepted a position with the Social Security Administration as a claims representative and returned to Ohio, living and working in Dayton.

The year 1962 remained a period of transition for Zelazny as he wound up his graduate work and applied, without success, for teaching jobs in Ohio.[25] Yet this period also marks the true beginning of Zelazny's career as a professional fiction writer and the start of a demanding but relatively stable lifestyle that he would maintain for the next seven years: working full-time by day for the Social Security Administration while writing at night and on weekends. Essentially, he returned to the systematic work habits of his teen years. He resumed the extensive reading of science fiction that he had largely abandoned in college (concluding that the field "hadn't changed much since [he'd] been away"),[26] wrote prolifically, submitted his stories to sf magazines methodically, analyzed rejections carefully, adjusted accordingly, and submitted more.

He did not have long to wait. On March 28, 1962, Zelazny made his first professional sale to a science fiction magazine when editor Cele Goldsmith bought his story "Passion Play" for *Amazing Stories* (hereafter *Amazing*). Encouraged, Zelazny began submitting "A Rose for Ecclesiastes," selling it to *Fantasy and Science Fiction (F&SF)* in July 1962. Meanwhile, he continued to submit work regularly to *Amazing* and its sibling magazine *Fantastic Stories of Imagination* (hereafter *Fantastic*) with significant success. By the time "Rose" appeared in the December 1963 issue of *F&SF*, Goldsmith—who also acquired the first stories of Ursula K. Le Guin and Thomas M. Disch—had published an astonishing eighteen stories by Zelazny in *Amazing* and *Fantastic*, so many that several appeared under the pseudonym Harrison Denmark.

It is fair to say that none of these early stories was as memorable as "A Rose for Ecclesiastes," and readers encountering Zelazny's work as it was published saw a talented young writer racing through a quick apprenticeship before producing an early masterpiece. Yet the stories published by Goldsmith are, in their own way, audacious. Indeed, the first two stories to appear—"Passion

Play" and "Horseman!," published in the August 1962 issues of *Amazing* and *Fantastic*, respectively—immediately displayed the formal techniques and thematic concerns that would mark Zelazny's more mature work.

In "Passion Play," a short–short story set in the twenty-second century, sentient machines gather annually at Le Mans to reenact a twentieth-century racing disaster—specifically, the 1961 crash that killed driver Wolfgang von Trips and seventeen spectators. As the title indicates, the event serves as a religious festival: "After the season of Lamentations come the sacred stations of the Passion, then the bright Festival of Resurrection, with its tinkle and clatter, its exhaust fumes, scorched rubber, clouds of dust, and its great promise of happiness" (1:85).[27] The narrator is a machine that enacts the "stations of the Passion," enthusiastically sacrificing itself in honor of "the ancient masters" who "left us these ceremonies, in commemoration of the Great Machine" (1:86). "Horseman!" describes a fearsome warrior riding from village to village seeking his companions; by story's end, the horseman is revealed to be one of the Four Horsemen of the Apocalypse, all of whom are, apparently, mythically transformed humans who have landed on another planet: "The ship from Earth settled upon the plain, and the wondering villagers watched. . . . The four horsemen waited upon the hilltop" (1:155). Thus these two stories, approximately a thousand words each, premiere many of the major themes and formal strategies of his later work: in "Passion Play," the supplanting of humanity by machines and the spectacle of the car crash; in "Horseman!," the sword-wielding superwarrior, adrift but determined to find his bearings, probably at the expense of any lesser being who gets in his way. In both, the remixing of religion and mythology in future landscapes and the poetic impulse manifest in vivid, repeated metaphor and, frequently, single-sentence paragraphs that could be lines of poetry.

> When he was thunder in the hills the villagers lay dreaming harvest behind shutters. When he was an avalanche of steel the cattle began to low, mournfully, deeply, and children cried out in their sleep. ("Horseman!" 1:153, opening paragraph)

> My hearing-mechanism still functions weakly.
> Now there is a great horn sounding, and metal bodies rush across the fields. Now. Now is the time for me to turn off all my functions and cease. ("Passion Play," 1:87)

Two decades after its publication, Robert Silverberg singled out "Horseman!" as the early work that "defined [Zelazny's] . . . method" with its "immediate, idiosyncratic" imagery and "bold use of metaphor."[28]

If these early stories lack the emotional weight of "A Rose for Ecclesiastes," they also lack the narrative development of Zelazny's breakthrough story: as reprinted in *Collected Stories*, most of the stories that appeared in *Amazing* and *Fantastic in* 1962 are fewer than six pages long. (The one novelette of the group, "Nine Starships Waiting" [*Fantastic*, March 1963], draws directly on Zelazny's graduate work in its science-fictional recasting of the plot of *The Revenger's Tragedy*, but three years after its publication Zelazny dismissed it as "doubtless the worst thing I've written.")[29] But the stories' brevity was, arguably, a specific strategy employed to a deliberate end. When "Passion Play" was reprinted in the Winter 1978 issue of *Unearth* as an installment of the magazine's First Sale feature, Zelazny provided a retrospective introduction in which he found the failure of his earlier stories to sell to have been due in part to "overexplaining . . . describing settings, events, and character motivations in too much detail." Once he decided to "avoid the unnecessarily explicit . . . to draw [himself] up short whenever [he] felt the tendency to go on talking once a thing had been shown"—an impulse clearly present in "Passion Play" and "Horseman!"—the stories started selling.[30]

Zelazny's determination not to talk down to his audience apparently did not have its intended effect on some readers, who, in the letter columns of Goldsmith's magazines, complained that the new author's stories were "confusing, nonsensical strings of words," "offbeat," and "all but incomprehensible."[31] Nonetheless, Goldsmith reported that "most readers seem to like Zelazny,"[32] and the sheer number of stories by him that she published proves her regard for his work. That Zelazny's initial burst of professional activity was for the most part well received is also supported by his inclusion, with the likes of Isaac Asimov, Ray Bradbury, Arthur C. Clarke, Harlan Ellison, and Robert Silverberg, in a list of sf authors surveyed by Lloyd Biggle Jr. for an article published over the course of three issues of the prominent fanzine *Double:Bill* in 1963 and 1964.[33]

The clearest early signal of Zelazny's impact, however, may be *F&SF* editor Avram Davidson's positively joyful acceptance letter for "A Rose for Ecclesiastes": "You have done a difficult and rare thing—taken a much-used (and a much-abused) theme, and done a new and good thing with it. All the equipment for cliché and bathos is in your story . . . but you have avoided absolutely any trace of either . . . send us more, send us more."[34] Davidson was a writer as well as an editor; in 1962 he had already won a Hugo Award for short fiction, and his later work included some of the most idiosyncratic and demanding of science fiction and fantasy texts. His effusive praise forecasts another aspect of Zelazny's later career: the author's standing as a writer's writer whose colleagues were as awestruck as his readers.

Davidson underscored his enthusiasm by making "Rose" the cover story for the December 1963 issue and commissioning for the cover a painting by the legendary sf artist Hannes Bok. The story was received with equal enthusiasm by readers, who voted it a finalist for the Hugo Award for Best Short Fiction of 1963. Although this was only the first of many award nominations and wins for Zelazny, "A Rose for Ecclesiastes" has remained perhaps his most highly regarded individual work of short fiction. In 1970 it ranked sixth on a list of the greatest pre-1965 sf novelettes and short stories as voted on by the members of the Science Fiction Writers of America, and in the 2012 *Locus* poll of the greatest sf stories of the twentieth century, it ranked third in the Best Novelette category, behind Isaac Asimov's "Nightfall" (#2) and Daniel Keyes's "Flowers for Algernon" (#1).

By 1964, then, Zelazny had a secure day job that provided both adequate support and time to write and a writing career taking off so rapidly and successfully that he could begin seriously considering abandoning his day job to write full-time.[35] He also seemed to have put his relationship with Hedy West behind him, becoming engaged to Sharon Stebrel and planning an October wedding.[36] In the last four months of the year, however, Zelazny underwent a series of traumatic events. On September 27 he and Stebrel were involved in an automobile collision near Mansfield, Ohio, that occurred when Zelazny, who was driving, did not realize the one-way road they were on had become two-way. Both were hurt, but Stebrel's injuries were much more severe, requiring six weeks' hospitalization. With his wedding postponed and his fiancée still recovering from the accident, Zelazny suffered another blow when his father died unexpectedly from a heart attack on November 25. The loss left Zelazny devastated. He and Stebrel finally wed on December 5. The accident had left Zelazny, still mourning his father, consumed with guilt, however, and Stebrel emotionally as well as physically damaged.[37] They separated in the summer of 1965,[38] and Zelazny transferred to the Woodlawn Social Security office in Baltimore, Maryland. When he moved to Baltimore in September 1965, he had lost his father and his marriage. He had also just published the novelette and the novella, and was about to publish the novel, that marked the end of his apprenticeship and the beginning of his stardom.

CHAPTER 2

EVERYBODY LOVES A WINNER
1964–1968

After the breakthrough of "A Rose for Ecclesiastes" Zelazny continued to publish steadily in American science fiction magazines, with seven stories appearing in 1964 and another seven in 1965. While still selling to *Amazing*, *Fantastic*, and *F&SF*, he published in a widening range of markets including fanzines such as *Double:Bill* and *Kronos* as well as major professional magazines such as *Galaxy*. Although a number of these stories were the kind of short, sharp pieces that had appeared in *Amazing* and *Fantastic*, this period also saw him stretching into longer fiction—once again, consciously and deliberately. As he wrote two decades later, "[The short early stories were] practice which I knew I needed while I figured out what it was that I really wanted to say when I found my voice and moved on to greater lengths."[1] He learned quickly, and 1965 proved a genuine *annus mirabilis*, previewed by the novella "The Graveyard Heart," opening with the novella "He Who Shapes," continuing with the novelettes "The Doors of His Face, the Lamps of His

Mouth" and "The Furies," and concluding with the magazine serialization of his first novel, . . . *And Call Me Conrad*. In these stories Zelazny found his voice as he built on and brought under greater control what he had achieved in "A Rose for Ecclesiastes."

In "The Graveyard Heart" (*Fantastic*, 1964), Alvin Moore has conceived a great passion for Leota Mason, a prominent socialite in "the Set" (1:96),[2] an elite group living at the dawn of the twenty-first century whose members, through regular retreats into suspended animation, enjoy significantly extended lifespans. After gaining the approval of Mary Maude Mullen, the "Doyenne" who controls admission to the Set, Moore enters into the decadent lifestyle of the near-immortals, wins Leota, and convinces her to leave the Set and live out a continuous normal lifespan with him. But before that can happen, Leota is brutally assaulted and almost killed by Wayne Unger, a group member who, rejected by Leota, sees her as the embodiment of the seductive but hollow lifestyle of the Set, a "vampire . . . luring men aboard her Flying Dutchman to drain them across the years. . . . She is the future— a goddess on the outside and a thirsting vacuum within" (1:138). Moore, in turn, tries to murder Unger, and the story concludes with Leota and Moore in suspended animation, awaiting a future cure for Leota's injuries, while the recovered Unger remains a part of the endless, empty existence of the Set.

Zelazny's first published story of novella length bears a superficial resemblance to "A Rose for Ecclesiastes" in its portrait of an arrogant young man forced to confront an imposing, long-enduring system in order to possess the woman he loves—a system whose access, as in "Rose," is controlled by an enigmatic matriarch. And in "The Graveyard Heart" literary allusion and playful prose style are even more pronounced. Scarcely a character fails to drop the occasional evocation of Shakespeare or the English Romantics, and at one point the author describes Moore's nighttime walk through a garden to a beach in a four-hundred-word-long sentence (1:126–127). Alvin Moore is not a poet but an electrical engineer, however, and his desire for Leota, at least to begin with, seems more calculation than passion. When Moore asks himself why he wants to marry Leota, he answers, "Because she is beautiful . . . and the future will be lovely. I want her for my beautiful wife in the lovely future" (1:96). The story focuses not so much on what Moore does or does not feel for Leota as on the theme to which Zelazny would return in later stories and novels: the psychology and lifestyle of the immortal. Moore soon acknowledges that what he wants more than Leota herself is "an in to the Set . . . to ride high, like those gods of old who appeared at the rites of the equinoxes, slept between processions, and were remanifest with each new season, the bulk of humanity living through all those dreary days that lay between" (1:104). What Moore does not understand is that a generous life-span requires a correspondingly generous perspective. Early in the story, the Doyenne warns Moore that if he enters the Set and lives only for days while years pass, he "will have to develop a Buddhist's attitude toward the world. . . . That world will change from day to day. Whenever you stop to look at it, it will be a different world—unreal" (1:109). By story's end she lays the blame for the double attempted murder not on the system itself but on Moore and Unger's toxic masculinity, "a male antagonism of the mutually accelerating variety" (1:145).

"The Graveyard Heart" does include a poet, but the poet is Wayne Unger, disappointed lover and disillusioned quasi-immortal. Unlike that of Gallinger in "Rose," Unger's poetry is not a factor in solving a problem but an expression of the problem itself, as poems with such titles as "Our Wintered Way Through Evening, and Burning Bushes Along It" and "In the Dogged House" articulate what Unger regards as the sterility and meaninglessness of the Set's lifestyle.[3] The lines of poetry attributed to Unger are in fact taken from Zelazny's own poetry, revised from poems included in *Chisel in the Sky*, the manuscript he submitted for the Yale Younger Poet's Prize and the title of one of Unger's books (1:116). It is tempting to read this story of an engineer who winds up with at least a chance of getting what he wants, and a poet who ends up with nothing, in terms of Zelazny's own turn away from poetry back to science fiction. At the same time, as Lindskold points out, Unger is in some ways a more memorable character than Moore,[4] and though his de-monization of Leota is misguided at best, his critique of the Set is, arguably, correct: "People join the Set for a variety of reasons . . . but the main one is exhibitionism. . . . Attracting attention to oneself gets harder and harder as time goes on" (1:119).

Whereas "The Graveyard Heart," like "A Rose for Ecclesiastes," takes place within the solar system and during the twenty-first century, "The Furies" (*Amazing*, June 1965) ranges into the far future and deep space for the story of three special talents—Sandor Sandor, who knows all locations in the mapped galaxy, Benedick Bendict, who can psychically read people and objects, and Lynx Links, a preternaturally effective assassin—tasked with hunting down and eliminating Victor Corgo, a rogue space captain who has turned against humanity with a series of near-genocidal raids. Along the way we learn that Corgo has his reasons since humanity has "marked for death" the Drillen, an alien species who rescued Corgo after he lost his ship and crew to pirates, because they "refused relocation to a decent Reservation World" (2:28).[5] Yet his desire for justice has become an indiscriminate rage: "People are all alike, all the same. . . . The guilt is equally distributed," he says. "Mankind is commonly culpable" (1:50). After much frantic action and equally frantic dialogue, the three special talents finally accomplish their mission and kill Corgo—an inevitable outcome, we are told in the concluding paragraph, for Sandor's, Benedict's, and Links's "real names . . . are Tisiphone, Alecto, and Megaera. They are the Furies. They arise from chaos and deliver revenge; they convey confusion and disaster to those who abandon the law and forsake the way" (58).

If "The Graveyard Heart" stands as an early consideration of one of Zelazny's main preoccupations—immortality—"The Furies" offers an early glimpse of two recurrent concerns of Zelazny's later work: the outlaw-terrorist whose violence emerges from the collision of human and alien cultures, and classic mythology as a template for the science fiction story. "The Furies" also continues Zelazny's stylistic explorations as it alternates between an omniscient narrator and long stretches of vernacular dialogue with enough exclamation points for any self-respecting comic book. Kovacs, in fact, asserts that "The Furies" is intended to honor "the comic book heroes that [Zelazny] loved,"[6] while Samuel R. Delany views the story as an homage to Cordwainer Smith and cites "The Furies" as the inspiration for his own homage to Zelazny, "Lines of Power" (1968).[7]

The story yielded a split decision from two of the most prominent sf writers of the day. Theodore Sturgeon called "The Furies" a "tour de force," noting that Zelazny "makes you believe it all the way, and walks off breathing easily leaving you gasping with a fable in your hands." Frederik Pohl, however, at that time the editor of *Galaxy Magazine*, rejected the story on the grounds that, despite the heavy-handed explication of its conclusion, it was simply confusing: "Since the subject matter [of sf and fantasy] can be pretty far-out, a far-out style is multiply confusing . . . the story becomes difficult to follow, and maybe not worth the trouble—and I have the feeling that something like that happened here."[8] Sturgeon's and Pohl's differing takes on "The Furies" encapsulate what would become a long-term debate about Zelazny's fiction. Was the author fully, and brilliantly, in control of his materials, or not? Was he so carried away with colliding genre tropes and high literary language that he forgot to ensure it all made sense, or was he simply a wizard whose magic required no explanation?

"The Doors of His Face, the Lamps of His Mouth" (F&SF, March 1965) made a strong case for wizardry. Zelazny wrote "Doors" only a little over a year after writing "A Rose for Ecclesiastes,"[9] and, as Theodore Krulik notes, the later story is in some ways a "companion piece" to the earlier.[10] Both feature planetary settings that, in the early 1960s, were already scientifically outmoded: in "Rose," a Mars populated by humanoid Martians, and in "Doors," a Venus with oceans that can be fished. (Zelazny was well aware of this, stating in a 1982 interview, "Our knowledge of the solar system had changed so rapidly . . . I realized that was the last point in time that anyone could write that kind of story. . . . But they ["Rose" and "Doors"] were both, in a way, my tribute to a phase in the genre's history which had just closed and expressed my feelings towards it."[11]) Both stories also feature protagonists who need to prove themselves to the world and who tell their stories in the allusive, slangy first-person narration that, by the time "Doors" was published, had already become a Zelazny trademark.

But whereas the narrator of "Rose," Gallinger, is an arrogant, impulsive young genius whose story ends in professional triumph and personal heartbreak, Carlton Davits, the narrator of "Doors," is a more mature figure who has already been humbled by failure. A "baitman" who once had the opportunity to help land an "Ichthyform Leviosaurus Levianthus, generally known as 'Ikky'"(1:258),[12] a gargantuan creature that inhabits the Venusian ocean, Davits froze when confronted by the creature's giant eyes, losing the catch and suffering serious injury to both his body and his reputation. Offered a chance at redemption by his ex-wife Jean Luharich, a cosmetics mogul and media celebrity determined to land Ikky, Davits resumes the hunt, confronts his fears, and, finally, captures his prey.

As Carl is a calmer, more controlled character than Gallinger, "Doors" is a calmer, more controlled story than "Rose." Whereas the allusions and metaphors of the earlier story maintain and support a tone of earnest anxiety, the language of "Doors" is more relaxed and, on occasion, aware of itself. The story's opening sentences simultaneously invoke and satirize literature as Carl announces: "I'm a baitman. No one is born a baitman, except in a French novel where everyone is. (In fact, I think that's the title, *We Are All Bait*. Pfft!)" (1:255). He then interrupts a metaphor-laden description of landing on Venus with what seems almost an apology: "When you break into Cloud Alley it swings its silverblack bowling ball toward you without a warning. . . . You are caught like an infield fly at the Lifeline landing area . . . but afterwards—shaking off the metaphors—you descend to scorched concrete and present your middle-sized telephone directory of authorizations to the short, fat man in the gray cap" (1:256). Like "Rose," "Doors" maintains an energetically lyrical tone, but not via bursts of figurative language as much as via the rhythms of the sentences, what Delany has identified as "the intensifying technique" of "mak[ing] a sentence parallel, in its syntax, what it represents in its semantics,"[13] as in this description of Carl and Jean's swimming beneath their boat:

> Beneath us, black. Immense. Deep. The Mindanao of Venus, where eternity might eventually pass the dead to a rest in cities of unnamed fishes. I twisted my head away and touched the hull with a feeler of light; it told me we were about a quarter of the way along. (271)

The relationship between Carl and Jean is also more nuanced than the relationship between Gallinger and Braxa. Whereas Braxa is, to Gallinger, an object of erotic desire who ultimately betrays and abandons him, Jean, even as seen through Carl's weary and self-accusing gaze, is clearly an intelligent, successful, autonomous individual who is well aware of her ex-husband's predicament and determined to help him get out of it. In her analysis of the story, Lindskold argues that Carl's two rescues of Jean—saving her from potentially deadly miscalculation during the underwater swim quoted above, and, when she is on the verge of reenacting his own failure, urging her on as she successfully lands Ikky—are less a matter of Carl's becoming the hero who saves the damsel in distress than of Jean's conscious efforts to give her ex-husband a chance to redeem himself.[14] Like Braxa, Jean knows exactly what she's doing; unlike Gallinger, Carl seems content with Jean's manipulations. And though "Rose" ends with a devastating metaphor of heartbreak, "Doors" ends with the promise of reconciliation: "No one is born a baitman, I don't think, but the rings of Saturn sing epithalamium the sea-beast's dower" (1:285). This somewhat puzzling statement, centered on the Latin for "wedding song," might seem a lapse in the stylistic control discussed above. But even as the flip reference to French literature that begins the story runs deeper than it seems at first glance—Davits's initial succumbing to the existential terror of the sea creature's blank gaze suggests that Zelazny not only had read his Sartre but taken it to heart—this concluding outbreak of lyricism perhaps signals that, fish caught and protagonist redeemed, it's all right to sing.

The other major work of short fiction that Zelazny published in that year, the novella "He Who Shapes" (*Amazing*, January and February 1965), was his longest work of fiction to date[15] and his first serialized publication. It tells the story of Charles Render, a near-future psychiatrist who, as a "neuroparticipant therapist" or "Shaper," uses technology that allows him to enter and control his patients' dreams. One such patient, Dr. Eileen Shallot, has a seemingly insoluble problem. She wishes to become a Shaper herself but, blind since birth, might not be able to construct complete and effective scenarios for her patients and might also be subject to trauma from the visual content of patients' dreams. Render agrees to help Shallot learn how to see within a Shaped dream, but the therapy quickly becomes a contest of wills between Render and Shallot for control of the dream scenarios. Confident of his abilities and ignoring reminders from colleagues that a Shaper who loses control risks becoming trapped in a patient's dream, Render continues to work with Shallot but, during an emergency session to bring Shallot out of a severe depression, does, in fact, become trapped within her dream.

Render's story is that of a great man whose pride leads to his downfall, and Zelazny acknowledged that "He Who Shapes" was "the only story [he] wrote where [he] intentionally, consciously, set out to create a character in the traditional form of the classical tragedy figure."[16] Certainly, Render is a more sharply focused protagonist than those of Zelazny's other early stories. Brilliant and aloof, he is internationally famous in his chosen field; he is also a widower who, having lost his wife and daughter in an auto accident, is extremely protective of his ten-year-old son Peter. Before taking on Shallot's case he enjoys a normal and apparently satisfying relationship with his girlfriend, Jill DeVille. Neither immortal nor seeking immortality, Render veers in the opposite direction in his preoccupation with a neighbor's suicide and, arguably, engages in potentially suicidal behavior in his high-risk work with Shallot.[17]

If Render is an atypical Zelazny protagonist, Shallot is Zelazny's most complicated female character thus far. Lindskold argues that there is a strong and intentional element of seduction as she draws Render deeper into her dreams,[18] but Shallot enters into her relationship with Render seeking professional advancement, not romance and, eventually, control over the new experience of seeing. Even so romantically laden a gesture as, in one of the dream scenarios, clothing Render in a suit of armor becomes another exercise in control as Render comments, "You stuffed me into [the armor]. . . . You're a strong-willed woman" (1:425).[19] Late in the story, when Shallot tells Render that Jill has paid her an accusing visit, she seems far less affected by jealousy than by the continued gap between her ambitions and her actual accomplishments as a Shaper (1:466). Unlike Braxa or Jean, she neither betrays nor rescues Render; her goal is not to possess him but to control her own mind and destiny.

It is this issue of control more than any other that lies at the heart of "He Who Shapes." Render is the Shaper and has absolute confidence in his mastery of the tools of his profession. As he decides to take Shallot's case, in part because doing so would "make therapeutic history" (1:411), he tells himself, "The day a better neuroparticipant began practicing would be the day that a troubled homo sapiens was to be treated by something but immeasurably less than angels" (1:412). But, of course, Render's very name means both to piece together and to tear asunder. One of the more interesting elements of the story is the practice of "blindspin," in which the operators of self-driving cars can enter random coordinates and zoom to an unknown destination, temporarily giving themselves a sense of losing control without actually doing so. At Shallot's suggestion, she and Render conduct their initial conversation about her possible treatment while in a blindspin, during which she strenuously defends her desire to become a Shaper against his equally strenuous arguments to the contrary. Thus, their initial struggle for control takes place within an environment that, on one hand, is out of their control but, on the other, is absolutely under control.

If the speeding automobile and the tension between avoiding and falling victim to collision is an apt metaphor for what unfolds between Render and Shallot, it is an equally apt expression of a young author's attempts to control his ambitious and complex story.[20] In addition to being Zelazny's longest story to date, "He Who Shapes" is also the most heavily freighted with mythological and literary allusion. The story opens with Render shaping the dream of a neurotic politician into Julius Caesar's assassination, and when the patient questions his diagnosis, Render has to restrain himself from citing Dante (1:397); a memory of snow calls to mind "novels by Thomas Mann" (1:400). Eileen Shallot's name invokes the doomed lover of Sir Lancelot; Render's decreasing control over Shallot's therapy is conveyed with reference to the Norse legend of Ragnarok, "the howl of the Fenris Wolf as it prepared to devour the moon" (433); and the final dream, in which Render loses control, reinforces the earlier references to Arthurian myth with imagery from the story of Tristan and Isolde.[21] With an opening out of Shakespearean tragedy and a closing out of Wagnerian opera, "He Who Shapes" is an early apotheosis of Zelazny's allusiveness, a tendency in his work that concerned even his admirers. Lindskold, discussing the story in its expanded novel form, found it "almost too heavily allusive," and Theodore Sturgeon, referencing Zelazny's work in general, suggested that "even so deft a wordsmith as Zelazny can forget from time to time that such a creation can keep a reader from his speedy progress from here to there, and that his furniture should be placed out of the traffic pattern."[22] But if the story contains perhaps one too many mythological allusions or untranslated German phrases, it also remains the purest example of the sheer glee with which Zelazny "rendered" his own stories in terms of the literature he loved. Or, as the singer-songwriter Patti Smith wrote half a century later in her densely referential memoir M Train, "Writers and their books. I cannot assume the reader will be familiar with them all, but in the end is the reader familiar with me? . . . I offer my world on a platter filled with allusions."[23]

Allusiveness notwithstanding, "He Who Shapes" also contains some of the most vivid and effective writing Zelazny produced, before or after, as in this description of Render, in his auto-controlled car, reminded of the loss of his family by the landscape rushing by:

> He could remember a time when he had loved snow, when it had reminded him of novels by Thomas Mann and music by Scandinavian composers. In his mind now, though, there was another element from which it could never be wholly disassociated. He could visualize so clearly the eddies of milk-white coldness that swirled about his old manual-street auto, flowing into its fire-charred interior to rewhiten that which had been blackened; so clearly—as though he had walked toward it across a chalky lakebottom—it, the sunken wreck, and he, the diver—unable to open his mouth to speak, for fear of drowning; and he knew, whenever he looked upon falling snow, that somewhere skulls were whitening. But nine years had washed away much of the pain, and he also knew that the night was lovely. (1:400)

With a colorless landscape that seems drenched in color, repeated dashes that propel rather than hesitate, the apt grotesque, and the culture-check of literature and music that concerned Sturgeon, "He Who Shapes" is one of Zelazny's most challenging stories, but it is also one of the most rewarding. It takes more risks than anything he had written up to that time, and by and large it succeeds. A little more than a year after " Rose" and only a month before " Doors," "He Who Shapes" demonstrated clearly Zelazny's increasing confidence and expertise as a writer, his increasing ability to control the car without losing speed.

The miraculous year of 1965 concluded with the serial publication of . . . *And Call Me Conrad* in the October and November issues of *F&SF*. Zelazny's first novel is a far-future tale of a ruined Earth, interplanetary politics, exotic aliens, and a hero who may or may not be immortal. The title narrator, happily married to the beautiful Cassandra, is the "Commissioner of Arts, Monuments, and Archives for the planet Earth"(2:372)[24] who has been assigned to escort a prominent alien journalist, Cort Myshtigo, on a tour of "what's left of Earth" (2:374). A brief atomic war known as "The Three Days" has decimated Earth's population and left its civilization in ruins. Most of the survivors have relocated to the home worlds of Myshtigo's race, the Vegans, where they lead a comfortable existence as, essentially, support staff to the Vegans; the humans who remain on Earth, like Conrad, function mainly as caretakers and tour guides. As he reluctantly leads the touring party, which includes his old acquaintances Phil Garber, the poet, and Hasan the Assassin, "the last mercenary on Earth" (2:386), he learns that some members of the party are connected with Radpol, a resurgent terrorist group whose members want all humans to return to Earth. To this end, they attempt to assassinate Myshtigo, forcing Conrad to protect the alien visitor against threats from an organization to which Conrad had once belonged. Complications mount as he goes temporarily mad on receiving word of the death of his wife in an earthquake, engages in one-on-one combat with Hasan, and tries to determine exactly what Myshtigo is really up to and who is really trying to kill him. Eventually, a posthumous message from Phil Garber reveals that the Vegans in fact want to return control of Earth to humanity but are opposed by the human government-in-exile. By story's end, the Vegans have named Conrad "heir to the property commonly referred to as Earth" (2:501), and he is comfortably settled in a villa on a Greek isle with Cassandra, who survived the earthquake after all.

As this brief synopsis indicates, . . . *And Call Me Conrad* is busy even by the standards of the sf adventure tale. What holds it all together is the character and voice of Conrad. In his landmark critical history of science fiction, *Trillion Year Spree*, Brian W. Aldiss singles out Conrad as "one of many such [narrators] in Zelazny's work—a man skilled in the martial arts, blessed with cunning insight, and a poetic tongue."[25] If not universally applicable to Zelazny's protagonists,[26] Aldiss's description is certainly apt for Conrad. Here was the jaunty cadence and lyrical language of Gallinger and Carl Davits put in the mouth of someone who, like the narrators of "Rose" and "Doors," is brimming with powerful emotions and wounded by the past, but, unlike them, is a man of action who is not afraid of a fight. (If "He Who Shapes" gave Zelazny a chance to draw on his undergraduate training in psychology, *Conrad* gave him the chance to draw on his expertise in martial arts: The novel features two vividly detailed set pieces in which Conrad engages in hand-to-hand combat with Hasan.) When Gallinger loses his true love, he attempts suicide; when Conrad thinks he has lost his wife, he snaps, lashes out violently, is subdued, and then gets back to work. When Davits suffers a catastrophic setback, he sinks into indolence; when Conrad's political agenda is thwarted, he makes a new life for himself with a new identity.

This is not to say that Conrad is an uncomplicated good guy. In his earlier career as founder of the Radpol he was "Karaghiosis the Killer," a terrorist, and while as "Conrad" he may have renounced violence, he has not repudiated it: Early in the novel, when Cassandra asks him if he is sorry that Karaghiosis "bombed resorts," he replies, "No" (2:377). Later, when asked by Cort Myshtigo why he ordered the disassembly of the Great Pyramids, he replies, "To needle Vega. . . . [If] you do manage to take [Earth] away from us, you'll get it in worse shape than it was after the Three Days. . . . We'd burn the rest of our history. Not even a scrap for you guys" (2:493). Conrad's willingness to pursue a literal scorched-earth policy ultimately earns the respect of the Vegan representative, who notes that "as Karaghiosis you inspired men to bleed for [Earth.] . . . Your ingenuity as well as your toughness, both physical and mental, is singularly amazing" (2:501). Karaghiosis/Conrad is, to anticipate a later Zelazny tale, a creature of darkness as well as light. Within Aldiss's formulation, Conrad's qualities are all manifestations of a shrewd maneuverer who is always figuring the odds and will try to talk his way through any given situation, but is perfectly willing to resort to violence if that's what it takes—all the while making sure that the world at large is never quite certain of exactly who he is.

If this description looks forward to other Zelazny protagonists such as Corwin of *Nine Princes in Amber* and the nameless narrator of *My Name Is Legion*, it also looks back to another Greek hero defined by calculation, addicted to disguise, swept up in a journey he'd rather not take, and prone to outbursts of violence, namely, Odysseus. It is no surprise that the author of "The Furies" and "He Who Shapes" should write a story that evokes Homer, but . . . *And Call Me Conrad* shows an even deeper commitment to exploring mythology within science fiction. In the first line of the novel, Cassandra playfully accuses Conrad of being one of the Kallikanzaroi, creatures from Greek mythology who live underground and emerge, in his own description, "every spring to spend ten days sawing at the Tree of the World, only to be dispersed at the last moment by the ringing of the Easter bells" (2:371). Lindskold suggests that Conrad, described as having a limp, also recalls Hephaestos, and, in "his empathy with the wild things of the earth," Pan, a comparison reinforced by Conrad's playing the syrinx, or panpipe—not to mention Conrad's description of the Kallikanzaroi as "Pan-like" (ibid.).[27] Does his longevity, which may be immortality, derive from his status as a god? Or is it all a result of atomic mutation? More than a decade after the novel's first publication, Zelazny wrote, "I wanted to leave it open to several interpretations . . . either Conrad is a mutant or he is the Great God Pan. The book may be read either way."[28]

After three years of steady professional publication Zelazny was well-recognized as a strong, innovative new voice in science fiction. In 1966 this status was solidified with his first book publications and his first awards. In accepting *Conrad* for publication in *F&SF*, editor Edward Ferman steered Zelazny toward the magazine's consulting editor, Robert P. Mills, who was also a literary agent. Mills submitted the novel to book publishers and, after several rejections, it was accepted by Ace Books, a paperback house with a strong track record of publishing original and reprint science fiction. And even before his first novel began making the rounds, Zelazny was occupied with turning "He Who Shapes" into his second novel at the urging of Damon Knight, sf author, editor, critic, and founder of the Science Fiction Writers of America. Although the expanded story was rejected by Knight's suggested publisher, Berkley, Mills eventually sold the book to Ace. Both novels appeared in 1966 under new titles imposed by the publisher: . . . *And Call Me Conrad* was retitled *This Immortal*, and "He Who Shapes" became *The Dream Master*.[29] Zelazny preferred the original novella "He Who Shapes" to its novel-length expansion, and Delany thought the additional material, although "beautifully done," disrupted "the original dramatic unity of the whole."[30] There is no reason to disagree with either assessment.

A year later, Ace published Zelazny's first collection of short fiction, *Four for Tomorrow*, also as an original paperback. The book contained the four novelettes that had by 1965 confirmed his reputation with sf magazine readers— "The Furies," "The Graveyard Heart," "Doors," and "Rose"—along with a lengthy and enthusiastic introduction by Theodore Sturgeon. As noted previously, Sturgeon expressed reservations about the degree to which Zelazny's poetic, densely allusive prose might prove a barrier for some readers, but these concerns did not keep Sturgeon from declaring "Rose" to be "one of the most beautifully written, skillfully composed, and passionately expressed works of art to appear anywhere, ever."[31] In its combination of skepticism and near-idolatry, Sturgeon's introduction well represents the passionately engaged reaction of readers and writers to Zelazny's early work.

With three books published in the space of a year, Zelazny's work was now subject to review by professional magazines and newspapers. The response to *This Immortal*, *The Dream Master*, and *Four for Tomorrow* in such outlets was both more critical and less gushing than Sturgeon's but, on the whole, positive. Writing in *Galaxy*, Algis Budrys found *This Immortal* "extremely interesting and undeniably important" and regarded *Four for Tomorrow* as evidence that Zelazny was, at the beginning of his career, writing at a level that would mark a career pinnacle for other writers. In her *F&SF* review of *This Immortal*, Judith Merril noted Zelazny's distinctive prose style, embrace of mythology, and "occasional philosophical insights" but declared the book "disappointing as a novel." Whereas the *Times Literary Supplement* thought the "intelligent and basically simple story" of *The Dream Master* was undercut by Zelazny's "obtrusive style" and "too many fragments of older legend," the *London Tribune* praised Zelazny's "assured knowledge of myth" and thought *This Immortal* "far above any run-of-the-mill adventure yarn." These early reviews set the tone for much of the critical response that would follow: mingled awe and reservations about the author's confident embrace of mythology and elevated prose style, but also keen awareness that a strong, new, and highly distinctive voice had emerged from the world of science fiction.[32]

As critics scrutinized Zelazny's books, his magazine fiction received increasing acclaim. The year 1966 marked the first Science Fiction Writers of America's Nebula Awards; in March "The Doors of His Face, the Lamps of His Mouth" and "He Who Shapes" won in the categories of Best Novelette and Best Novella, respectively. ("He Who Shapes" tied with "The Saliva Tree" by Brian W. Aldiss.)[33] "Doors" was also a finalist for the Hugo Award, and at the World Science Fiction Convention, held over Labor Day weekend in Zelazny's home base of Cleveland, . . . *And Call Me Conrad* won the Hugo for Best Novel in a tie with Frank Herbert's *Dune*. Delany, who attended the Cleveland convention, saw a newcomer's brief serialized novel tying with a massive landmark work by a much better-known writer as "astonishing" evidence of "the extraordinary excitement that the verbal electricity of Zelazny's prose had generated in the three years since he'd been publishing science fiction."[34] Equally astonishing was Zelazny's reception at the convention. Delany recalled:

> During the opening ceremonies when the names of the various SF writers present were announced, while older and more popular professionals such as Isaac Asimov, Frederik Pohl, and Poul Anderson drew a perfectly respectful amount of applause, when Roger Zelazny's name was read out, it was greeted with a standing ovation in a hall filled with almost a thousand attendees—an ovation which went on and on and *on!*[35]

Delany himself was a young writer who had burst onto the sf scene in the early 1960s with works that carried their own verbal electricity. He and Zelazny together were among the fastest to win acclaim in the history of the field. Over the course of the ensuing five years they won between them a total of three Hugos and six Nebulas as they became the most widely discussed American writers associated with the New Wave movement within English-language science fiction.

The term *New Wave* had currency both before and after its application to sf in the 1960s, before as the *nouvelle vague* of French cinema in the 1950s, after as an all-purpose label for punk-influenced rock music of the 1970s and 1980s. It had been applied as early as 1961 by the reviewer P. Schuyler Miller to describe work by British sf authors such as Aldiss and John Brunner.[36] By the time the Cleveland Worldcon took place, the idea of a New Wave in sf had gained currency from Judith Merril's *F&SF* book review columns and *Year's Best SF* anthologies and from *New Worlds*, the venerable British science fiction magazine that, edited by Michael Moorcock beginning in 1964, turned toward "a kind of SF which is unconventional in every sense."[37] Within the next two years, two anthologies—Harlan Ellison's *Dangerous Visions* (1967) and Merril's *England Swings SF* (1968)—hailed a new era of sf that rejected the unartful naiveté of the pulp tradition in favor of a style that was more sophisticated, mature, often experimental, sometimes overtly political, and more accurately reflecting the increasingly chaotic and complex world of the late twentieth century. In the words of J. G. Ballard, the British writer who became both the best-known and most radically experimental of the writers associated with the New Wave, "The biggest developments of the immediate future will take place, not on the Moon or Mars, but on Earth, and it is *inner space*, not outer, that needs to be explored."[38]

This sense of movement and change within science fiction did not, however, bring with it any consensus as to what exactly was moving and changing, or if it should. Writing a year-end summary for the *WSFA Journal*, a fanzine published by the Washington, DC, Science Fiction Association, the fan critic Banks Mebane put it succinctly: "Everybody is talking about a 'New Thing' in sf. No one agrees on what it is."[39] Like most identified literary trends, the New Wave resisted any comprehensive description or uniform categorization. The fiction writers and critics of the day and the scholars of later generations disagreed, often vehemently, concerning the degree to which New Wave texts were dependent on the politics of the present or on the artistic innovations of the past, whether the key innovations were thematic or stylistic, and the degree to which such texts actually broke from genre traditions. And, unsurprisingly, most, if not all, of the writers associated with the New Wave denied that they were a part of it or of any other movement. In a note to his contribution to *England Swings SF*, Aldiss wrote, "I'm no part of the new wave . . . the whole idea of a new wave is a publicity stunt, based among other things on a lack of perspective."[40] Years later, Delany saw himself as separate from the New Wave owing to his "sf conservatism," noting, "I was interested in space operas and hardware at precisely the point when they, with great vigor and energy, were turning away from such writerly pursuits as puerile."[41] In 1967 Ellison introduced *Dangerous Visions* (which included work by Aldiss, Ballard, Delany, and Zelazny) as "a thirty-three story demonstration of the 'new thing'—the *nouvelle vague*, if you will[,] of speculative writing . . . constructed along specific lines of revolution." But by 1969 he had decided, "I do not believe that there is such a thing as 'New Wave' in speculative fiction[;] . . . this richness of new voices is *many* waves: each composed of one writer."[42]

Whether or not one wishes to enforce a category of 1960s science fiction called New Wave, during this period there were a number of writers within the genre, most in their twenties and thirties and most associated with either Ellison's anthologies (including the 1972 sequel *Again, Dangerous Visions*) or

Moorcock's magazine, whose work demonstrated, in varying combinations and to varying degrees, an interest in literary style and characterization, a skepticism concerning technological progress (including the achievements of the U.S. space program, a frequent theme of Ballard and the American writer Barry N. Malzberg), a willingness to portray explicitly human violence and sexuality, and an overall desire to push sf in a different direction. By the time of the Cleveland Worldcon, even with much of his most ambitious work yet to appear, it was no surprise that the author of " Rose," "Doors," "He Who Shapes," and . . . *And Call Me Conrad* was one of the authors labeled New Wave.

And it is also no surprise that the author himself was dubious of such a label. In a 1969 letter he acknowledged his personal as well as professional friendships with Delany and Ellison but added, "I doubt very much that we have influenced one another . . . we are all very independent spirits."[43] Two years later, he labeled the experiments of the New Wave "a temporary phenomenon . . . already beginning to pass" in favor of "a new synthesis . . . wherein form and content are more proportionally balanced."[44] In a 1975 letter he dismissed the New Wave altogether as "just a popular tag slapped on a number of writers . . . who had very little in common other than temporal proximity and some interest in stylistic and structural experimentation. . . . I have never considered myself part of any sort of movement—and neither did Delany the last time I asked him."[45] By 1990 he was willing to admit that he and other science fiction writers of the 1960s were reacting to "the sf of the '40s & '50s, which . . . was not particularly noted for the quality of the writing" but noted that the formal ambition of much of the New Wave was "old hat in general fiction." Echoing both his and Ellison's earlier observations, he concluded, "Most of us deny there was such a thing as a New Wave 'movement'[;] . . . we are all sufficiently individualistic to dislike being categorized."[46]

As Zelazny's diligent self-development began to pay off, his nonwriting life settled into place. His new position in the Social Security Administration offices in Baltimore not only continued to provide a baseline of financial stability but also enabled a significant personal development when he began dating one of his co-workers, Judith Alene Callahan. On August 20, 1966, two months after his divorce was final and less than a year after moving to

Baltimore, Zelazny married Callahan at Baltimore City Hall.[47] Soon afterward, *The Dream Master* was published with the following dedication:

To Judy,
of the hurst of oaks
with a wolf issuant therefrom
to the sinister all proper.
"Fidus et audax."[48]

The couple lived quietly in Baltimore, both continuing to work full-time at the Social Security offices for the next three years.[49]

This combined personal and work stability was apparently a good fit for Zelazny's writing ambitions, as his fictional output continued unabated. He continued to publish at a rapid pace in the sf magazines, with ten new stories appearing in 1966 and nine in 1967. In significant contrast to the author's initial burst of published fiction, few of the stories that appeared in this period were short, clever exercises; they were, instead, well-developed, fully resonant stories. They included a novelette, "Death and the Executioner" (*F&SF*, June 1967, later incorporated into Zelazny's third novel, *Lord of Light*), and a novella, "Damnation Alley" (*Galaxy*, October 1967), that would later appear, expanded, as Zelazny's sixth published novel.

Of the stories of 1966–1967, four novelettes in particular stand out. In "This Moment of the Storm" (*F&SF*, June 1966) Godfrey Judson Holmes has achieved extreme longevity by means of repeated travel between the stars in a state of suspended animation: with an apparent age of thirty-five, he is in fact almost six hundred years old. Now centuries removed from the cause of his travels, his attempt to escape his grief over the death of his wife, Holmes has made a life for himself on Tierra del Cygnus, a watery planet with a single large continent that serves as a "stopover . . . on the way out to other, more settled worlds" (2:196).[50] He is a "Hell Cop" supervising an extensive network of surveillance cameras and drones designed both to prevent human crime and to monitor the planet's often lethal fauna. He is also in a comfortable romantic relationship with Eleanor Schirrer, the mayor of the coastal city of Beta-Prime. Holmes seems to be on the verge of ceasing his travels, settling down with Eleanor, and living out the rest of his life in normal time. After surviving a gigantic storm and flood that nearly destroys Beta-Prime and witnessing the enormous material and human cost of the catastrophe, he decides that Cygnus may indeed be where he should remain—only to lose Eleanor to the random violence of a post-storm looter, a loss that sends him back into cold sleep in search of a new life in a new time and place.

Zelazny's fascination with longevity enabled by suspended animation is also on display in "The Keys to December" (*New Worlds*, August 1966). In the far future, humans are able to modify themselves physically to inhabit any given planet and to make the same arrangements for their planned offspring. The parents of Jarry Dark choose the planet Alyonal, but when it is destroyed, Jarry is raised by the corporation that owned Alyonal in a controlled enclosure replicating the destroyed planet's environment. As he grows up, Jarry discovers that he has "a knack for making money" (2:257)[51] and, after amassing a great fortune, acquires a planet that can be terraformed into Alyonal II. He lives on the new planet, remaining in suspended animation for most of the millennia-long process of altering the planet into a hospitable environment, awaking every 250 years to check on the project's progress. When many cycles later, Jarry concludes that a race of beings native to the planet is sentient and will be destroyed by further terraforming, he attempts to halt the project. When the corporate directors refuse, he spends his current awake cycle destroying the project's various installations until the directors agree to stop. The story concludes with Jarry's refusing to go back into hibernation and living out the rest of his life among the planet's indigenous inhabitants, who revere him as a savior.

The events of "For a Breath I Tarry" (*Fantastic*, September 1966)[52] also take place over the course of many centuries. Humanity has placed in Earth orbit Solcom, an artificial intelligence "invested with the power to rebuild the world" (2:22).[53] When an atomic war destroys the human race, Solcom is damaged and repairs itself, but not in time to prevent Divcom, another AI, placed beneath the Earth's surface as a backup to Solcom, from coming online. The two entities are then in continual dispute as to which should be in charge. In the meantime, Solcom has established two machine intelligences to supervise the planet: "Frost" at the North Pole and "the Beta-Machine" (2:82) at the South Pole. When Solcom temporarily malfunctions, Frost comes online and develops a highly individualized consciousness that is deeply curious about the departed human race, to the point where "Man [becomes] his hobby" (2:83). Frost's curiosity becomes a part of the struggle between Solcom and Divcom when Mordel, a mobile AI under Divcom's control, challenges Frost to gather and process enough information to achieve truly human self-awareness, including experiencing emotional responses. For centuries Frost and Mordel explore what remains of human civilization, Frost finally constructing and inhabiting a human body. By the end of the story Frost is a Man with dominion over both Solcom and Divcom, and he offers his counterpart, the Beta-Machine, the opportunity to assume human form as a female.

In "This Mortal Mountain" (*If*, March 1967), the renowned mountain climber Jack Summers, while on the planet Disel, attempts to scale "The Gray Sister, the highest mountain in the known universe" (3:22).[54] As Summers and his team make their way up the mountain, they are periodically blocked by "a bird-shaped thing . . . all fire and static" (3:29), while Summers has recurrent visions of a young woman who urges him to go back. Undaunted, he continues to the summit, losing several of his companions along the way. At the summit, he discovers that the young woman of his visions is Linda, a member of the planet's original colony, whose scientist husband left her in cryogenic sleep when she contracted the plague that killed the colony. Both she and the "bird-shaped thing" were images generated by a "defense-computer" (3:56) programmed to protect Linda and keep any future colonists from being exposed to the plague. The story concludes with Linda awake and symptomatic as Jack hopes that the expedition's doctor has the necessary serum to cure her.

All four of these stories explore Zelazny's recurrent themes of the fundamental narratives of mythology, the allure of immortality, the quick-witted but ultimately disappointed protagonist and also provide an interesting double pair of Zelazny's two main approaches to narrative point of view: in "This Moment of the Storm" and "This Mortal Mountain," the romantically displaced, archly allusive first-person narrator previously on display in "Rose," "Doors," and *Conrad*; in "Keys to December" and "For a Breath I Tarry," the rhapsodic third-person omniscient voice of "The Furies" and "He Who Shapes." But in these stories Zelazny grapples with his obsessions in ways that show his rapid evolution as a writer. "This Moment" appeared only two years after "Graveyard Heart," in which the depiction of cold-sleep near-immortality served a clever but easy critique of the superficiality of those who would seek such an existence. In the later story, Zelazny does not linger over Holmes's relatively straightforward motivation of escaping grief. Instead, the author ponders the implications of such an extended lifespan, implications that bear out Kovacs's observation that the story "presents aspects of existentialism."[55] Holmes may want to believe that there is "a time and place best suited for each person who has ever lived" and that "the Renaissance of [his] days" may be yet to come (2:214). Not only do "a hundred years of travel . . . not bring a century of forgetfulness" (2:213), however, but the sought-after renaissance is inevitably subsumed within the "moment of the storm": the brute reality of material existence in the form of both grand natural catastrophe and petty human violence. Indeed, the story opens with Holmes remembering the time when his "old philosophy prof" defined man, in the existentialist tradition, solely in terms of action or inaction: "Man is the sum total of everything he has done, wishes to do or not to do, and wishes he had done, or hadn't" (2:189, 190). Like "Rose," "This Moment" ends with a highly figurative description of its narrator looking out from the viewport of a spaceship. But whereas the romantic egoist Gallinger sees the environment of space in terms of his own subjective drama, Holmes sees a universe that is distant, indifferent, and ultimately beyond his grasp: "It is cold and quiet outside and the horizon is infinity. There is no sense of movement. There is no moon, and the stars are very bright, like broken diamonds, all" (2:218).

If the dilemmas of existential philosophy underlie "This Moment," "This Mortal Mountain" returns to more classical points of reference. Kovacs reads the story as a retelling of Dante's *Purgatorio*, suggesting that the story's seven sections correspond to the seven sections of Mount Purgatory and remarking that, even as Dante's story ends with the protagonist's seeing stars that foreshadow his ascent to heaven, Zelazny's concludes with the protagonist's desperately hoping to see stars as a sign that Linda will be saved,[56] a reading supported by the awakened Linda's informing Summers that the mountain's original name is Purgatorio (3:56). Lindskold notes that the name Gray Sister "evokes the Gorgons of Greek mythology."[57] It is crucial that, whereas Holmes's battle with the overpowering forces of nature, and indeed his travels through space and time, are part and parcel of his running away from his grief-stricken past, Summers's actions move toward a goal. Holmes's storm is to be resisted, but Summers's mountain is to be conquered and, ultimately, embraced. As he explains to the revived Linda, "Each mountain is a deity, you know. Each is an immortal power[;] . . . a mountain may grant you a certain grace" (3:57). The image of the stars that concludes "This Moment" signifies emptiness and loss in an indifferent universe; the stars that Summers yearns to see at the end of "This Mortal Mountain" represent for him, as they did for Dante, the promise of rescue and redemption: "(Stars. Oh let there be. This once to end with. Please.)" (ibid.).

Whereas "This Moment" and "This Mortal Mountain" demonstrate Zelazny's deepening consideration of basic themes and increased control of his first-person voice, "For a Breath" and "Keys" offer, from an omniscient perspective, both a subtle interrogation of these themes and an expansion into new ones. "For a Breath" is, on one level, as firmly grounded in the canon of European literature as "This Mortal Mountain" in its retelling of the legend of Faust (Frost/Faust, Mordel/Mephistopheles)[58] while also echoing other sources, from the Books of Genesis and Job to *Frankenstein* and the poetry of A. E. Housman. Frost's education in what it means to be human begins with books (including Housman's *A Shropshire Lad*, source of the story's title), but after scanning "all the existing books of Man" (2:92) and surveying all the surviving artifacts of the human race, Frost is still unable to grasp the essence of humanity. Not until Frost is downloaded into a physical human body does he become human, and then his humanity is defined not by his knowledge of art and science but by his experience of fear and despair (2:113).

If "For a Breath" concludes that the human condition is more than poetry and machines, "The Keys to December" suggests that we should be more careful to acknowledge conditions other than our own. Zelazny had already shown a nascent awareness of the downside of exploring new worlds in "A Rose for Ecclesiastes." But "Keys" takes this awareness a significant step further when Jarry Dark discovers that the inhabitants of the planet his corporation is slowly terraforming are at risk of extinction and says, "We're the ones who made them evolve, cursed them with intellect" (2:274). When his board of directors counters that the indigenous race might well have evolved on their own, Jarry replies, "It doesn't really matter how it happened. . . . We have some responsibility to an intelligent race . . . at least to the extent of not murdering it" (2:274–275). Jarry is, by his own admission, motivated to destroy key parts of the project not only by compassion for the aliens but also by his self-identification as their savior: "I am their god. . . . They have told my story for two and a half centuries. . . . I am powerful and wise and good, so far as they are concerned. In this capacity, I owe them some consideration" (2:277). Jarry's pride in assuming a role that one hopes twenty-first-century readers would find obnoxious—the Great White Savior—complicates but by no means contradicts the story's status as an early example of both Zelazny's interest in environmental issues[59] and, more striking, his willingness to consider violent resistance as a workable strategy, a stance that was already on display in *Conrad* and that would appear in several works of the 1970s.

Zelazny's readers, including his fellow writers, responded enthusiastically to these increasingly thoughtful stories, all four of which were award finalists. Indeed, Zelazny wound up competing with himself, as "This Moment" and "For a Breath" were both finalists for the 1967 Hugo Award for Best Novelette, while "This Mortal Mountain" and "Keys" were both finalists for the 1968 Nebula Award in the same category. "This Moment" was also a finalist for the Nebula Award. The four have remained among Zelazny's most highly regarded stories, with "For a Breath" and "Keys" ranked thirty-first and forty-seventh, respectively, in the Best Novelette category of the 2012 *Locus* readers' poll of the best science fiction of the twentieth century.

As his writings gained greater and greater acclaim, Zelazny became a more prominent public figure within the science fiction community. Most of the writers associated (however problematically, from their perspective) with the New Wave of the 1960s entered the field from outside, rather than from within, the sf subculture. Writers such as Ballard, Delany, Thomas M. Disch, Le Guin, Joanna Russ, and Norman Spinrad came to sf as readers but not as fans; although aware of the artistic and commercial traditions of the genre, they were relatively unconcerned with the social and ideological traditions of genre fandom. Zelazny, however, had been active in science fiction fandom as a teenager and had met the twenty-one-year-old Harlan Ellison (who, even more than Zelazny, was active in sf fandom as a young man) at the 1955 WorldCon.[60] It is no surprise, then, that when Zelazny returned to writing sf several years later and rapidly became a star, he reentered the world of fandom and conventions. As the novels and stories that made his initial reputation appeared in the mid-1960s, he attended conventions as a highly regarded professional writer, including appearances as the guest of honor at the 1966 Marcon in Toledo and the 1967 Ozarkcon in St. Louis.[61] When he made his triumphant appearance at the 1966 Worldcon he was coming home not only to Cleveland but also to the science fiction community, a place where he was, by all accounts, very comfortable and as well received personally as he was professionally.[62]

It was while attending an sf convention that Zelazny first conceptualized the story that became his most famous standalone novel. On the last morning of the 1965 Disclave, a regional convention in Washington, DC, after cutting himself shaving, Zelazny fantasized about being able to switch into a body that, during a public appearance, would not display an obvious shaving cut. This train of thought led to his pondering the transmigration of souls and, in turn, realizing that little, if any, sf and fantasy had drawn on Hindu mythology.[63] While driving back to Ohio with his friend Ben Jason, Zelazny "pretty much roughed out the whole story in [his] head."[64] The story was *Lord of Light*, which Zelazny worked on steadily for the rest of 1965 and early 1966,[65] as the stories that solidified his star status were appearing regularly in the sf magazines and while still working a full forty-hour week for the Social Security Administration.

Many readers have seen *Lord of Light* as a "science fantasy" novel that blurs genre lines; Zelazny encouraged this reading. A decade after the novel appeared, he claimed he wrote it in order to leave "intentional ambiguity. . . . [He] wanted it to lie somewhat between both camps [sf and fantasy] and not entirely in either."[66] Yet the core of the story is very much a science fiction narrative: The crew of the interstellar spaceship *Star of India*, traveling from "Urath" (i.e., Earth), discovers and colonizes an inhabited planet, conquering and in some cases destroying the planet's various indigenous races, "the Rakasha and the Nagas, the Ghandarvas and the People-of-the-Sea." (156).[67] In so doing, the crew members use hyperadvanced technology to assume "Aspects" (images of gods and goddesses from the Hindu pantheon), employ "Attributes" (superpowers that extend and amplify the individual's will), and transfer individual personalities to new bodies as needed. "The First"—the original crew members—keep themselves continually renewed while still reproducing normally, resulting in a hierarchy within which they maintain their status as "gods" but also severely limit their descendants' access to mind-body transfer and prevent any significant technological advancement. In short, the crew of the *Star of India* use technology to replicate the great figures of Hindu mythology, enforce a caste system, and enable the transmigration of souls.

Enter Sam, one of the First, an active participant in the subjugation of the planet's populace. As the First grow increasingly dictatorial, Sam embraces the doctrine of "Accelerationism," which argues that the descendants of the First are entitled to advance as rapidly as they are capable. He recants his earlier activities against the native inhabitants and rebels against the other gods. Assuming the Aspect of Siddhartha, he spreads the teachings of Buddhism in an attempt to undermine the authority of the First, who maintain their Hindu Aspects. Kali, goddess of destruction, sends the executioner Rild to dispatch Sam, but Rild instead becomes Sugata, the Buddha's most devout follower and proselytizer. Yama, god of death, appears, kills Rild/Sugata, and attempts to kill Sam, who escapes. Sam then releases from bondage Taraka, lord of the Rakasha, and enters into an alliance with him to battle the gods. The alliance fails when Taraka takes control of Sam's body and postpones battling the gods while he indulges in the pleasures of the flesh. Sam eventually reasserts control and frees other demons to wage war, but the gods keep the demons at bay, capture Sam, and confine him to the enclave known as Heaven. Meanwhile, Kali and Yama marry, and Brahma, the supreme god, has been murdered by an unknown party. The upper levels of the pantheon decide that Kali must replace him, but in order to do so she must reincarnate as a man, thus ending her marriage to Yama. Sam, whose merger with the demon has left him able to survive outside his body, reappears in the guise of the lesser god Murugan and recruits allies, including Yama, who is deeply wounded by what he regards as Kali's betrayal. The gods defeat Sam and his allies in the massive battle that follows, but many of the gods are killed, badly undermining the stability of Heaven. Because Sam, apparently, can no longer be killed, he is projected into the Bridge of the Gods, the ion ring that surrounds the planet, where he achieves, for all intents and purposes, Nirvana.

After an unspecified amount of time, Yama, with the assistance of Tak, ex-archivist of the gods who has been reincarnated as an ape as punishment for his participation in the previous rebellion, and Ratri, goddess of night, use a radio device to bring Sam back to the planet and return him to a physical body in order to resume their struggle against the gods. Sam is not pleased at having to leave Nirvana but eventually agrees to resume the rebellion. They attempt an alliance with Niritti, the Black One, the Christian chaplain of the *Star of India* who has his own reasons for wanting to destroy what remains of the First in their Hindu Aspects. But the duplicitous actions of the demon Taraka prevent the proposed alliance, and the rebels instead join with Brahma (the reincarnated Kali) to defeat Niritti. The gods prevail, but at great cost, including the life of Brahma / Kali. The novel concludes with the hegemony of the First shattered, the forces of Accelerationism ascendant, and Sam, the Lord of Light, disappearing into the world at large, with at least four conflicting myths to account for his ultimate fate.

Zelazny's interest in mythology and religion had been on display since "A Rose for Ecclesiastes," and with the publication of *Lord of Light*, for many readers his name became as closely associated with mythologically based science fiction as it was with stylistic flamboyance. Zelazny's use of myth also lay at the center of much of the critical response, positive and negative, to his future work. In the first book-length study of Zelazny's publications, Carl Yoke suggests that myth serves an anchor and organizing principle in the early works, noting the author's "abundant use of myth and legend . . . to structure his stories" as well as to give "a deeper, richer, and broader meaning to them."[68] Krulik similarly notes Zelazny's use of myth and ancient religion "in order to rework ideas and concerns that he cares deeply about. . . . Creating characters who have an established mythic origin is a clever way in which he uses metaphor to reveal some of those personal concerns."[69]

What some saw as a strength, however, others saw as a weakness. Critics such as Franz Rottensteiner and James Blish challenged the very notion of using the fixed, enduring structures of mythology in science fiction, a literature that almost by definition foregrounds a basic notion of change. In a 1970 review of the British editions of *Four for Tomorrow* and *Isle of the Dead*, Rottensteiner dismisses Zelazny's mythic structures as "crutches for an unoriginal mind turning to the past because it is either unwilling or unable to come to grips with the realities of the present or a probable future," while Blish, discussing *Creatures of Light and Darkness*, condemns Zelazny's "mytholatry" as "dangerously ill-conceived" and argues that myth's concern with "eternal forces which are changeless" is "antithetical to the suppositions of science fiction, which center around the potentialities of continuous change."[70]

In the context of such critiques, the speech that Zelazny gave as the guest of honor at Ozarkcon 2 in 1967 is of particular interest. In the speech, Zelazny begins an argument for the distinctive nature of science fiction by discussing the origins of drama in religious myths that mirrored the cycles of the natural world by invoking the death and rebirth of gods.[71] Drawing on the renowned literary critic Northrop Frye's *Anatomy of Criticism* (1957) and its model of literary modes, Zelazny argues that, whereas literature since the nineteenth century has been given over largely to the Low Mimetic mode (stories of ordinary people who are not superior to nature or to other people) and, increasingly, to the Ironic (stories of people who are inferior to both nature and other people), science fiction continues to employ the High Mimetic. In this mode, he states, "we have characters who are greater than ordinary men . . . people who exercise some measure of authority, characters who still have a slight trace of the Mythic Mode about them . . . someone who is greater than other people and can sometimes have a reputation for slaying a monster, or controlling some natural force" (2:514).[72] While acknowledging that not all sf fits this model—he cites, approvingly, J. G. Ballard's work as an example of science fiction in the Ironic mode—he concludes that, to the degree it employs the High Mimetic Mode, sf will remain distinct from mainstream literature. He offers Theodore Sturgeon's *More Than Human* and Arthur C. Clarke's *Childhood's End* (both 1953) as examples of sf stories that could "come close to" producing "genuine tragedies and comedies, in the strict classical sense of the word" (2:514).

Zelazny's summary of Frye's High Memetic Mode well describes the space-travelers-become-gods of *Lord of Light*, and Zelazny's embrace of Frye's analysis might serve as Exhibit A for Rottensteiner and Blish's objections. But these characters, like most of Zelazny's, do not enact the cyclic rise-and-fall or birth-death-rebirth of Frye's archetypes. Their journeys tend to be more unstable and uncertain, mythic overtones or no, as described by Zelazny scholar and bibliographer Joseph L. Sanders:

> Rather than clinging to a myth for security, Zelazny boldly shatters myth and throws away many vital parts; rather than holding to a fixed sense of character and morality, his stories rejoice in the invigorating, mind-straining process of self-discovery and moral growth that myth can stimulate. . . . If [Zelazny's characters] cling to myth they always destroy themselves.[73]

The characters in *Lord of Light* who "cling to myth"—the members of the First who battle to hold onto their identities and status as gods—ultimately fail. Sam, who succeeds, may be greater than other humans and in control of powerful forces, but he doubts that there is "some one thing constant and unchanging in the universe" (179), is at one point described as "a bomb-throwing anarchist" (184), and, neither elevated in triumph nor crushed in defeat, exits the story in a fashion for which no one can account. In Sanders's terms, Sam uses the power of myth without clinging to it, suggesting that myth does not necessarily have to reinforce existing ways of looking at the world but can instead point to new ones.

Zelazny's use of myths not to retell old stories and reaffirm old values but to interrogate and destabilize them was not the only level on which he challenged his audience. *Lord of Light* was his most ambitious work since "He Who Shapes" and, like the earlier novella, one that made substantial demands on its readers. About three hundred pages in most editions, the novel was by far Zelazny's longest work to date, but given the large cast of characters and active plot, and compared to most twenty-first-century fantasy fiction, it compresses a lot of material into a relatively short length. The novel also plays with structure and chronology: The first and last chapters narrate Yama and Tak's reclaiming Sam from the Bridge of the Gods, Sam's reentry into the material world, and the final battle that breaks the rule of the First; the five chapters in between are a flashback beginning with the early stages of Sam-as-Siddhartha's campaign against the gods and ending with his defeat and transmission to the Bridge of the Gods. What is, chronologically speaking, the first part of the story—the arrival of the *Star of India*, the crew's assumption of the personas of the Hindu pantheon, and the subjugation of the aliens—is revealed only as backstory in bits and pieces throughout the novel. By the final pages Zelazny's readers know everything they need to know, but only if they pay close attention.

It is not surprising that Zelazny's adventurous structure is matched by equally adventurous prose. On one hand, the novel employs the omniscient once-upon-a-time narration on display in "For a Breath I Tarry" and "Keys to December," including two-part introductions to each chapter that briefly synopsize the events of the chapter in the voice of scripture ("It is said that, when the Teacher appeared, those of all castes went to hear his teachings"

[83]) and then add what appear to be quotations from actual Hindu and Buddhist texts. These excerpts are, in fact, what Zelazny later called "Lowellian imitations" after the U.S. poet Robert Lowell's collection *Interpretations,* in which the poet recasts writings from another language in his own voice.[74] As in earlier stories, paragraphs may consist of single sentences or multiple pages—or, on one occasion, both (76–77)—each having the effect of poetry, while dialogue frequently assumes the high formality of the fantasy epic: "'You have presumed too much, Lord Krishna,' she told him, 'and offended against the sanctity of Night. For this, I shall punish you by leaving this darkness upon Heaven for a time'" (195).

On the other hand, these strutting gods are, or, at least, were, human beings who once lived on Earth, as Zelazny reminds us by occasionally having them lapse into more prosaic dialogue. Sometimes this takes the form of specific references to human culture, as when Sam requests a musician to play "The Blue Danube" (46) or when one minor god dismisses another by declaring, "You fertility deities are worse than Marxists. . . . You think that's all that goes on between people" (175). At other times characters simply speak informally. When, for instance, one of Sam's allies offers Sam a drink and he asks, "You make that yourself?" the character replies, "Yep. Got a still in the next room" (56).

This back-and-forth between the elevated rhetoric of high fantasy and the down-to-earth exchanges of regular human beings well reflects the novel's protagonist, known as the Lord of Light but also simply as Sam. Like the title character of *. . . And Call Me Conrad,* Sam is a mysterious figure of considerable power, more than willing to employ spectacular levels of violence to achieve his goals. But he is a more ambivalent crusader than is Conrad; to use Delany's formulation, he is an adventurer who is deeply unsure of himself.[75] When pondering the Firsts' original defeat of the aliens and subsequent construction of the City of the Gods, he considers the city's "beauty and its rightness, its ugliness and its wrongness. . . . He [knows] that he would never feel either wholly right or wholly wrong in opposing it" (156). He is also conscious of the degree to which, as the First use their Aspects to hold on to power, he uses Buddhism and the willingness of others to believe in it as a strategy against his enemies: "I am not the saint the Buddhists think me to be," he declares, "and I am not the hero out of legend. I am a man who knows much fear, and who occasionally feels guilt. Mainly, though, I am a man who has set out to do a thing" (143).

The thing Sam has set out to do is to destroy the power of the gods, thereby giving greater freedom to the descendants of the First and, along the way, perhaps rectifying the injustice done to the planet's original inhabitants. During Sam's initial attempt to enlist the Rakasha in the battle against the gods, Traka points out, "You stole our world. . . . You chained us here" (131), a claim that Sam later conveys to members of the First: "It was their world first. We took it away from them." Referring to the humans' calling the Rakasha demons, Sam continues, "To them, we are the demons. . . . Nothing really wanted us here and everything disputed our coming" (166, 178). Unquestionably, Sam regrets his active participation in the subjugation of others by "an immortal aristocracy of willful hedonists who played games with the world" (187).

But if contemporary debates concerning colonialism and multiculturalism have taught us anything, it is that admitting such transgressions and attempting to repair the damage do not automatically secure the rights, protect the autonomy, or acknowledge the inherent value of others. Although Sam is notably described more than once as having dark skin, for the twenty-first-century reader he may come across as yet another Great White Savior, swooping down to rescue the natives, perhaps genuinely compassionate but ultimately concerned only with his own agenda—not unlike, some might argue, the white American author who rewrites the myths of another culture to suit his own purposes. Some recent commentators have been relatively sanguine in their responses to this aspect of the book. The novelist Rajan Khanna, writing in two separate essays published in 2012, considered *Lord of Light* "one of Zelazny's finest works . . . a treasure of ideas," and, while acknowledging that the author also "took freely from these mythologies for his own purposes" and wondering when such borrowings "cross the line into cultural appropriation," concludes that Zelazny "honored the original stories." And the novelist Jo Walton, writing in 2009, suggested, "If someone wrote this book today, we'd probably call the use of Hindu mythology and Indian trappings cultural appropriation. In 1967, I think we call it getting points for being aware that the rest of the world existed."[76]

Such issues were, of course, scarcely front and center in the critical response to the novel at the time of its publication. What was of concern to the critics then was Zelazny's attempt to write a different kind of science fiction in a different kind of voice. The *Times Literary Supplement* called the novel a "weird allegorical fantasy . . . far-fetched" and disliked Zelazny's mix of high and low style, while the novelist Edmund Cooper, writing in the London *Sunday Times*, found parts of the novel "hazy" but other parts "brilliant and written with impact." A longtime reviewer for the sf magazine *Analog*, P. Schuyler Miller, called the novel "a unique blend of myth and mirth, legend and jarring anachronism," while Paul Redfern, writing in *New Scientist*, found the novel "long and tortuous . . . original and highly imaginative . . . demanding of time and patience."[77]

Perhaps the most thoughtful response to Zelazny's novel, and still one of the most thoughtful it has received, was the review in *F&SF* by Joanna Russ, who is often cited with Zelazny, Delany, and Disch as a leading U.S. figure of the New Wave and also a critic deeply familiar with both sf and mainstream literature. In contrast to the reviewers cited above, Russ approves of both Zelazny's myth-mining and style, calling the novel brilliant and praising "the manner in which the mimicked Hindu culture is both splendidly described and splendidly explained in the purest science fiction terms; Zelazny can write like the Ramayana while discussing incendiary grenades or the flush toilet[;] . . . The two worlds never conflict; they are always at one, and that is a triumph." More problematic for Russ is the lack of any detailed presentation of the original conflict between Sam and the other members of the First and the resulting sense that Sam's motives are unclear: "Behind the exciting surface movement of the book is a tale of outsiders fighting entrenched insiders. . . . But Sam / Siddhartha / Buddha never rises above the personal adventurousness of a kind of combative instinct." She concludes with a question that remains perhaps the most concise statement of a critical concern that followed Zelazny throughout his career: "Will Zelazny ever write the inside stories of his stories? Can he?"[78]

One could address such a critique by returning to Zelazny's embrace of the High Mimetic, within which the exterior actions of grand figures and the results of those actions are more important than internal motivations and struggles. But it is hard to argue against Russ's diagnosis that we never have a full sense of the source of the antagonism between Sam and the other gods beyond the take-it-or-leave-it portrayal of his ambivalence toward authority and his guilt concerning the Firsts' treatment of the planet's native population. In the same discussion in which she defended Zelazny's use of Hindu mythology, Jo Walton echoed Russ's observations when she declared the book "a cold intellectual exercise. . . . None of the characters feels real. . . . Sam's motivations are obscure, the other characters['] even more so."[79] Like Russ four decades earlier, Walton longed for the story inside the story.

The anonymous reviewer for the *Times Literary Supplement* went so far as to wonder whether *Lord of Light* was intended as a parody. It is difficult to believe that Zelazny was that unconcerned about the actual story he was telling. But when one considers the degree to which the novel refuses to stand still, constantly shifting from high drama to low comedy and back again and featuring a protagonist who is constantly doing things while seemingly uncertain whether there is, in fact, anything that can be done, one can see the novel operating not only as a critique of genre tradition but also as self-critique. After delivering an extended and eloquent lecture to Sam about the burdens and responsibilities of godhood, Yama observes, "It appears that our minds will never meet on this subject," and Sam replies, "If someone asks you why you're oppressing a world and you reply with a lot of poetic crap, no. I guess there can't be a meeting of the minds" (167). Later, Sam says, "Poetic truth differs considerably from that which surrounds most of the business of life" (204).

Such sentiments may, of course, be read as merely another expression of Sam's antiestablishment belligerence. Yet in a letter to Damon Knight dated July 19, 1965, when he was writing *Lord of Light*, Zelazny admitted to second thoughts about the strategies of his early work:

> [I] go back over my old tales and wince at the over-writing and just plain verbal garbage of which I have been so frequently guilty. I think I have now passed the fork in the trail where I stood hesitating for a time—that place where I asked myself whether I wanted to do pretty writing or story-telling—and decided that the subject was not just a thing to heap up words upon.[80]

The tensions that so spectacularly energized Zelazny's most famous stand-alone novel and that to this day continue to challenge and provoke its audience were perhaps not solely an artistic choice but also an artistic problem that the author was working through even as he wrote. If Zelazny's readers were struggling, then so, apparently, was he.

In that context, Zelazny's final major work of short fiction from the period 1966–1967, the novella "Damnation Alley," is especially instructive. Displaying none of the structural and few of the stylistic flourishes that marked *Lord of Light* and the major novelettes, it is a straightforward story told in a straight line, "a nice, simple action-adventure story," as the author later described it.[81] The story is set in a United States that has been almost destroyed by nuclear war, with only the northeastern and southwestern regions of the country reasonably intact. When a plague breaks out in the surviving city of Boston, the only hope is a vaccine manufactured in the other major surviving city, Los Angeles. But unceasing high-altitude winds make air travel impossible, while ferocious storms, mutated monsters (including giant bats, snakes, and spiders), and areas of high radioactivity make ground travel difficult and potentially lethal. Hell Tanner, an outlaw biker and multiple felon, is coerced into driving one of three armed and armored ground vehicles attempting to transport the vaccine across the country in the hope that at least one will make it to Boston. Tanner undertakes the mission not to help his fellow citizens—"What did they ever do for me? Nothing" (3:126)[82]—but to earn a full pardon for his numerous crimes. As the journey progresses, however, Tanner rethinks his indifference, deciding, "I'd hate to see the whole world get dead" (3:135). His decision to continue is supported by the kindness and hospitality of residents of rural Pennsylvania when his vehicle becomes stuck in the mud, as well as by his brief but passionate interlude with Cornelia, a young woman who joins him after he fends off an attack from a biker gang to which she was attached. The nearer he gets to Boston, the more frequently such attacks occur; in the last stages of the journey he loses his vehicle, his lover, and, almost, his life. But the mission succeeds, and the story concludes with the grateful citizens of Boston erecting a statue to Tanner—only to have it obscenely defaced, with the implication that Tanner himself did so before disappearing in a stolen car "without leaving a forwarding address" (3:186).

In later comments on the story, Zelazny referred to Tanner as an "anti-hero . . . someone who had been sort of trapped into being a hero and reaching a point where he couldn't turn back."[83] As with most Zelazny protagonists, there is more going on than can be summarized in a quick phrase. On one hand, Tanner is clearly intended, at least at first, to be an unsympathetic figure; the official who sends him on his mission tells him, "You have a big dead spot somewhere inside you where other people have something that lets them live together in society and be neighbors" (3:113). On the other, he is in a line from heroes such as Conrad and Sam, oppositional figures who in their younger days were willing to employ violence to achieve their goals but who wind up performing heroic deeds on behalf of others, the difference being that Tanner's transgressions were committed in his own service and not on behalf of a greater cause. Damon Knight would not grant Tanner the relative glory of the anti-hero, writing to Zelazny, "Your characters are usually loners, but Hell does not fit that pattern. . . . a Hell's Angel without other angels is not an Angel, he's a bum."[84]

What really distinguishes Tanner from Zelazny's other loners is the degree to which he is contradictory but never really conflicted. He is a criminal but not a sociopath; he is capable of empathy but almost always expresses it through violence. Before setting out on the run to Boston he prevents Denny, his younger brother, from risking his life as one of the drivers by assaulting Denny and leaving him with broken bones that prevent his driving. When Greg, Tanner's co-driver, decides the mission is doomed and tries to turn back, Tanner beats him into submission and then, during the bucolic interlude in Pennsylvania, seeks medical treatment for him. He saves Cornelia from the wastelands, but only after killing all the men in her gang. He successfully completes his mission, and then—like Sam—disappears on his own terms. For Krulik, Tanner's rejection of gratitude proves that the outlaw "may have been affected by his experiences" but "doesn't seem to have changed much." Lindskold, however, concludes that the "real journey" of the story is not the run through Damnation Alley but "the journey within Hell's emotional life, a journey that teaches him to transfer his small, personal loyalties to the larger community."[85]

Has Tanner in fact found redemption? Zelazny hints at an answer in two offhand remarks by Tanner that appear early and late in the story. When told that part of his responsibility during his mission would be to kill any drivers of the other vehicles who try to turn back, Tanner says, "That might be fun" (3:113). Yet on the verge of completing his journey, after he uses his vehicle's weaponry to mow down members of an attacking biker gang, Cornelia says, approvingly, "You're taking the whole damn club!" Tanner replies, "It ain't that much fun" (3:172). In Flannery O'Connor's 1953 short story "A Good Man

Is Hard to Find," an escaped killer who calls himself the Misfit declares that, in a world without the certainty of Christ, there is "no pleasure but mean-ness"—but, after committing the supremely mean act of murder, concludes, "It ain't no real pleasure in life."[86] It is likely that Zelazny, the English major and omnivorous reader, would have encountered O'Connor's most famous work. Perhaps this subtle moment in an unsubtle story—a story that other-wise lacks the literary referentiality that marked so much of Zelazny's major early work—is a hint that, although he may not yet be ready to accept public acclaim as a hero, Tanner, like O'Connor's Misfit, has also been pushed to at least the possibility of reevaluating his own actions.

As his writing career continued to accelerate, Zelazny was increasingly occupied with not only the craft but also the business of writing. The literary agent Robert P. Mills had handled the sales of Zelazny's first three books to Ace, but Zelazny negotiated the sale of *Lord of Light* to Lawrence Ashmead at Doubleday without involving Mills. This omission led Mills, in late 1966, to suggest that Zelazny no longer needed his services. Why Zelazny would not have relied on his agent is unclear. Kovacs's speculation that Zelazny didn't want to have to pay for the services of an agent that he didn't think he needed seems quite plausible given the unwavering independence that the young author had already showed in his development as a writer. Within a year, however, at the urging of Robert Silverberg, Zelazny signed with the Henry Morrison Agency.[87]

At the same time as Zelazny's status as a professional writer solidified, in terms of the business of writing and his increasing fame among science fiction readers, he raised his profile among his fellow sf writers by serving, beginning in June 1967, as secretary-treasurer of the Science Fiction Writers of America. The inevitable experience of the first-time administrator, to be overwhelmed with paperwork, was intensified by upheavals in the lives of the organization's president (Robert Silverberg) and vice-president (James Blish) that led to Zelazny's having to attend even more continually to the demands of countless authors, editors, and agents. He stepped down after one term.[88]

His involvement in the administration of SFWA also led to his editing the anthology *Nebula Award Stories Three*, containing works published in 1967 by Nebula Award winners and finalists. Zelazny included two stories that were not on that year's final ballot: J. G. Ballard's "The Cloud Sculptors of Coral D," a representative entry in the author's elegantly decadent Vermillion Sands sequence, and Gary Wright's "Mirror of Ice," a lean, efficient example of the subgenre of the science fiction sports story. In his introductions to the stories Zelazny praised Ballard as "one of the greatest cloud-sculptors I have ever witnessed in action" and approvingly categorized Wright's entry as "a story of freedom, violence . . . as cold and clean as a bottle of akvavit frozen in a block of ice, or the winds that lash the highest mountains."[89] These comments may explain Zelazny's decision to push the limits of editorial discretion by including the two stories, given that the comments could just as readily describe the twin impulses of his own work toward language-soaked fantastic landscapes and toward violent revolt against systemic restraint.

Zelazny apparently had expressed his admiration directly to Ballard, and the feeling was mutual, as Ballard indicated when he granted permission to reprint his story:

> Many thanks for taking The Cloud-Sculptors for your anthology. Thanks too for all the complimentary remarks. For what it's worth, I have always tremendously enjoyed your science fiction. I remember reading a long story in Amazing a good many years ago, Starships Waiting, I think it was called, which was a sure sign that a brilliant new talent had appeared in an otherwise dull sky.[90]

Ballard's enthusiasm for Zelazny's work is echoed throughout the latter's correspondence during his rise to fame in the mid-1960s. In 1965 Michael Moorcock wrote, "I have read little of your work in American magazines, but what I have read has shown a potential talent that gleams out like a life-saving beacon to one wading through quicksands"; in that same year, Judith Merril, editor of the annual *Year's Best SF* anthologies, urged Zelazny to inform her of any of his stories that might be appearing outside sf magazines. A young James Sallis, one of the most distinctive voices in sf short fiction before becoming an acclaimed crime novelist, recalled *Conrad* "exciting me as a reader, intimidating the writer part of me" and conveyed Disch's desire "to relay his respect and admiration." The author of *Psycho*, Robert Bloch, wrote, "I have been reading you, of course, and with pleasure, these past several years," and Philip K. Dick declared, "At this point I have no doubt that you will—or have already—displaced Bradbury as the finest sf and fantasy writer. You will be remembered the most, out of all of us." Harlan Ellison perhaps summed up the response of Zelazny's colleagues most succinctly: "You have been at it such a short time yet are so much better than all the rest of us."[91]

By the time of the 1968 Worldcon, held over Labor Day weekend in Oakland, California, Roger Zelazny had completed the first half-dozen years of his career as a professional science fiction and fantasy writer. In that time he had published three novels, a collection, an edited anthology, and approximately sixty works of short fiction. He had been nominated for the Hugo Award eight times and the Nebula Award seven, winning each award twice—including, at the Oakland Worldcon, his second Hugo for Best Novel for *Lord of Light*. Of equal significance to the writer who began studying the literary marketplace in grade school and turned away from writing poetry in part because one couldn't earn one's living at it, his books were beginning to be not only popular but financially successful. Lawrence Ashmead reported the sale of paperback rights to *Lord of Light* for $5,000 (approximately $36,800 in 2020 dollars) to be "unusually high for a science fiction book." This statement was confirmed by Zelazny's new agent, Henry Morrison, who informed his client, "I don't think Doubleday has ever had a science fiction novel that earned that kind of money before."[92] Although Zelazny's increasing concentration on novels had finally caused his output of short fiction to wane, with only five standalone stories appearing in 1968, the shift in focus was paying off. Through Morrison he had contracts for four new novels with three different publishers, and, for the first time, his income from writing equaled his income from his job with the Social Security Administration.[93]

In May 1969 the thirty-one-year-old Zelazny and his wife Judy both resigned from their jobs. Zelazny was now supporting his household solely with his writing income, a fact that led him, for the rest of his career, to devote most of his time and creative energy to writing novels rather than short fiction. How this new distribution of labor would affect the quality of his writing remained to be seen.

CHAPTER 3

DO QUIT YOUR DAY JOB
1969–1971

Zelazny's move to full-time writing required a practical emphasis on books rather than short fiction, and he had in fact been working steadily on novels since finishing *Lord of Light* in early 1966. In the three years between completing that landmark work and resigning from his job, Zelazny completed three new novels and expanded "Damnation Alley" to novel length. As these books appeared during his first year as a full-time writer, it became apparent that his ambition and innovation were now matched by an equal degree of unpredictability. In a little more than a year readers were greeted with *Isle of the Dead* (1969), a carefully modulated far-future science fiction story and the first Zelazny novel that did not incorporate work previously published in magazines,[1] the myth-drenched, overtly experimental *Creatures of Light and Darkness* (1969), *Damnation Alley* (1969), a straightforward, near-future post-apocalyptic sf adventure, and *Nine Princes in Amber* (1970), a heroic fantasy drawing on Arthurian legend.

The novel-length version of *Damnation Alley*, which Zelazny expanded from the original novella at the suggestion of his agent, provides more explanation of how its protagonist Hell Tanner became the outlaw he is.[2] On the whole, the additional material nonetheless slows the momentum of the original story, particularly when Zelazny allows himself lyrical interludes, typical of his earlier work and often quite striking in themselves, which are significantly different in tone from the rest of the narrative. There is little reason to disagree with Krulik's conclusion that the additional material does not "really satisfy the simple requirements of an action-adventure tale" or with Zelazny's stated preference for the novella version.[3] The other three novels of the 1969–1970 period are significant achievements that, collectively, mark the conclusion of the first period of Zelazny's career while also looking ahead to the work that would follow in the 1970s.

Given the wide range of both subject matter and tone among these works and what, over the years, became received wisdom concerning Zelazny's motivations in writing them, it is worth noting that the sequence of composition does not match the sequence of publication. Beginning with *Lord of Light*, Kovacs establishes the order of composition as follows:

Lord of Light: written May 1965–March 1966; published September 1967
Nine Princes in Amber: written c. April 1966–February 1967; published June 1970
Creatures of Light and Darkness: written "intermittently" summer 1966[?]– March 1967; published September 1969
Isle of the Dead: written c. April 1967–mid-1968; published February 1969

The publication of *Nine Princes in Amber* three years after *Lord of Light* and a year after Zelazny became a full-time writer led some to conclude that the first Amber novel was a deliberate shift toward more commercial writing. Both the novel that many consider Zelazny's finest and the novel that became the opening volume of his greatest popular success were, however, written consecutively.[4] Zelazny wrote *Nine Princes in Amber* not because of a market imperative but from a desire to try something different—while working on *Creatures of Light and Darkness*.

As the timeline above indicates, *Isle of the Dead*, the first novel to appear after *Lord of Light*, was actually the last of the novels to be composed in this time frame. Zelazny's fourth published novel appeared, as did the first three, as a paperback original from Ace Books, this time as part of the renowned series Ace Science Fiction Specials edited by Terry Carr. For the series, named to evoke the television specials of the era (one-time events that stood out from regular programming),[5] Carr solicited original novels and reprinted recent work from well-established writers (Clifford D. Simak, James Blish, and Philip K. Dick), rising stars (Ursula K. Le Guin, Michael Moorcock, and Joanna Russ) and less famous but equally distinctive voices (Alexei Panshin, John Sladek, Keith Roberts, and D. G. Compton). The cover of each novel consisted of original artwork by Leo and Diane Dillon, whose paintings, "similar to wood-block prints: rough, sometimes semi-abstract shapes powerfully assembled,"[6] stood largely outside the traditions of genre illustration, and the back covers featured endorsements from other sf authors that often went well beyond the normal "cover blurb."[7] As Malcolm Edwards and John Clute have noted, Carr showed an "extraordinary capacity to commission or purchase work which, once published, seemed inevitable. His authors seemed to speak to the heart of their times."[8]

Zelazny's contribution to the series is narrated by Francis Sandow, born in 1965 but, thanks to the time-dilating effects of repeated interstellar travel combined with ongoing medical advances, still alive almost a thousand years later. Sandow is a "worldscaper," the only human practitioner of the religion of the alien Pei'ans, whose adepts, bonded with a specific deity, become telepaths with the power to modify and create new worlds. Over the centuries he has also become "one of the hundred wealthiest men in the galaxy" and lives in luxury on the planet Homefree, also known as Sandow's World (12).[9] Sandow's splendid isolation is interrupted, however, by a series of unexpected communications: mysterious envelopes containing pictures of individuals in his life who he thought were dead, a request for immediate aid from Ruth Laris, an old friend, and a request for a visit from Marling, his Pei'an mentor. After failing to find Ruth, he is visited by an agent of Earth's "Central Intelligence" who seeks his aid in recovering stolen "Recall Tapes," downloads of individual minds and personalities, all corresponding to the figures in Sandow's life whose pictures he has received. Sandow refuses to cooperate and, after receiving another message from Marling, departs for the planet Megapei. Marling tells Sandow that the mysterious pictures are from Gringrin, a Pei'an who, after failing the final test to become a worldscaper, is enraged that the Earthman Sandow passed and seeks revenge. After participating telepathically in his mentor's death ritual, Sandow travels to Illyria, the planet he formed that contains the Isle of the Dead, intending to defeat Gringrin once and for all.

On Illyria, Sandow finds Gringrin badly wounded and learns that Mike Shandon, a human telepath and corporate spy whom Sandow thought he had killed back on Earth, has convinced Belion, the sworn enemy of Sandow's patron deity Shimbo, to abandon Gringrin and bond with Shandon instead. Reluctantly allied to defeat their common enemy, Sandow and Gringrin sail downriver to the Isle of the Dead, where the gods Shimbo and Belion force a final showdown between Sandow and Shandon, their Earthmen proxies. Sandow finally kills Shandon for good, but only after seeing two of the downloaded figures from the pictures, including his late wife Kathy, die in front of him. Exhausted, heartbroken, and convinced that, gods or no, the human condition is "rubbish and pain" (174), Sandow refuses to rescue Lady Karle, another of the downloaded figures, who is trapped in a cave. But he makes peace with Gringrin, who, before he dies, reveals the location of the still-missing Ruth Laris. After accompanying Gringrin on his mystical death journey, Sandow has a vision of the many worlds he has created and realizes, "I had done something, and I knew how to do more" (186). He then frees Lady Karle and leaves Illyria, determined to rescue his friend Ruth.

Zelazny acknowledged that *Isle of the Dead* draws on both the themes and the voice of his novelette "This Moment of the Storm,"[10] and the novel does include many now-familiar elements: the jaunty yet lyrical first-person voice, the hero with a history of violence who nonetheless just wishes to be left alone and whose near-immortality seems to make every loss that much harder to take, the enduring power of religious myth. *Isle of the Dead* provides a notably different reading experience than do Zelazny's previous novels, however. Francis Sandow possesses the comprehensive literacy we would expect from a Zelazny protagonist and is not above the occasional reference to British poetry or jazz, but there are fewer such allusions than in earlier works. The signature stylistic moves—paragraphs that can go on for two pages or consist of a single sentence, intensely metaphoric and personifying descriptions of landscape (e.g., "Outside, the sun, an amber giant now, was ambushed by a wispy strand which gave up in less than a minute and swam away" [15]), long stretches of unattributed dialogue—are balanced by straightforward procedural narrative as Sandow discovers bit by bit the information he needs. The plot, although as busy as that of *This Immortal* or *Lord of Light*, feels more pared-down and under the author's control. If Sandow is an expert at building worlds, by this point Zelazny is an expert at pacing his narratives.

The novel also represents Zelazny's most nuanced treatment to date of the theme of immortality. Delany notes that Zelazny's early work, unlike the classic view of immortality as more curse than blessing, suggests that within an infinitely long life, "each moment becomes infinitely fascinating because there is so much more to relate it to; each event will take on new harmonies as it is struck by the overtones of history and like experiences before. . . . No other writer . . . can evoke so much hunger for the stuff of living itself."[11] Sandow's reflections on his own immortality certainly display a "hunger for the stuff of living," but in a context not of enjoying its presence as much as fearing its loss: "the longer one exists the more strongly one becomes infected with a sense of mortality" (22). A search of Ruth's abandoned apartment leads him to consider "how life redistributes what once was meaningful amidst the always to be foreign, killing its personal magic, save in a memory you carry" (43). A later reflection on his path to near-immortality reveals that he sought training from the Pei'ans because it was "the one thing that might save [him] the feeling of being the last survivor of Atlantis walking down Broadway" (74). In an extended aside, after noting that "the longer you've been around, the more of them [memories] you have," Sandow asserts that he values sleep insofar as it "puts brackets around each day": "When I have been swamped emotionally, I sleep. When I awaken, thoughts of other days come forth[;] . . . sleep gives memory a chance to rev its engine and hand me back my head each day" (101–102). For the near-immortal, processing the stuff of living— "joy, sorrow, love, hate, satiation, peace" (102)—is an unceasing task, one that weighs more heavily with each passing decade.

Sandow, nonetheless, neither seeks nor longs for death. Near the end of the novel, convinced that he has lost everything, he remains stubbornly committed to his own survival: "I intend to rage against the dying of the light, fighting and howling every damn step of the way. . . . I would never opt for the easy way out. I wanted to live, pain and all" (184). Having evoked Dylan Thomas's "Do Not Go Gentle into That Good Night," Sandow then cites *Fruits of the Earth*, which André Gide wrote shortly before his death: "You could tell that [Gide] was saying goodbye and did not want to go, despite everything. That is how I feel about it" (184). Sandow's concluding epiphany—that all the worlds he has created meant that he "had hurled something into the pit . . . [and] when [he] walked that Valley, they would remain after [him]" (186)—leaves little doubt that the major decisions of his life have been products of his hunger for the stuff of living, from the day-to-day impulse to stay home in order to avoid potentially lethal conflict to the more long-term and profound decision to embrace an alien religion that will enable him to create worlds.

Also distinguishing *Isle of the Dead* from Zelazny's previous novels is the degree to which the story comments on contemporary real-world issues. Zelazny indicated on more than one occasion both his disinclination to reveal his own political leanings in his fiction and his disdain for fiction in which the story was subsumed within the politics.[12] This does not mean that he had not previously, in Delany's words, used "images that vibrate sympathetically with the times," be it the general anti-establishment inclinations of Conrad, Sam, or Hell Tanner, or a specific point such as one of Render's patients in "He Who Shapes," a politician with a morbid fear of assassination in a story written the year after the assassination of President Kennedy.[13] Nonetheless, the book was written and published in the late 1960s, the era of the Vietnam War, the civil rights movement, the initial expressions of modern feminism and environmentalism, and, more generally, the eruptions of a youth culture determined to reject institutions it considered at best boring and at worst repressive. Perhaps it is no surprise, then, that a novel written in this era by an author who did not respond well to "anyone or anything capable of exercising power over [him]"[14] and published as part of a series whose authors seemed to speak to the heart of their times would, however obliquely, reference the issues of the day. One of *Isle*'s earliest mentions of Sandow's past is the traumatic memory of his service, and the loss of his younger brother, in "a small and neatly contained war in Asia" (6). Although he has profited in the extreme from an intergalactic entrepreneurial capitalism, he has no reverence for either money or the mechanisms of its acquisition, imagining money as the leaves and branches of "a Big Tree as old as human society. . . . There are names written on these leaves, and some fall off and new ones grow on, so that in a few seasons all the names have been changed. But the tree stays pretty much the same" (13). When another wealthy individual assumes that Sandow is traveling in order to secure a new business deal, he is insulted: "All that bastard thought about . . . was stacking up his wealth. He automatically assumed I spent my time the same way" (51). Negotiating with a representative of Earth's Central Intelligence Department, he condemns bureaucracies as "neuter machines" that "parody their own functions" as they combine "the worst of both father-image and mother-image—i.e., the security of the womb and the authority of an omniscient leader" (62). Even the novel's most idiosyncratic sidebar concerning social issues—an extended complaint about service-industry expectations of tipping—may be read, in context, as a gripe about a system in which everything is predicated not on principles of service but on money changing hands.[15]

The novel's most fully developed evocation of the issues of its day, and a sign of things to come in Zelazny's work, is its foregrounding of environmentalism. *Isle* opens with Sandow's declaration that life reminds him of "the beaches around Tokyo Bay," which he recalls as "a terrible expanse of dirty water . . . smelling and slopping and chill close at hand, like Time when it wears away objects, delivers them, removes them" (5). There follows a catalog of detritus to be found in the bay, Sandow's first statement about his dead brother, and the observation that "sometimes, I suppose, things that are taken away might, by some capricious current, be returned to the beach" (6). By the end of the two-page paragraph he has introduced both plot (hearing unexpectedly from figures thought long buried in the past) and theme (how to cope with the accumulated memories of an abnormally long life) through the image of a polluted body of water. Later, when he arrives at Illyria, he dwells on the damage done to the planet's—his planet's—landscape by the "Green Development Company," a front for his adversary Gringrin: "The trees were different, the animals were. . . . The insects all had stings and the flowers stank. There were no straight, tall trees. They were all of them twisted and squat. . . . Judging from the sky, a quarter of the world was on fire" (107–108). When he concludes, at novel's end, that his worldshaping had in fact "hurled something into the pit," he returns to the image of Tokyo Bay to make his point: "Whatever the Bay claimed, I had made some replacements, to thumb my nose at it. I had done something, and I knew how to do more" (186). Such imagery previews the environmental concerns of later novels such as *Bridge of*

Ashes and *Eye of Cat*. It also suggests that, if the Ace Science Fiction Specials did speak to the heart of their times, the character of Francis Sandow—damaged by war, contemptuous of mere material acquisitiveness, alarmed by environmental degradation—is very much of those times.

The critical response to *Isle of the Dead* showed the same range of responses and concerns as with his previous work, with one reviewer condemning its *"mélange* of irrelevant high-school cultural reference" and "mediocre plot," another praising its "wholly new, alien, *[sic]* mythology," and still another calling it Zelazny's finest work to date. Reviewers also noted how the character of Sandow fit into the tradition of the wealthy amateur detective, with one specifically comparing the novel to John D. MacDonald's tales of the private detective Travis McGee.[16] The novel earned Zelazny his eighth Nebula Award nomination.

Within a few months of *Isle's* publication, Zelazny's next novel, *Creatures of Light and Darkness*, appeared. In what appears to be a departure from his carefully cultivated professionalism and acute market awareness, Zelazny claimed that he wrote *Creatures* primarily for his own amusement while working on other projects and, at least initially, without any thought of publication.[17] *Creatures* in fact sat on the shelf for almost a year until, after Zelazny mentioned the novel to Delany, the latter in turn mentioned it to an editor at Doubleday, who then asked to see the manuscript and, eventually, bought it.[18] Its dedication reads: "To Chip Delany, Just Because."[19]

It is easy to see why the editors at Doubleday, the publisher of *Lord of Light*, were drawn to *Creatures*. Like the earlier work, *Creatures* not only uses non-Western mythology to tell a far-future science fiction story that has the feel of fantasy but also lyrically presents epic confrontations among gods who try and, ultimately, fail to maintain control over their worlds. *Creatures*, however, marks a more radical departure from conventional narrative than does *Lord of Light* and Zelazny's most wholehearted embrace of the techniques of literary modernism.

A recent survey of American literature identifies a "key formal characteristic" of modernism as "its construction out of fragments. . . . Modernist literature is often notable for what it omits: the explanations, interpretations, connections, summaries, and distancing that provide continuity, perspective, and security in earlier literatures. . . . The effect may be shocking and unsettling;

the experience of reading will be challenging and difficult."[20] One would be hard pressed to find a more accurate description of *Creatures* with regard to both the author's formal choices and the effect of those choices on the reader. Whereas *Lord of Light* presents a story focused on its protagonist and unfolding over the course of seven long, detailed chapters, *Creatures*—two thirds as long as the earlier work—presents a large cast of characters in forty-one sections that range from chapters of more than twenty pages to fragments of fewer than fifty words. Conventional transitions between major scenes are almost nonexistent, a key flashback is presented in the form of an eight-page poem, the novel's conclusion is presented as a play script, and—unusual for a work of genre fiction at this time, even at the height of the New Wave—the entire novel is narrated in the present tense.[21]

The novel's most sustained narrative section is its opening, "Prelude in the House of the Dead," in which Anubis, Master of the House of the Dead, summons a nameless individual who has served him for a thousand years. Anubis names his servant Wakim, forces him to submit to a series of physical mutilations resulting in the replacement of body parts by machines, leads him through a Socratic dialogue regarding the nature of life and identity, and explains how the "Middle Worlds" are held in balance between the House of Life and the House of Death, each house keeping balance and order by either granting life or taking it away as needed (22–25). After Wakim proves himself by defeating a creature named Dargoth, Anubis orders him to seek out and kill "the Prince Who Was a Thousand," one of 283 immortals who roam the Middle Worlds (33).

A brief, seemingly disconnected section titled "The Waking of the Red Witch" is followed by the next sustained narrative, "Death, Life, the Magician and Roses," which moves the story to Blis, one of the Middle Worlds, where death is so rare that a man's suicide serves as a sideshow attraction. We are introduced to two immortals: Madrak the preacher, who in the past served the Prince Who Was a Thousand, and Vramin the poet-magician, formerly the "Angel of the Seventh Station" (46). We also meet the nurse Megra of Kalgan and the Steel General, "one of the very few masters of temporal fugue in the entire universe" (43). Wakim arrives, publicly fights all comers, and embraces Megra—observed, at an unexplained distance, by the Red Witch. After the brief "Interlude in the House of Life," where Osiris sends his son Horus on the same mission as Wakim, and an even briefer glimpse of a "Dark Horse Shadow" in the House of the Dead, we return, in "The Changing of the Tide," to Blis, where death has arrived in the form of a plague. Wakim fights Madrak, who is astonished that Wakim is in fact a "genuine fugue master" (62) who can instantly travel back and forth among different points in time. Madrak responds by summoning the Steel General, who has the same power.

After these opening sections, comprising approximately a third of the novel, the story unfolds in increasingly short, disjointed fragments. Alliances are formed, battles fought, true identities discovered, background explicated. Wakim is revealed to be Set the Destroyer, whose weapons of destruction are scattered across the worlds after a failed attempt to destroy a malevolent force identified as The Thing That Cries in the Night. The Prince is Thoth, who formerly ruled over all of existence but, distracted by his own struggles to contain The Thing That Cries in the Night, was overthrown by the Angels of the Stations. Thus, Anubis's and Osiris's campaigns to destroy the Prince, and Anubis's determination to keep Set/Wakim ignorant of his true identity, are attempts to hold onto power as controllers of the Houses of Life and Death. The Red Witch is Isis, mother of Horus, variously wife of both Osiris and Set—the latter of whom, via temporal fugue, is Thoth's father and son. Accounts of confrontation and battle are interspersed with episodes and fragments grandiose, absurd, and occasionally grotesque: Thoth maintains the consciousness of his wife, Nephytha, on a world where the ocean hovers over the sky; the recovery of Set's weapons involves, among other things, stealing a pair of sacred shoes whose worshipers supplicate the objects to "lighten our hearts and uplift our soles" (126); Megra of Kalgan has been fused with a prognosticating machine so that, as an "electrical- mechanical-biological votary of the god Logic" (158) still human from the waist down, she can answer questions if provided with sufficient sexual pleasure. By the end of the novel, both Anubis and Osiris are dead, Thoth has regained control of the Middle Worlds, Horus and Vramin respectively rule the Houses of Life and Death, Madrak leaves on a "pilgrimage of repentance" (189), and Set has disappeared into the many worlds, continually battling monsters created by Thoth in order to keep the Destroyer occupied and, therefore, the universe in balance.

Modernist fragmentation notwithstanding, within this swirl of gods and monsters are many of the same themes and concerns that we have seen in

Zelazny's other novels. Most obvious, and most similar to *Lord of Light*, is Zelazny's use of non-Western mythology to tell a story of fantastic confrontations between gods in science-fictional terms: Wakim, Megra, and the Steel General are mixtures of human and machine; births in the city of Kalgan are often the result of "a gene pattern . . . constructed to satisfy the parents' specific wishes" (44); the description of Skagganauk Abyss, a "chasm in the sky" whither the Thing That Cries Out in the Night is ultimately dispatched, matches that of a black hole (155). But whereas Zelazny presents the gods of *Lord of Light* as human beings clearly matched to their Hindu models and operating, however spectacularly, in a measurable universe, he never confirms whether the characters in *Creatures* are human, alien, or something else, and his application of the ancient Egyptian pantheon is, depending on one's perspective, either playful or erratic, mixing and matching the relationships among the major figures as suits the purposes of his story (e.g., in actual Egyptian tradition, Set was never partner to Isis or father to Thoth).

Creatures also diverges from *Lord of Light* in its consideration of power, rebellion, and the dangerous relationships between gods and ordinary beings. The characters in the novel who are represented as Egyptian deities scramble to control their domains as frantically, and as violently, as the humans who assume the personae of Hindu deities in *Lord of Light*. Both Sam in *Lord of Light* and Wakim/Set in *Creatures* battle the prevailing power structures, but Wakim's main goal, unlike Sam's, is not to dethrone the gods but to reclaim his own identity.[22] If Sam is fighting for the overall good, Wakim/Set is fighting for himself. *Creatures'* truest figure of rebellion is the Steel General, the eternally reconstituted idealistic revolutionary, who survives from the twentieth century: "He flew with the Lafayette Escadrille. . . . He helped to hold Stalingrad in the dead of winter. . . . He was beaten in Little Rock, had acid thrown in his face in Berkeley . . . again he fought the rebel battle . . . his ideals mean more to him than his flesh" (76). And like Sam, who, by the concluding pages of *Lord of Light*, speaks in favor of "negotiation, rather than unnecessary bloodshed" (280), the Steel General demonstrates at least some awareness of the consequences of the actions of superbeings. In support of the Prince, the Steel General engages in a "fugue battle" with Wakim that threatens to destroy the planet Blis. When Vramin, witnessing the battles, pleads with them to stop before they "lay waste to the entire world," the Steel General acknowledges that "civilians are dying," but Wakim laughs and asks, "What difference does a uniform make in the House of the Dead?" (88). The gods, in Zelazny's view, are as oblivious as they are omnipotent.[23]

An anonymous UK newspaper review that called the novel a "bizarre coagulation" signaled what would prove to be a mixed critical response. Reviews in fanzines of the day reflected this divided opinion: *Luna* considered the characters remote and noted the novel's lack of a true central character with whom readers could empathize; *Renaissance* found it "uneasy in tone"; *Science Fiction Review* claimed a "curious hollowness" in the prose but noted approvingly the author's obvious joy in writing; *Phantasmicom* proclaimed *Creatures* "Zelazny's best novel." This lack of consensus is starkly displayed in the comments in the two most prominent sf magazines by the two most prominent contemporary reviewers (and two of the most respected sf writers). As noted in Chapter 2, James Blish strongly disapproved of Zelazny's application of myth to science fiction; his review of *Creatures* in *F&SF* dismissed the novel as "a flat failure" with an inconsistent tone and confusing narrative. In contrast, Algis Budrys, reviewing the novel in *Galaxy*, declared the novel "full of adventure and poetry . . . possessing a nearly perfect clarity"—but also noted that the book was "lacking guideposts" and suggested that one such novel was plenty.[24] Perhaps the clearest evidence for the novel's mixed reception—and a reminder of the extraordinary response Zelazny's work had received to date—is the fact that *Creatures of Light and Darkness* was the first of Zelazny's novels that, either as novel or novella, was not a finalist for the Hugo or Nebula awards.

Was the novel, in fact, a failure? The publisher that acquired *Lord of Light* clearly did not think so; neither did Delany or Budrys. Yet the *Luna* and *Renaissance* reviews accused Zelazny of self-parody, a charge also leveled by at least one review of *Lord of Light*. Based on Zelazny's own comments, the *Luna* and *Renaissance* reviewers may have been right. In a 1969 interview Zelazny said that he "intended [*Creatures*] to be a parody of what is sometimes referred to as the 'New Wave'"; three years later, he claimed, "I discovered it was a self-parody." We have already seen, in Zelazny's 1965 letter to Damon Knight, the young author wondering if he was undervaluing pure narrative; in the 1972 interview he acknowledged publicly that, after *Creatures*, he "was getting tired of this sort of thing."[25]

But if the novel was in fact self-parody, it was, as the author eventually acknowledged, "more than a piece of self-indulgence. . . . It was also a learning book."[26] In rejecting the novel for Ace Books, Terry Carr complained that "the outcome of each battle seems to depend on the author's whim" as opposed to the actual skills and power of the characters.[27] One might counter that such seeming arbitrariness reflects the author's theme of the arbitrariness of the uncaring gods. What is more, *Creatures*, into which the author admitted he "threw everything but the kitchen sink,"[28] is a novel whose tumult and seeming slapdash is inextricably bound up with the question of identity. Even as Wakim/Set is trying to discover his personal identity—whether he is a servant of the gods or a god himself—the author is trying to discover his literary identity—whether he is fundamentally a wordsmith or a storyteller.

The 1970 publication of *Nine Princes in Amber* seemed to answer in the affirmative for storytelling. The timeline for the novel's publication indicates, however, that, for the author, the question may still have been open. Although Zelazny had completed the novel in early 1967 and had editors interested at both Doubleday (Lawrence Ashmead, who had acquired *Lord of Light*) and Ace (Terry Carr, who wanted the novel for the Ace Science Fiction Specials), Zelazny did not submit it until a year later, and then only at the prompting of a second Doubleday editor, Mark Haefele, who had been told of the project by Delany.[29] The novel finally appeared from Doubleday in June 1970, three years after Zelazny finished writing it.

In a 1968 letter to Haefele, Zelazny referred to *Princes* as "something a bit lighter than my usual fare, sort of sword-and-sorcery and something which I would have fun writing."[30] The novel is certainly more straightforward and accessible than either *Lord of Light* or *Creatures*; however, unlike the determinedly pull-the-plow storytelling of *Damnation Alley*, the first Amber novel, though inarguably within the epic fantasy tradition, takes many liberties with that tradition even as it exemplifies Zelazny's well-established approaches, themes, and concerns.

Like *Creatures*, *Princes* begins with a character who does not know who he is. Unlike *Creatures*, the story is told in the first person by the amnesiac narrator, who wakes up on page one not in a fantasy landscape but in a hospital in New York State in the author's present day. Escaping from the hospital, the narrator learns that his name is Carl Corey, he was hospitalized after an auto accident, and his sister is paying for his care. He also immediately begins to display both an instinct for survival and a willingness to resort to violence. He makes his way to the home of his sister, Flora, where he discovers a deck of cards fashioned after the Tarot but containing Trumps bearing unique images of exotically dressed and posed men and women—including one with his own image. He recognizes the eight men and four women by name: they are his brothers and sisters. He also recalls for the first time the word "*Amber* . . . charged with a mighty longing and a massive nostalgia . . . the name of a place I once had known" (19).[31]

Corey takes pains to hide his amnesia as he meets more members of his family: his brother Random, who takes him to Amber in a journey that begins as a ride in Flora's Mercedes but turns magical as the landscape changes around them; his brother Julian, guardian of the Forest of Arden, who reveals that another brother, Eric, has taken control of Amber; and his sister Deirdre, who is fleeing from Eric's rule and for whom Corey feels a particularly strong affinity. Corey, Random, and Deirdre, at Random's urging, travel to Remba, an undersea city that (as its name implies) is a mirror image of Amber and where, Random believes, his brother can recover his memory. After he walks a reversed image of the Pattern that lies at the heart of Amber, Corey's memory is restored. Corey is in fact Corwin, a prince of Amber, "the greatest city which had ever existed or ever would exist. . . . Every other city that existed was but a reflection of a shadow of some phase of Amber" (60). He has been living on Earth, another shadow of Amber, since the reign of Elizabeth I, exiled by Eric, and robbed of his memory. Now understanding his goal, which is to defeat Eric and claim the throne for himself, he uses the Pattern to transport himself to Amber.

Once there, Corwin quickly regains control of his powers, including the use of the Trumps, through which members of the royal family can both communicate and teleport. He forms an alliance with another brother, Bleys, to depose Eric, and recruits a navy of warriors from various shadow worlds to complement Bleys's army. The two brothers move against Eric but the campaign fails, in part because Eric has acquired the "Jewel of Judgment," which grants him many powers. Eric takes Corwin prisoner, blinds him, and throws him into a dungeon; Corwin pronounces a curse on Eric and languishes for three years, consumed by hatred and despair bordering on insanity. Corwin, who had displayed extraordinary powers of healing on the shadow Earth, eventually regains his sight, however. He then receives a sudden, magical visit from Dworkin, the mad wizard/artist who designed both the Pattern and the Trumps, and escapes by simply walking through a picture he tricks Dworkin into drawing on his cell wall. After a long recovery Corwin discovers that the curse he pronounced from the dungeon has manifested in Amber: The "peaceful valley of Garnath" has become a dark, malformed place, "a symbol of my hate for Eric," but also a new gateway to Amber through which shadow forces can enter. The novel concludes as Corwin sails "into Shadow" (119), already plotting his revenge.

One need go no further, perhaps, than Zelazny's reference to *Princes* as "sort of sword and sorcery" for an immediate sense of the novel. The apparatus of the story—a magical world beyond our own, strange beasts to be encountered, forces of evil to be subdued, a more or less medieval European aesthetic, and plenty of swordfights—places it clearly within an epic fantasy tradition going back through Tolkien and Robert E. Howard to Arthurian legend, a tradition that, at the time of the novel's publication, had been recently explored in Fritz Leiber's Fafhrd and the Gray Mouser series and the stories of Elric of Melnibone by Zelazny's contemporary and sometime editor Michael Moorcock.

As Zelazny and his commentators have noted, however, the novel's deeper points of reference lie not in heroic fantasy but in science fiction and mainstream literature. The author cited the influence of "earlier science fiction" in his decision to open in the here and now before sending his protagonist off on fantastic adventures[32] and of Philip José Farmer's World of Tiers series of science fiction novels (1965–1993), with its "pocket universes" and "bickerings of immortal lords."[33] Lindskold notes the similarities between *Princes* and Henry Kuttner's *Dark World* (1946), whose first-person narrator is, like Corwin, "haunted by memories of a world he cannot quite recall."[34] And Zelazny acknowledged the influence of the British novelist Lawrence Durrell's *Alexandria Quartet* insofar as the Amber novels "comment on the nature of reality and people's perceptions of it."[35] Indeed, Zelazny originally intended to tell his story as Durrell told his, from the points of view of several different characters, but decided not to as his interest in Corwin grew.[36]

It is Corwin, and in particular Corwin's voice, that most distinctively sets the Amber series, and its first volume in particular, apart from more traditional high fantasy. Corwin is immediately recognizable as the glibly erudite, cynical, physically gifted but emotionally challenged protagonist of "The Doors of His Face," . . . *And Call Me Conrad*, and *Isle of the Dead*. But this is not a character or voice normally associated with the high fantasy tradition. As in *Lord of Light* and *Creatures*, the novel's dialogue alternates between the slangy and the Shakespearean. When Random tries to persuade Corwin to abandon his campaign against Eric, Corwin replies, "''Fraid I can't do that'" (80); a single page later, responding to another brother's demand for surrender, Corwin announces, "'Pray hear me, brother Caine, . . . and grant me this then: give me your leave to confer with my captains till the sun stands in high heaven'" (81). But Corwin's overall tone is much more like the world-weary voice of hardboiled crime fiction than the triumphant narratives of classic sword and sorcery, as in this description of a duel with Eric:

> I knew I still couldn't take him: he was a better man than I was, when it came to the blade. I cursed this, but I couldn't get around it. I tried three more elaborate attacks. . . . He parried me and made me retreat before his own attacks.
> Now don't get the wrong idea. I'm damn good. It's just that he seemed better. (65)

To the faithful Zelazny reader this was familiar territory; to the devotee of high fantasy the effect was, arguably, jarring—as it was to no less noteworthy a reader than Ursula K. Le Guin, who, in a famous assessment, took exception to "being jerked back and forth between Elfland and Poughkeepsie" and suggested that Zelazny was not taking his fantasy seriously.[37]

Ironically, one of the strongest defenses of this aspect of the novel came from the same critic who had harshly dismissed *Creatures*. Reviewing *Princes* in *F&SF*, James Blish not only praised the novel as "an adventure story with real originality and zest" but also declared that Zelazny's "mixture of poetry and slang . . . is not jarring here, since it makes a perfect fit with the hero's double life."[38] Zelazny's grounding his story in the here and now may be an homage to earlier science fiction, and the hero with amnesia may be a less-than-innovative narrative device (in one of the few negative comments in his review, Blish dismisses Corwin's amnesia as the stuff of "soap-opera").[39] But in arranging the story around the protagonist's move from the real world to a fantastic world—or, from the perspective of the royals of Amber, from a shadow world to the real world—Zelazny provides a structure that, as Blish indicates, both justifies and controls the language. In general, the dialogue becomes more formal and the descriptions more lyrical as Corwin returns to Amber, most notably in the memorable sequence describing Corwin and Random's auto trip from present-day New York State to the Forest of Arden and beyond. But even as Corwin lapses into slang while in Amber, his Earthbound language from the beginning hints at a broader erudition, as in his perceptions after waking up in the hospital: "It was dark outside and a handful of stars were standing naked beyond the window. I winked back at them. . . . In the State of Denmark there was the odor of decay. . . . I saw the Old Moon with the New Moon in her arms. . . . The night was bargaining weakly with the sun" (2, 4). Whether in Amber or in Shadow, Carl Corey, resident of Earth and popular songwriter, is also Corwin, Prince of Amber.[40]

If the novel's language reinforces the duality of Corwin's character, the move from Corey to Corwin is also, to employ the sort of pun Zelazny was fond of, a double-edged sword. Early on, when he realizes that his hospitalization stemmed not from an accident but from an attack, he states: "An anger, a terrible one, flared within the middle of my body. Anyone who tried to hurt me, to use me, did so at his own peril . . . I felt a strong desire to kill . . . and I knew that it was not the first time in my life I had felt this thing" (17). This capacity not merely for violence but for bloodlust and vengeance reaches its peak when, after his blinding and imprisonment, Corwin curses Eric, ensuring that his brother "would never rest easy on the throne, for the curse of a prince of Amber, pronounced in a fullness of fury, is always potent" (100).

Yet as he rediscovers his capacity for violence and revenge, Corwin also shows himself capable of mercy, from his refusal to kill Julian during their initial confrontation in the Forest of Arden—a refusal that astonishes Random—to his efforts, however futile, to minimize casualties during the military campaign against Eric. These impulses force him to admit, "My centuries on the shadow Earth had changed me, softened me perhaps, had done something to me which made me unlike my brothers" (82). When Corwin assesses the recruits for the army that will attempt to overthrow Eric, he notes, "[They were] loyal, devoted, honest, and too easily screwed by bastards like me and my brother. . . . Most of these troops were destined to die. I was the agent responsible for much of this. I felt some remorse" (71–72). As Bleys continues to recruit their army in the shadow worlds, Corwin's description of the process focuses on the horrific casualties of the warfare that Bleys encounters, including "nineteen thousand dead or missing in action as they passed through the jungles of a place [Corwin] didn't recognize, when the napalm fell upon them from the strange buzzing things that passed overhead" (77). And as he surveys his troops on the eve of battle, Corwin feels "tears come into [his] eyes, for the men who are not like the lords of Amber, living but a brief span and passing into dust, that so many of them must meet their ends upon the battlefields of the world" (87). As noted above, Zelazny wrote *Princes* in 1966 and early 1967, during the escalation of both the Vietnam War and public protest of that war. In its foregrounding of the true cost of war—loyal troops giving their lives in service to powerful men who may or may not deserve their loyalty—this fantasy adventure is as much a document of its time as is the science fiction novel Zelazny wrote immediately afterward, *Isle of the Dead*. For all that the author may have felt that his first novel-length foray into epic fantasy was lighter than his usual fare (and with due notice to the brilliance of . . . *And Call Me Conrad,* as well as the ambition and achievement of *Lord of Light*), *Nine Princes in Amber* stands with *Isle of the Dead* as Zelazny's most thoughtful book up to that time. And although by the end of the novel his story is not merely unresolved but is just beginning, Corey / Corwin is arguably Zelazny's most fully realized character yet and certainly the author's most effective match of voice to action.[41]

Now officially writing full-time, Zelazny managed to complete one more novel by the end of the 1960s, although it was not published until 1971.[42] Having begun his take on the heroic fantasy tradition, he returned to blending science fiction and fantasy with *Jack of Shadows*, a novel set on a nameless, tidally locked planet whose light side is subject to the rules of science but whose dark side is controlled by magic. Unlike other darksiders, whose powers are linked to specific locations, the title character, a legendary thief, "is himself a Power—one of the few mobile ones" (52).[43] Constrained in either full light or total darkness, Jack's abilities, including teleportation, are activated only in the shadows of the "Twilight Lands" (3) between the planet's light and dark sides. As the novel opens, Jack is in the Twilight Lands at the

Hellgames competition. Accused of planning to steal the competition's prize, the Hellflame jewel, he is summarily executed. Darksiders, though they lack souls, possess multiple lives, so Jack will return to the world after making his way back from the planet's Western Pole through the Dung Pits of Glyve. Enraged by both the physical pain and public humiliation of his execution, he expends almost as much energy plotting excruciating revenge on those responsible for his death—in particular, his old enemy the Lord of Bats—as he does on making the miserable journey through the Dung Pits.

Back in the world, and after an encounter with his former lover Rosalie, Jack is taken prisoner by the Lord of Bats but eventually escapes by forging his name in the Book of Ells, a logbook of darksiders who maintain the Shield that keeps their planet's dark side from completely freezing. In falsifying the book he breaks the compact that supersedes all other darkside concerns and disputes, causing the Lord of Bats to declare him an outcast. Unconcerned, Jack flees, pausing to visit his only friend, Morningstar, partly frozen into a twilight land mountainside so as to always face a sunrise that never arrives. Jack decides to solve his problems not merely by escaping but by conquering the dark side altogether.

Relocated to the light side of the planet, Jack assumes the identity of Jonathan Shade, a university professor, and gains access to computers in order to locate Kolwynia, the Key That Was Lost, which is necessary to his plans. On his return to the dark side Jack assumes total control of the dark regions of the planet. He enacts horrific revenge on all his enemies and forces Evene, the woman he loves, who had taken up with the Lord of Bats, to become his consort, keeping her enthralled with a magic spell. He claims High Dudgeon, the Lord of Bats' compound, as Shadow Guard, the retreat to which he had promised to bring Rosalie. But when she reappears and offers him his soul, which he had abandoned in the Dung Pits, he refuses, and she leaves him for good.

When Jack discovers that he can neither force those who maintain the Shield to do so nor maintain the Shield on his own, he descends to the center of the world and destroys the Great Machine that has maintained the planet's tidal lock. The planet begins to rotate; there will be no more light side and dark side. As the violent physical forces unleashed by the planet's rotation destroy everything around him and erase his powers, Jack accepts his soul and feels remorse for his actions. The novel concludes with Jack's fall from the collapsing walls of Shadow Guard; Morningstar, who has been released from his captivity by the planet's rotational forces, swoops down to rescue him, but it is not clear "whether he would arrive in time" (207).

Jack of Shadows was the first novel Zelazny produced as a full-time writer, the last one he completed in the 1960s, and the first of his standalone novels to be published in the 1970s. As such, it serves as a bridge between the first and second decades of his career, looking back to the explosively creative 1960s and forward to the more settled, prolifically commercial 1970s. He finished writing it in December 1969, well after *Princes* but before that novel was published,[44] and one can readily see the common elements of both: magic jewels, empowering shadows, contrasting worlds of science and magic in which time passes at different rates. Both Jack and the Lord of Bats enable their spells by drawing patterns on the ground. And as *Princes* draws consciously on the work of sf precursors such as Henry Kuttner and Philip José Farmer, Zelazny publicly acknowledged the indebtedness of *Jack of Shadows* to the work (and byline) of Jack Vance.[45]

Yet *Jack of Shadows* is quite a different story from the first Amber novel, and that difference is rooted both in form and in character. Whereas *Princes* is a first-person narrative that shifts gradually but precisely between hardboiled and high fantasy language depending on whether Corwin is in Amber or on the shadow Earth, the third-person narrative of *Jack of Shadows* maintains a consistent tone throughout, one largely lacking the rhetorical flourishes, bantering slang, and literary allusiveness of earlier Zelazny works. Like *Princes*, the novel unfolds in a straight chronological line, avoiding the nonlinear narrative of *Lord of Light* or the modernist fragmentation of *Creatures*; unlike *Princes*, there is no real mystery to be solved: We know from the beginning exactly who Jack is, what he wants, why he wants it, and what he does to obtain it. On almost every formal level, the greater parallel to other Zelazny novels is not *Princes* but *Damnation Alley*.

The similarities between Zelazny's first book-length attempt at a straightforward adventure story and his first standalone novel of the 1970s extend to the protagonists as well. In his cover endorsement of a 2016 reprint of *Jack of Shadows*, George R. R. Martin calls Jack "a worthy brother to Corwin of Amber and Sam of *Lord of Light*," but in her study of Zelazny, Lindskold discusses Jack and *Damnation Alley*'s Hell Tanner together under the heading "More Villain Than Hero" (108).[46] It is difficult to disagree with Lindskold's assessment. Like Tanner, and unlike Corwin, Jack is strong and skilled but neither charming nor clever. Like the protagonists of almost all Zelazny's novels to this point, Jack is perfectly willing to use violence to achieve his goals, even when said violence leads to extensive casualties and collateral damage. But unlike Conrad's, Sam's, or Corwin's, and more than Tanner's, Jack's violence is sadistically indulgent. He wants not only to remove his enemies, but to do so in a manner that will both make them suffer and display his complete control over them. Hence his promised (but not shown) rape of Evene, his compelling one of the Lord of Bats's henchmen to perform a "Helldance" until his heart bursts, and his ordering Evene's father to commit suicide by slashing his wrists and then giving him detailed instructions on how to accomplish his task. In his review of the novel in *F&SF*, James Blish, who had been generally favorable toward the first Amber novel, finds Jack, compared to Corwin, "a completely unattractive man" with a "passion to defile and wreck everything he touches."[47] It is little wonder that Evene refers to him as "Jack of Evil" (143).[48]

Although in *Princes* Corwin's actions are profoundly self-interested, they are rooted in an absolute loyalty to Amber; in contrast, Jack, like Tanner, is loyal mostly to himself and scornful of the society that produced him. When the Lord of Bats is incredulous that Jack would break the compact that protects the dark side from completely freezing, Jack declares, "The world is of little use to a madman, which is what you would have had me; and I spit on the Contract." And to the lord's declaration that Jack can now "count no darksider as friend," Jack replies, "I never have" (79). As Lindskold points out, Jack's enemies, however violent, at least occasionally behave in ways that earn them the loyalty of others.[49] The only characters for whom Jack seems to feel any regard are Rosalie and Morningstar, and neither stands by him. Rosalie ultimately refuses Jack's offers of protection, and Morningstar sets Jack on the course that destroys the Great Machine, arguably not from concern for Jack but as a means to free himself from his captivity. If Jack is the most unqualifiedly villainous of Zelazny's protagonists, he is also the most completely alone.

Still, as Hell Tanner eventually gained some degree of redemption by succeeding in his appointed task, Jack has, by the end of the story, accepted responsibility for his actions. He apologizes to Evene and considers, even as his world literally collapses around him, the possibility that the violent change he has caused, "the succession of light and darkness[,] would be a new order of things, and he felt that this would be good" (206). That he clearly owes this change in perspective to his acceptance of his soul, as proffered by Rosalie, may seem overly easy. But any change at all is a more significant achievement for Jack that it might be for another character, given that those from the dark side, who lack souls, have no need to change. Earlier in the novel he pondered the changes he witnessed while living on the light side and contrasted them with his own stasis: "They [light side residents] change and we do not. . . . We have no need to change. . . . What value is there in change, anyway?" (123–124). That Jack would go on to change the fundamental nature of the physical world he inhabits and conclude that "a new order of things . . . would be good," is such a profound shift in both thought and action that it almost doesn't matter whether Morningstar catches him before he falls. What matters is not whether he continues to live but what he has become before his death—one that, with his reclaimed soul, will be final.

Jack of Shadows received perhaps the most mixed critical reception of any Zelazny novel up to that time. As noted above, Blish found the title character beyond the pale and compared the novel as a whole unfavorably to *Princes*. The noted fantasy writer and anthologist Lin Carter accused Zelazny of "sloppy plotting, inadequate motivation, [and giving] no background information," while Jeff Clark noted (correctly) that the book's "mood is different from almost anything Zelazny has done before . . . [it has] a graceful somberness." Bruce Gillespie, writing in *SF Commentary*, complained that "Zelazny asks us to participate in Jack's great moral traumas, while all the time we wish that Jack would commit a few entertaining crimes."[50] Nonetheless, the novel was popular with readers, earning Zelazny his ninth Hugo nomination and finishing fourth in the Novel category of *Locus* magazine's annual best-of-the-year poll.

Two years after the novel's publication, Zelazny acknowledged that he should have "expanded it more in the final third, producing a stronger overall effect."[51] And in a 1989 introduction to a reprint, he noted matter-of-factly,

"This was not one of my experimental books. . . . This was a more workman-like job in that I knew exactly what I wanted to do and how to do it."[52] The statement could serve as an epigraph for the phase of Zelazny's career that followed *Jack of Shadows*, when he alternated between the workmanlike and the experimental to an increasingly mixed critical response but almost always, seemingly, knew exactly what he wanted to do.

CHAPTER 4

A SERIES OF DIFFERENT ENDEAVORS
1972–1979

Although Zelazny wrote novels at a remarkable pace even before quitting his day job, after turning to full-time writing he felt, as Lindskold notes, "a greater awareness of the pressure to produce for a market."[1] As early as 1972, when his agent relayed a request from *Analog* editor Ben Bova for new short fiction, Zelazny replied, "I would like to give it a try sometime, but would prefer holding off on doing short fiction again until I'm more caught up in the novel department."[2] By 1980 he acknowledged that his shift away from short fiction to novels in the preceding decade was "mainly economic. . . . It is a fact of writing life that, word for word, novels work harder for their creators when it comes to providing for the necessities and joys of existence," adding, as if anticipating the accusation of abandoning art for commerce, "I enjoy writing novels, too."[3] But a letter to the writer Mack Reynolds written in May 1969, the month in which he quit his Social Security job, shows his uncertainty about giving himself over completely to the marketplace: "I'm scared shitless over the whole thing. . . . I've never been solely dependent on my writing before . . . I keep wondering, 'What if I dry up? What if my next couple of books are no good?'"[4]

Despite these anxieties, Zelazny plunged into this new phase of his career with the same kind of pragmatic ambition that had marked his rise to fame in the 1960s. Indeed, *pragmatic* may be insufficient to describe Zelazny's meticulous attention to the freelancer's bottom line: A 1973 letter to his agent notes that the publisher's royalty statement for *Jack of Shadows* erroneously lists the cover price of the paperback edition at $0.75 instead of the correct $0.95.[5] Perhaps as a sign that his confidence ultimately outweighed his anxieties, in early 1971 he and Judy Zelazny bought a new and larger home in the Roland Park neighborhood of Baltimore, an event followed in December by the birth of their first child, Devin Joseph.[6] By midyear, he informed a correspondent, "I have been writing full-time for a little over two years now, and am very happy with this form of existence."[7] Zelazny was firmly on the path that he would follow for the rest of the decade, largely abandoning short fiction to concentrate on the novels that would pay the mortgage and support his young family. *Abandon* is, of course, a relative term; from 1970 to 1979 Zelazny published fifteen works of short fiction, a respectable output for most authors, but from 1962 to 1969 he had published about seventy.[8]

As if to remind Zelazny's audience of the impact his short fiction had had, in the same year he moved into his new home, Doubleday published *The Doors of His Face, the Lamps of His Mouth and Other Stories*, a fifteen-story sampling of his 1960s magazine fiction that included many of the works that had made his reputation,[9] such as "A Rose for Ecclesiastes," "This Mortal Mountain," "This Moment of the Storm," "The Keys to December," and the title novelette. A pre-publication notice in *Kirkus Reviews* encapsulated the stories' impact on science fiction readers with its observation that Zelazny "somehow manages to give old themes new twists to accomplish something bordering on the extraordinary."[10]

Also bolstering Zelazny's confidence was the continuing high regard in which he was held by the science fiction and fantasy community. Through the early 1970s he was associated with the Guilford Gafia,[11] a writer's workshop that met in the Baltimore area and included such rising sf stars as Joe Haldeman, George Alec Effinger, Jack Dann, and Gardner Dozois. Independent as ever, Zelazny did not submit his own fiction to the workshop or participate in the manuscript critiques but, rather, "advised the budding writers as mentor and friend."[12] The "budding writers" were clearly in awe of him; in the words of Jack Dann, Zelazny "was the grand old man of the workshop[;] . . . at the end of [the weekend workshop] would be 'the party,' and the party would be Roger. . . . There I was on a Sunday night sitting around with Roger Zelazny. What would be better?"[13] Zelazny also remained a sought-after guest at conventions, and in 1974, little more than a decade after his first published sf story, he was the guest of honor at that year's World Science Fiction Convention, Discon II, in Washington, DC. In what must have been a welcome acknowledgment of the origins of his literary career, the convention issued *Poems*, a limited-edition chapbook of his poetry, including a number of pieces from *Chisel in the Sky*.[14]

In short, Zelazny's fears that he might dry up proved unfounded: In the decade that followed his letter to Reynolds, he published fifteen books. *Nine Princes in Amber, Jack of Shadows*, and *The Doors of His Face* were followed by *My Name Is Legion* (1976), a collection of three linked novellas; *Deus Irae* (1976), a collaboration with Philip K. Dick that the authors had worked on intermittently since the late 1960s; *The Illustrated Roger Zelazny* (1979), in which several of Zelazny's stories are rendered as comics by Gray Morrow, with commentary by the author; the remaining four novels in what proved to be the first half of the Amber series (*The Guns of Avalon*, 1972; *Sign of the Unicorn*, 1975; *The Hand of Oberon*, 1976; and *The Courts of Chaos*, 1978); and five standalone novels: *To Die in Italbar* (1973), *Today We Choose Faces* (1973), *Doorways in the Sand* (1976), *Bridge of Ashes* (1976), and *Roadmarks* (1979). Throughout the decade, then, Zelazny not only remained a prolific fiction writer but also managed to balance his output almost evenly between the Amber series and a variety of science fiction novels.

Perhaps the best evidence that Zelazny's move to full-time writing paid off was that, by the early 1970s, he felt confident enough in his career to consider moving away from Baltimore, seeing no need "to remain where the fates had cast me when I could reside just about anyplace."[15] After considering various locations around the country, Zelazny purchased a recently built house on a one-acre lot near the Pecos Wilderness in Santa Fe, New Mexico, a location that seemed to have it all. "I either like to have mountains or water near me," he remarked. "I tire easily of large urban centers. . . . I had wanted to get back to a smaller town, but one which still had all the amenities, a good restaurant, theater, opera, lots of big stores. That's what appealed to me about Santa Fe."[16] In January 1975 he moved there with his wife and son; after two years, he declared, "[The city was] the most pleasant place I have ever lived. . . . I like it even better now than when I came."[17] By the end of the decade the Zelaznys had another son, Jonathan Trent, and a daughter, Shannon, and Zelazny's mother had relocated to Santa Fe and had a home nearby.[18] Zelazny remained in Santa Fe for the rest of his life.

Although the move clearly shows Zelazny's increasing sense of security in his career as a novelist, it is worth noting his claim that *"Damnation Alley* paid for this house"[19]—apparently a reference not to the novel but to the substantial payment he received in 1973 for its film adaptation.[20] Like most successful authors, Zelazny periodically received inquiries regarding film rights to his work; his correspondence with his agent during this period includes references to such queries regarding *Today We Choose Faces*, "For A Breath I Tarry," the Amber series, and even the unpublished *Dead Man's Brother*, not to mention a 1971 report that a young filmmaker named George Lucas was "developing a new science fiction project and would like to talk with [him]."[21] The record does not show whether that conversation ever took place; Zelazny, in contrast to contemporaries such as Harlan Ellison, Norman Spinrad, and David Gerrold, seemed uninterested in Hollywood beyond its money. When Gene Roddenberry offered him the chance to write a script for *Star Trek*, he declined.[22]

Released by 20th Century Fox in 1977, *Damnation Alley* was a big-budget, major studio release starring George Peppard, Jan-Michael Vincent, and Paul Winfield. The script, however, rewritten from an earlier version of which Zelazny approved, bore little resemblance to Zelazny's story, the film was reedited after production was completed, and the end result was a commercial and artistic failure.[23] Zelazny, ever the pragmatic professional, was philosophical: "All that remains of my story is the title and some of the special effects. Everything else, I disavow—except I took their money and I'd do it again."[24]

Four years later he had the chance to do just that when the same studio asked him for material to develop into a film. After rejecting two outlines, the studio bought a third that was based on *The Dream Master* but declined to pursue the project with Zelazny. The outline was finally developed into the 1984 film *Dreamscape*, but Zelazny's initial contribution was not credited.[25] The only other screen adaptation for which Zelazny received credit was George R. R. Martin's faithful and entertaining dramatization of Zelazny's 1979 novelette "The Last Defender of Camelot" for a 1986 episode of the rebooted *Twilight Zone* television series.

As Zelazny was demonstrating increasing facility in his writing and enjoying increasing financial success, critics and reviewers complained that his turn to full-time writing coincided with a reduction in the quality of his work. As the Amber novels grew more popular, they also grew more conventional; as his standalone novels continued to test the boundaries of narrative form, they also, for some, displayed a gap between ambition and achievement. Three novels from this period exemplify how the pressures of full-time writing affected Zelazny's decisions as a writer and how some of those decisions led to work that was less than it might have been.

There is some dispute as to exactly when Zelazny wrote *To Die in Italbar*. According to Yoke, the novel was written in 1965 when the author "was going through a very difficult personal crisis," but Lindskold and Kovacs cite Zelazny's claim that he wrote the novel in June 1969, immediately after quitting his SSA job.[26] The author and his biographer-critics agreed, though, that the novel was written hastily, was shelved, and eventually appeared only "to fulfill a contractual obligation."[27]

Supporting that notion is the degree to which it incorporates not only thematic and formal elements but also a character and setting from earlier work. Like *Creatures of Light and Darkness*, the story jumps back and forth between several different characters; like "The Furies," one of the main characters is an outlaw pursued by other humans and assisted by "a small furry alien."[28] Most notably, the entire story is set in the same universe as *Isle of the Dead*, where humans with extraordinary powers are in fact pawns of the deities of the alien Pei'an religion, and the narrator of the earlier story, Francis Sandow, appears as a supporting character. The central figure of the story, Heidel von Hymack, also called "H," is a "walking antibody"[29] whose blood can serve as a kind of universal vaccine, but only after a period during which anyone who comes in contact with him will fall ill and die. After using his ability to save the life of a young woman, he remains too long on her planet, reverts to his toxic state, and inadvertently causes numerous deaths. The locals' attempt to hunt him down and kill him proves a tipping point, after which he decides to use his abilities deliberately to kill as many people as possible.

As Hymack's story unfolds, we also follow the missions of two other main characters. Malacar Miles, literally the last man on Earth, wages a one-man guerrilla war against the "Combined Leagues" (6), the interstellar forces who defeated Earth, with the assistance of Shind, an alien to whom he is linked telepathically. Larmon Pels is a research scientist who keeps a fatal illness at bay by remaining in cryogenic suspension, permanently confining him to a spaceship. Both seek Hymack for their own reasons: Pels to use him as a research subject, Miles to use him as a weapon. Added to the chase is Francis Sandow, who believes that Hymack is linked to one of the Pei'an gods, as is Sandow. These main narrative threads parallel one another before intertwining and culminating in a deadly confrontation between Miles and Sandow, with both men, as in *Isle of the Dead*, surrogates for the Pei'an gods. Sandow's victory not only defeats Miles for good but also purges Hymack of his special abilities, returning him to normalcy.

Despite its busy plot and relatively large cast of characters, *To Die in Italbar* is Zelazny's most straightforward adventure tale since *Damnation Alley*, focused on the chase and narrated in what is, for Zelazny, a bare-bones style (although, as in the expanded version of *Damnation Alley*, he cannot resist the occasional lyrical outburst such as a description of a rainstorm conveyed in a 220-word sentence [157–158]). The novel continues from . . . *And Call Me Conrad* and *Isle of the Dead* Zelazny's consideration of the role of humanity in a universe populated with diverse alien cultures and what effect an extraordinary, long-lived individual can have on humanity's role in that universe.[30] And though Heidel von Hymack is the central figure of the story, the most significant character in the context of Zelazny's other work is Malacar Miles, yet another example of the recurrent figure of the political terrorist. Defending his guerrilla war against the Combined Leagues, Miles declares, "In reaching all the guilty one sometimes strikes the innocent as well. . . . It is the way of revenge." When a former subordinate points out that "if revenge is abandoned, a few generations will level both the guilty and the innocent[;] . . . [t]he new generation . . . will be totally blameless," Miles replies, "That's too philosophical an outlook to accept—for a man who has lived through some of the things I have" (85).

For its contemporary readers, however, *To Die in Italbar* seemed to suffer in comparison with the author's earlier, more ambitious work. The handful of reviews were equivocal at best: "A slender but nicely balanced tale . . . Zelazny at his not quite best is still better than most"; "It isn't the best Zelazny, but it has his color and wild surmise and all the other qualities that make it impossible for him to be dull."[31] The reviewer for *F&SF*, Sidney Coleman, found the novel "well written" with "fast action" and "colorful characters," but nonetheless felt the story to be an example of "reverse alchemy," lacking the verve, humor, and grace of Zelazny's earlier work. And after supplying as pithy and accurate an insight into Zelazny's work as we have—"For Zelazny's purposes, a solid world would be as useless an object as a solid violin. The function of the thing is to resonate"—Coleman concluded with one of the earliest and one of the most anguished expressions of disappointment in the perceived turn of Zelazny's work in the early 1970s: "We once had something unique and wonderful, and it is gone, and what we have in its place is only a superior writer of preposterous adventures."[32] A decade and a half later, Zelazny himself declared *To Die in Italbar* "the worst book [he'd] ever written."[33] Unfortunately, what the author considered a lapse the reviewer for the magazine that had published much of his most famous work saw as a pattern.

Another novel from this period also points to the negative impact of commercial commitments on artistic achievements. *The Dead Man's Brother* is a noir-inflected thriller whose narrator, an art thief turned art dealer falsely accused of murder, attempts to clear himself by going on an exotic mission for the CIA to investigate a priest who has embezzled money from the Vatican; it remains one of the very few examples of Zelazny writing outside the sf and fantasy genres. Apparently written under contract for Berkley, which cancelled the project due to a change in editors and a declining mystery imprint,[34] the novel made the rounds of other publishers but left editors unimpressed, one complaining, "It's a dull book. What's the matter with him? His sf is swell."[35] Zelazny admitted he had lengthened the story to fulfill the original Berkley contract and indicated to his agent that he would try to revise it, but he never did.[36] With other projects needing his attention, Zelazny may have seen rewriting as a case of diminishing returns. Whatever the author's reasons, the novel's failure to sell apparently cured Zelazny of trying to write outside the genres in which he made his reputation. With one exception—*Wilderness* (1994), a historical novel written in collaboration with Gerald Hausman—Zelazny never again left science fiction and fantasy. *The Dead Man's Brother* remained unpublished in Zelazny's lifetime, finally appearing in 2009 from Hard Case Crime, a mass-market paperback imprint specializing in "hardboiled" crime fiction.[37]

The issue of prior commitments also affected the composition of Zelazny's first collaborative novel, *Deus Irae*, written with Philip K. Dick. The novel is set in the United States after a nuclear holocaust that has produced widespread mutations and a new religion, the Sons of Wrath, whose followers bow to one Carleton Lufteufel, the individual who developed the weapon that led to the catastrophe. Tibor McMasters, a limbless mutated artist, is commissioned to paint a mural of Lufteufel, whose location is unknown; the novel follows McMasters as he searches for Lufteufel across a blasted America.

The co-authors had discussed the possibility of collaboration as early as 1967, when Dick wrote to Zelazny that he had an idea about "alternate present-day worlds" that could be the basis for such a project.[38] Dick's letter implies that the topic had come up in earlier correspondence, and he makes it clear that he sees collaborating with Zelazny as a boost for his own career, writing: "My work has somehow ceased to evolve. Can I, with your assistance, be pushed forward one notch? This is what I'm hoping for."[39] That scenario did not advance, but when in early 1968 Zelazny read an opening section and outline for another story that Dick had been unable to continue, he contacted Dick, and the two agreed that this work would be their co-written novel. But both writers had numerous other contractual obligations, and the novel proceeded intermittently for several years, the authors working on it when they could, alternating sections—but, according to Zelazny, without rewriting each other's contributions and without any final rewrite of the entire manuscript.[40] The novel finally was published by Doubleday in 1976.

Although Zelazny claimed to be satisfied with the end result,[41] reviewers, in general, were not. Richard E. Geis admired the novel's ambitious meditations on religion, but Don D'Ammassa and future Zelazny bibliographer Joe Sanders found that the independently authored sections ultimately failed to cohere and declared the book not the best of either author.[42] On reading the sometimes compelling, frequently grotesque, and pervasively gnarled chapters of *Deus Irae*, it is difficult to disagree with the latter two assessments, and one wonders whether the novel might have benefited from some of the rewriting it apparently never received.

If the increasing number of Zelazny's publishing commitments was likely a factor in his shelving *Dead Man's Brother* and his sporadic attention to *Deus Irae*, chief among these commitments was the continuation of the Amber series. Having set aside the second volume, *The Guns of Avalon*, after writing the first three chapters—apparently, and perhaps tellingly, at about the time he realized that what he had originally conceived as a trilogy might well extend to six volumes—he resumed work on the novel as *Nine Princes in Amber* was published, completing *Avalon* in November 1971. For the next half-dozen years, as Zelazny produced a steady stream of standalone sf novels, he was never far from Amber, beginning *Sign of the Unicorn* shortly after completing *Doorways in the Sand*, completing *The Hand of Oberon* the same year he was writing *Bridge of Ashes*, and, bowing to pressure from his publisher and his fans, setting *Roadmarks* aside in order to finish *The Courts of Chaos*.[43] By 1979, when the Science Fiction Book Club republished all five novels in a two-volume omnibus titled *The Chronicles of Amber*, Zelazny was perhaps as well-known for the Amber series as he was for the novels and short fiction of the 1960s.

The Guns of Avalon picks up immediately after the events of *Nine Princes in Amber* as Corwin travels toward Avalon, a shadow world he had created long ago and where he had lived happily. He quickly finds himself battling monstrous dark forces connected to the Courts of Chaos, a distant land beyond the shadow lands. In Avalon he reunites with his brother Benedict and meets Dara, Benedict's great-granddaughter, an expert swordswoman who questions Corwin about their family history. As he continues to gather information about his family (and begins an affair with Dara) Corwin pursues his true goal: to obtain a substance that can function as gunpowder in Amber, giving him an insurmountable advantage in any battle to retake the throne from Eric. He raises a shadow army and attacks Amber, only to discover that the city is under siege by creatures from the Courts of Chaos. Putting his loyalty to Amber first, he assists in the city's defense, his actions complicated by Dara's sudden appearance in Amber. After the dark forces are defeated, the mortally wounded Eric gives Corwin the Jewel of Judgment and places a death curse not on his brother but on "the enemies of Amber" (250).[44] Corwin then contacts Benedict via Trump, Benedict denies that Dara is a member of the family, and Corwin races to the family castle, where he discovers Dara walking the Pattern, an act that appears to turn her into something other than human. After completing the Pattern, the transformed Dara declares that "Amber . . . will be destroyed" (255) and disappears.

As *Sign of the Unicorn* opens, Corwin rules in Amber but immediately faces a crisis when his brother Caine is murdered. Convinced that he will be accused of the crime, Corwin consults his brother Random, whom he has more or less trusted since the latter returned from the undersea city of Remba. Random tells Corwin that, before their reunion back on the shadow Earth, he had answered a call for help from their brother Brand, imprisoned in yet another shadow world, but failed to rescue him. Corwin then convinces his siblings to combine their powers to bring Brand back to Amber via Trump. As soon as Brand appears he is stabbed, the attacker unidentified. Soon afterward, Corwin himself is attacked by an unknown assailant and escapes death only by the power of the Jewel. The wounded, unconscious Corwin then awakens in his old home on the shadow Earth, where he hides the Jewel and learns that it was Brand who committed him to the hospital from which he escaped (as detailed in the opening of *Princes*).

After returning to Amber Corwin confronts the recovering Brand, who admits his involvement in a complicated plot to seize the throne, a plot in which he, their sister Fiona, and their brother Bleys were aligned against their brothers Eric, Julian, and Caine. Brand insists that he tried to opt out when he learned his co-conspirators were attempting to employ the forces of the Courts of Chaos. Looking for answers, Corwin travels with Random and Ganelon (a former second-in-command who accompanied Corwin from Avalon) to Mount Kolvir and then journeys alone to the sky city Tir-na Nog'th, where he confronts ghostly versions of Dara and Benedict. On the return to Amber, a white unicorn leads Corwin, Random, and Ganelon to an open area where, instead of the family castle containing the Pattern of Amber, there is another Pattern which, Corwin realizes, is the true, original Pattern—meaning that Amber itself is a shadow world.

In *The Hand of Oberon*, Corwin, Random, and Ganelon grapple with the revelation that they have found "the true Amber" (369).[45] Their examination of the primal Pattern reveals a dark stain, which they determine is the blood of Random's son Martin—a stain, caused by Brand, that will draw out the forces of Chaos. After returning to Amber, Corwin has a crucial conversation with Random's wife, Vialle, that yields an epiphany: Although he remains loyal to Amber and willing to combat the forces that threaten it, he no longer wants the throne. For the remainder of the novel, through various journeys and conversations, Corwin learns more about the plots that lay behind the events of *Nine Princes in Amber* and confirms that it is in fact Brand who is the most immediate threat to Amber. Having failed to gain Corwin's support, Brand has again disappeared—as has the Jewel. Corwin and Fiona journey to the primal Pattern, which Brand is already walking; Corwin removes him without killing him, and Brand disappears. Corwin then finds Random and Martin reunited. Martin confirms that Brand attacked him. Convinced that Brand will once again attempt to walk the primal Pattern, Corwin coordinates a defense by means of which Benedict vanquishes Brand and recovers the Jewel. Corwin, skeptical that these events have played out on their own, convinces Benedict that they should try to contact via Trump their father, Oberon, who, as revealed in *Avalon*, did not abdicate but simply disappeared. They do—and Ganelon answers, revealing himself to have been their father in disguise all along.

In *The Courts of Chaos*, Dara reveals to Corwin their son, Merlin, and declares that she is once again loyal to Amber. When Corwin learns that Oberon is attempting to mend the damage to the primal Pattern, he seizes the Jewel from his father and attempts the repairs himself. Oberon stops Corwin and orders him on a hellride through the shadow worlds to carry the Jewel to the Courts. After numerous adventures and confrontations on this ride, Corwin, convinced that Oberon has failed, uses the Jewel to draw a new Pattern in a wasteland that separates him from the Courts of Chaos. Brand reappears and steals the Jewel yet again; Corwin uses the new Pattern to reach the Courts. There follows a violent confrontation between the forces of Amber and the forces of Chaos, at the end of which Brand plunges to his death, taking with him the Jewel and Deirdre, the one sibling Corwin truly loves. Dara reappears, condemns Corwin for killing her representative during the hellride, and deserts Amber for the Courts. Also reappearing is the unicorn, which presents the Jewel to Random, confirming him as the legitimate ruler of Amber. With the throne secure and the forces of Chaos defeated, Corwin begins telling his son Merlin about his adventures—a final explanation of the narrative device, begun in *Princes*, of Corwin's periodically interrupting his own story to address an unknown figure at the Courts of Chaos. Corwin concludes by offering summary comments on all his siblings, planning to revisit the Courts of Chaos that so he may lead Merlin to "walk . . . his Pattern and . . . claim his worlds" (576),[46] and promising to revisit the new Pattern the he drew before the final battle at the Courts of Chaos: "The way ahead intrigues me, from hell to hallelujah. . . . If [the new Pattern] leads me to another universe, as I now believe it will, I must go there, to see how I have wrought. . . . Good-bye and hello, as always" (576–577).

The revelation in the final pages of *Courts* that Corwin has been telling the entire story to his son underscores what is, after Corwin's first-person narration itself, the most immediate formal device of the Amber novels: the degree to which they tell an uninterrupted story, with none but the first standing independent of the others. It is, as Charles N. Brown immediately noted in his review of *The Courts of Chaos*, "a five volume novel,"[47] the most linear of Zelazny's major works, proceeding in an undeviating chronological line from Corwin's awakening in the hospital on Earth to his reunion with his son and settlement with his family; any flashbacks occur within the memory of the narrator.

On one hand, such a narrative yields the kind of deep-immersion experience that draws many readers to epic fantasy; on the other, such a storytelling choice may work against the artistic integrity of the individual volumes. As early as the appearance of *Avalon* some reviewers complained of excessive exposition,[48] and as the series progressed, Zelazny relied more and more on expository dialogue among Corwin and his siblings to fill in crucial points of the plot—points that, as still other reviewers complained, he sometimes struggled to keep straight.[49] It is hard to escape the feeling that, especially by the last two volumes, if the reader is eager to find out how things turn out, the author is equally eager to wind things up.

Nonetheless, the individual volumes and the series as a whole fundamentally cohere. As Krulik notes, each of the novels has its own organizing principle. *Nine Princes in Amber* is a tale of a stranger in a strange land who, in the tradition of the earliest pulps, moves from present-day reality into a fantastic realm. *The Guns of Avalon,* with its fairy rings, knights-at-arms, supernatural women, and referential character names (Lancelot, Oberon), is the most explicitly indebted to weird Britain in general and Arthurian lore in particular. *Sign of the Unicorn* is a mystery story as Corwin seeks to solve the locked-room puzzle of Who Stabbed Brand. *The Hand of Oberon* provides a turning point for both readers, who finally start getting answers to the questions arising from the first three installments, and the narrator, who for the first time begins to have a sense of what he really wants and what he doesn't. *The Courts of Chaos* largely turns away from family schemes and battlefields to linger on the deep strangeness and, on occasion, fundamental absurdity of Corwin's shadow journeys before racing to an ending that provides closure but leaves the door open for further adventures.[50]

More important to the coherence of *The Chronicles of Amber* is, of course, Corwin himself—his journey, his changing goals, his widening perceptions, and, most of all, his voice. In her award-winning novel *Among Others* (2010), Jo Walton—whose critique of *Lord of Light* was discussed in Chapter 2—employs her own distinctive narrator, a 1970s teenage sf fan who, after reading *Sign of the Unicorn* "all in one gulp" on a train ride, declares, "The thing I really love about those books is Corwin's voice, so very personal, making light of things, joking about them, and then suddenly so serious."[51] Corwin's voice is the Zelazny narrator at its most effective, moving from the earnest concerns and elevated diction of high fantasy to the irony and informality of the hardboiled crime novel. There is, unfortunately but undeniably, less and less of this as the *Chronicles* progress; the increased use of in-our-last-episode exposition not only interrupts the plot but also unavoidably flattens Corwin's voice.

But if Corwin's voice is diminished, his self-awareness grows. Having settled the question of his own identity halfway through the first volume, Corwin schemes, plots, and frequently kills in order to advance his revenge-fueled, power-grabbing agenda. He is a prince of Amber, royalty whose reputation always precedes him and who can command the loyalty of countless troops in his pursuit of the throne he believes to be rightfully his. But what good is any of that if "a Prince of Amber is part and party to all the rottenness that is in the world," when the best advice you can give to a young member of the royal family is "never trust a relative," and the troops under your command are simply "those whom I had exploited once before" (158, 188, 241)? Not to mention the incursion of dark forces triggered in *Princes* by Corwin's curse. What good is a victory that means presiding over a world that is literally falling apart as the result of one's own anger?

All of the quotations in the preceding paragraph are from *The Guns of Avalon*, perhaps the darkest of the novels, and the point where Corwin's self-interrogation comes closest to a shrug: after the apparent twinge of conscience over once again mining the shadow worlds for cannon fodder, he concludes, "The morality of it did not especially trouble me this time" (241). All that matters is killing Eric and regaining the throne. But even after Corwin does both, his siblings are still at each other's throats, and there are still monstrous forces threatening the land. In a letter discussing his plans for *Sign of the Unicorn*, Zelazny envisioned the novel as "almost static . . . in order to provide necessary background."[52] The book may not exactly be static, but it is a pause: Corwin, while sorting out the schemes of his siblings and straining after the Jewel of Judgement, seems more interested in solving problems and repairing his family than in indulging his power and defeating his enemies. He displays something approaching empathy toward Brand for the latter's imprisonment, deals nonlethally with threatening behavior from Gerard, and gratefully accepts help from Bill, an old friend from his time on Earth. When Corwin admits that he himself is not really human, Bill replies, "It doesn't make any real difference to me, but I thought it might to you—to know that someone knows you are different and doesn't care" (337).[53] This moment of simple decency and acceptance reminds Corwin that there are people in the world who need not be viewed through a paranoid lens. Another reminder is his discovery, in *The Hand of Oberon*, that the brothers he thought were out to get him—Julian, Caine, and the despised Eric—were not as interested in hurting him as they were in defending Amber against Brand and that Julian had in fact saved his life by having him imprisoned rather than executed. By the time Corwin has a private conversation with Random's wife Vialle, who wonders whether he might have been happier before regaining his memory and declares, simply, "I want to understand you" (397), he realizes that what he wants now is not what he wanted at the start: "Eric is dead and there is nothing left of what I felt then. The throne remains, but now I find that my feelings toward it are mixed. . . . I am hardly a dutiful son of Amber or of

Oberon." When Vialle observes, "Your voice makes it plain that you do not wish to be one," the epiphany is complete, and all Corwin can say is, "You are right" (398–399).

Vialle's insightfulness may exist primarily to help Corwin understand himself, but she possesses a degree of agency that is not the rule among the other female inhabitants of Amber. Although many female characters play prominent roles throughout the first five novels of the series, it would be difficult to argue that many are ever at parity with the male characters. Corwin's various sisters are as ruthlessly enmeshed in the quest for power and control as are his brothers, but it is the brothers whose actions propel the story, and none of the sisters is a serious candidate for the throne.[54] The women outside the royal family are, variously, forces of supernatural opposition, sounding boards for Corwin, or seductresses—in the case of Dara, all three.

Still, Vialle's compassionate perception provides a crucial turning point in the narrative. Thereafter, and for the remainder of the series, Corwin's goal is neither power nor vengeance but repair and preservation: stopping the dark forces of Chaos, stabilizing his family, and making Amber whole again. This shift in Corwin's priorities caught the attention of Alexei and Cory Panshin. In their *F&SF* review of *Sign of the Unicorn*, after condemning Zelazny's recent work as consisting of "one bad novel after another," the Panshins dismissed the first two Amber novels as, respectively, "morally sleazy and solipsistic" and "self-hating" (while admitting "the immediate egotistical hypnotic power of first-person narration"). But they saw *Unicorn* as a return to form, praising the "redemption" of the sequence with Bill, hailing the revelation of the true Amber as a rejection of solipsism, and going so far as to declare the novel "Zelazny's best book since *Lord of Light. Zelazny is back! Hooray! Hooray!*"[55] That two of the leading critics of the day would, on finding merit in a new Zelazny novel, erupt in cheers—language not far removed from Walton's teenage sf fan, who "squealed out loud" when she discovered the new Amber novel in a bookstore and swore she "would rather have *Sign of the Unicorn* than all the boys in the Valleys"[56]—demonstrates that Zelazny still mattered as much to the readers who used to love him as he mattered to those who still did.

The focus on Corwin, however, raises an interesting question: What about Amber? Throughout the series, almost as striking as the overpowering presence of Corwin is the absence of the city. As Gary K. Wolfe points out, we know "little about Amber itself," a place that "often seems to have no population other than its royal family . . . no streets, no economy, no network of social organization." For Wolfe, the fact that Zelazny presents Amber not as a constructed environment but as "an emotional archetype" is fully in keeping with fantasy literature's ability to "sustain our interest in impossible worlds simply by making these worlds emotionally meaningful to us."[57]

In this context, it is striking that much of the sense of physical setting we do have in these novels is not the world of Amber, much less its infrastructure, but the corridors between Amber and elsewhere: the shadow worlds through which Corwin periodically hellrides, early on to pursue his quest for power and vengeance, later to preserve Amber itself. These are the passages where, even in the exposition-laden later novels, Zelazny allows himself to get lost in language, as in this description, from *The Courts of Chaos*, of Corwin's journey to the Courts (all ellipses are in the original):

> Turning, pacing . . . Red now the ferns, wider and lower . . . Beyond, a great plain, pinking into evening . . .
> Forward, over pale grasses . . . The smell of fresh earth . . . Mountains or dark clouds far ahead . . . A rush of stars from my left . . . A quick spray of moisture . . . A blue moon leaps into the sky . . . Flickerings among the dark masses . . . Memories and a rumbling noise . . . Stormsmell and rushing air . . . (503)

That which in a different kind of book would have been mere "carpentry scenes"—transitional sections whose function is solely to move the action from point A to point B—Zelazny writes with the poetic fragmentation that was so often a signature of his early work. To apply Wolfe's concept, what matters is emotional meaningfulness—not how the cities function but how the journeys between cities feel.

The strategies used in these scenes also exemplify one of Zelazny's principles of fiction writing. As noted in Chapter 1, one of his most crucial self-critiques was his decision that he was "overexplaining" to the reader and should instead "avoid the unnecessarily explicit" and not "go on talking once a thing had been shown."[58] In a speech given at a 1967 science fiction convention he elaborated on this insight, declaring, "Literature, of necessity, contains shadows. . . . A writer never writes an entire story. . . . You live part of it yourself." He went on to identify these shadows, gaps that the reader fills in, with the fabled "sense of wonder" that, to science fiction readers, defines the texts they love:

> Writing involves your taking everything in through those little cryptic bugs that crawl across the page and construct things around them. This is where that strange thing called "sense of wonder" comes into play. . . . It sort of enfolds this shadow area. Into those shadows you project those things you are looking for.[59]

Krulik considers this determination to avoid overelaboration "a central philosophy" of Zelazny's writing.[60] But what Zelazny posits in his speech, and what remains foregrounded even in a linear, plot-heavy work such as *The Chronicles of Amber*, is that readers experience the magic of shadow, and thus the sense of wonder, through language. Readers can imagine the streets, the plumbing, the business models of Amber as they see fit; the "emotional archetype" of the fantasy novel derives from Corwin's story and how he tells it—both the words themselves and the ellipses that lie between.

Just as the reader experiences Amber through Corwin's voice, the fate of Amber lies in Corwin's hands, even after he decides he doesn't want to be in charge any more. The outcome of the first half of *The Chronicles of Amber* comes down to learning who among the scheming, self-involved members of the royal family can master the Pattern—can, that is, control and focus their actions to execute a careful plan in order to achieve a goal. By walking the Pattern, Corwin regains his memory and Dara assumes her true form; by failing to master the Pattern, Brand is defeated; by failing to repair the Pattern, the patriarch Oberon is doomed. And when Corwin gains access to the Courts of Chaos, enabling his ultimate victory, he does so not through the old, broken Pattern but by making a new one, a process that calls forth memories of a happy interlude in his past—on Earth in 1905 Paris—even as it demands an excruciating precision:

> I did not meet with the physical resistance that I did on the old Pattern . . . a peculiar deliberation had come over all my movements, slowing them, ritualizing them. I seemed to expend more energy in preparing for each step . . . than I did in the physical performance of the act. Yet the slowness seemed to require itself, was exacted of me by some known agency which determined precision and an adagio tempo for all my movements. (542)

Could there be a better description of the act of writing? If Zelazny began *The Chronicles of Amber* struggling to find his preferred artistic path, he ended the series's first half with a reminder of the difficult requirements of both creative process and practical accommodation, and, arguably, a more mature vision of both. For Corwin, if Amber is not what you thought it was, it is still worth preserving. If the Pattern you thought was your legacy no longer works, the only thing to do—the only way to defeat the forces of Chaos—is to draw a new Pattern of your own.

The four standalone novels that appeared after *To Die in Italbar*—*Today We Choose Faces* (1973), *Doorways in the Sand* (1976), *Bridge of Ashes* (1976), *and Roadmarks* (1979)—did not have the long-term impact of the Amber series. Indeed, for many reviewers they were additional evidence of Zelazny's fall away from the achievements of the 1960s, the work of a writer seemingly more intent on writing quickly, prolifically, and profitably than on blazing new and interesting literary trails. While all four novels bore marks of the incompleteness that Charles N. Brown noted in his 1995 obituary (none exceeded approximately 180 pages, with *Bridge of Ashes*, at approximately 150 pages, barely qualifying as a full-length novel) they also displayed, in varying degrees, Zelazny's ongoing interest in experimenting with narrative structure and permanent impulse toward punctuating even the busiest of adventures with outbursts of lyricism. Together with the three novellas that comprise *My Name Is Legion* (1976), these books make it clear that, even as he committed more deeply to fantasy, his interest in exploring the possibilities of the science fiction story remained undiminished. And though the protagonists of these novels, in particular *Doorways* and *Legion,* are still, for the most part, the smart, suspicious, free-ranging outsiders of his earlier work, they are also, like Corwin in the later Amber novels, willing to reflect on and rethink their motives.

Of the four novels, *Today We Choose Faces*, written from 1970 to 1972, is the earliest.[61] Part I opens with Angelo di Negri, a cryogenically preserved Mafia hitman who has been awakened for one last job. Although organized crime has largely abandoned violence, Angelo's descendants need his anachronistic skills to eliminate a scientist, Herbert Styler, who has hidden himself away in a fortress on a distant planet. Angelo carries out the contract in a prolonged assault on Styler's facility during which the scientist insists that a planet-wide war has destroyed Earth. After killing Styler, Angelo answers a ringing phone, only to hear the dead scientist's voice on the other end directing him to "the other building" (40),[62] where he can learn what is necessary to escape and carry out another, more profound mission.

Part II continues the first-person narrative, but it is not immediately clear who the narrator is as he moves rapidly through various sections of "the House," an elaborately constructed space to which humanity has apparently retreated after a planetary catastrophe. As the narrator is repeatedly pursued, killed, and resurrected, we learn that he is a "nexus" of psychically connected clones; when one dies, his memories are acquired by the next in line. As each nexus clone is hunted down by a mysterious figure named Mr. Black, a disembodied voice urges each one in turn to pull a specifically numbered pin. The nexus is revealed to be part of the campaign by the mysterious forces behind the House to rid humanity of the undesirable attributes, aggression in particular, which led to the catastrophe. As the elaborate chase continues, the narrator is accompanied by the adult daughter of a prominent scientist whose attempts to liberate humanity from the constrictions of the House led to his death. The narrator finally confronts and kills Mr. Black, only to discover that Black, too, is a clone, able to transfer himself to another member of the nexus. After a prolonged battle in the post-apocalyptic ruins outside the House (the site of Negri's attack in Part I), the transferred Black dispatches the narrator, the last pin has been pulled—and we jump to Part III, a six-page coda returning to the narrative of Part I. Now the narrator is Black, who was in fact fighting to liberate humanity from the House and was also a clone derived from Angelo di Negri. The story concludes with Black/Negri shutting down the central computer that has controlled the entire enterprise and rejecting a phone call from the scientist Styler.

The dedication of *Today We Choose Faces* reads "To Philip K. Dick, electric shepherd" (5), and it is easy to see how Dick's visions of paranoid existential dread influenced a novel whose narrator at one point comments, "The first thing I did was try to relax and decide who I was" (57). The novel's frantic, one-trapdoor-after-another narrative, with transitions frequently driven by explosive violence and one key sequence represented in eccentric typography, also recalls Alfred Bester, while both the narrative pacing and the underlying tale of libertarian revolt against oppressive social engineering evoke the work of A. E. van Vogt. To these classic genre influences Zelazny added his signature thematic and formal concerns: the twentieth-century man caught in the far future who struggles to negotiate its systems, violence as a means of political resistance, experimentation with narrative structure, playful puns (the names of all the clones are variations on the name of Angelo di Negri, "Black Angel"),[63] literary allusiveness both classic and modern (the narrator quotes William Blake and references Thomas Wolfe, and the story as a whole, in the view of one critic, evokes both Dante and Milton),[64] and the occasional three-hundred-word sentence (19). Indeed, Zelazny's toying with structure was more pronounced than usual, as he originally intended the novel to start with Part II as an extended flashback, only to be overruled by his editors on the ground that doing so would be too much for the average reader.[65] And, perhaps more than any other Zelazny novel of the period, the stylistic and structural experiments were very much in service of the novel's deep issues: the fragmentation of human culture and human identity, the role of the individual within the elaborated systems of society, and the degree to which violence may be part of what it means to be human.[66]

In short, *Today We Choose Faces* was as thoughtful, ambitious, and audacious as any of Zelazny's work from the 1960s. But though the book had its admirers—Richard E. Geis declared it "the finest novel Roger Zelazny has written in years,"[67] and it was ranked #9 in the *Locus* poll for best novel of 1973—others were less enthusiastic. Zelazny bibliographer and commentator Joe Sanders wondered "how [the] hero's attempt to change humanity has had any effect," while Jeff Smith worried that the emphasis on the "mystery element" reduced both this and other Zelazny stories of the time to "superficial puzzles."[68]

There are at least two factors at work in the novel's reception, one being the structural uncertainty that Zelazny's editors identified. To a greater extent than *Creatures of Light and Darkness*, *Today We Choose Faces* is challenging to follow on a page-by-page level. But the three sections present difficulties no matter their order. Had Zelazny followed his earlier plan, the opening flashback of Part II would have taken up 123 pages of a 174-page novel; in its published form, the three sections are still so disparate that what should be suspense verges on confusion. One wonders what the effect might have been of simply ordering the novel in consecutive chapters rather than further disrupting an already disruptive reading experience by placing chapters within parts. The other factor is that Zelazny was now competing with himself in the world of novels as he previously had with short fiction. *Today We Chose Faces* and *To Die in Italbar* were published not only in the same year, but in consecutive months.[69] A new Zelazny novel had been published in each of the preceding three years, and over the course of the following three years, six new ones would appear, four in 1976 alone. It is hard not to conclude that, in addition to the novel's structural issues, part of the problem was simply that, in the ever-increasing tide of Zelazny novels, it never quite made it to shore.[70]

The experimentation continued in *Bridge of Ashes*. After an opening series of impressionistic fragments focusing on unidentified individuals from different periods of history (and prehistory), the scene shifts to modern-day New York, where, in the context of a pending speech calling for strong action on environmental issues, the author quickly sets up the novel's basic conceit: Human evolution was triggered by aliens whose long-term goal was to have humanity alter the Earth's environment—that is, pollute it—until it was suitable for habitation by the alien race. Ever since, the aliens have periodically intervened in order to prevent developments that might thwart their plan. The scene shifts again to northern New Mexico in the early twenty-first century, when telepathy exists as an observable and usable phenomenon. Thirteen-year-old Dennis Guise is possessed of unprecedentedly powerful telepathic abilities that have left him catatonic from the onslaught of others' thoughts; attempting to shield their son, his parents, also telepaths, have moved the family to this remote location. After federal agents employ Dennis's abilities in order to hunt down and kill a fugitive member of the eco-terrorist group Children of Earth, Dennis begins to display the personality of Quick Smith, another member of the group. Taking on more and more different identities, he has become a global telepath who can "reach anywhere in the world, regard anyone's thoughts with total absorption" (78).[71] As a last resort, Dennis's father arranges for him to leave Earth altogether for a medical facility on the moon.

Dennis's treatment leads to some improvement, but he once again begins to communicate with the language and personality of someone else—specifically, Leonardo da Vinci. By the time Dennis paints the *Mona Lisa*, his therapist is forced to conclude that Dennis can connect telepathically through time. After accepting his identity as a single entity who has existed in time through various individuals, Dennis convinces his therapist he has fully recovered, returns to Earth, reunites with his parents, reconnects with his original childhood therapist Lynda Dimanche, and meets Quick Smith in person. He learns that Lynda is connected not only to Smith and the Children of Earth but also to the aliens' opponent, introduced in the novel's opening sequence and now known as "the dark man." On the coast of Somalia Dennis and Smith meet the dark man, who believes that the planet's only hope is for Dennis to permit himself to be examined by the aliens to "convince them that their plan is failing, that mankind is more complex, has become less responsive to their promptings" (146). The aliens' ship rises from the ocean and Dennis boards it, carrying with him the figures from the past whom he had telepathically channeled, "all of those who had been defeated in the name of man . . . suppressed men of learning, broken geniuses . . . I was the dark man, who bore all names" (149). After Dennis tours the ship and leaves, the alien craft rises from the water and departs, presumably signaling a victory for Earth and humanity. But the aliens' departure is followed by a "dark form" taking the shape of a horned beast rising from the waters: "Our ancient oppressors had departed, but they had left this final doom for their greatest enemy" (152). The dark man and Smith kill the beast, but not before it gores the dark man. Lynda reappears and orders Dennis and Smith away. As Dennis leaves, he connects telepathically with the dark man one last time, feeling himself lying wounded with his head in Lynda's lap, reproducing the prehistoric moment that opened the novel.

Although Zelazny hinted in 1972 at moving away from mythology in his science fiction,[72] *Bridge of Ashes* begins and concludes with evocations of the myth of the Fisher King, a reference that Zelazny directly acknowledges: As Dennis goes to be judged by the aliens, he makes "the final leap back, to become the dying god-king who will be resurrected" (149). The novel most deeply evokes more recent stories, however. If *Today We Choose Faces* recalled the classic science fiction of Bester, Dick, and van Vogt, *Bridge of Ashes* pays direct homage to Theodore Sturgeon and Arthur C. Clarke. In the same convention speech in which he discussed science fiction in relation to the theories of Northrop Frye, Zelazny cited Sturgeon's *More Than Human* and Clarke's

Childhood's End (both 1953) as sf novels that "come close" to classical notions of literature as they reach for catharsis, pity, and the tragic fall.[73] Sturgeon's novel focuses on the idea of gestalt intelligence—many minds contained within a single consciousness—and, in its middle section (previously published as the novella "Baby Is Three"), depicts a teenage boy with potentially extraordinary powers undergoing psychotherapy; Clarke's novel describes all-powerful aliens intervening in humanity's evolution. In *Bridge* Zelazny is clearly indebted to both, although he employs their tropes to different ends. When the aliens depart, humanity's fate is not, as in Clarke, transcendent metamorphosis but freedom and self-determination: "The world is ours once more . . . with no one to blame but ourselves for whatever follows" (151). And Dennis's channeling of multiple personalities through history, as opposed to Sturgeon's here-and-now gestalt, does not establish a new kind of community in space but instead connects different communities through time: "The past is not lost to us, is not a bridge that has been burned, leaving only ashes, but rather is an open way, that all of history is there to be explored, learned from" (147).[74]

More than for its use of classical myth and modern literature, *Bridge of Ashes* is noteworthy as Zelazny's most detailed exploration of environmental themes. Ecological issues cropped up in earlier works such as "The Keys to December" and *Isle of the Dead*, but *Bridge*, one of the first novels that Zelazny wrote after moving to Santa Fe, both foregrounds and explicitly links them to his recurrent presentations of political violence. The novel's basic premise is inextricable from ecological issues because the success of the aliens' program depends on the environmental degradation of Earth. The central event of Part I is a UN resolution on environmental issues whose passage or defeat could alter history (an intriguing forecast of the 2015 Paris climate accords). Part II of the novel is structured as a third-person narrative, but in it Zelazny devotes a significant number of first-person scenes to the storyline involving Roderick Leishman, the fugitive eco-terrorist, and Children of Earth, scenes in which Leishman muses on the convictions underlying his violent resistance: "The world comes at you through the senses. . . . I have it inside me here. . . . Though the world is greater than I am, I know that it can be hurt" (35). He is convinced that his pending attempted assassinations of two governors constitute "some positive thing to protect [the Earth]"; if he dies in the attempt, he will have "rendered the Earth [his] mother some payment for [his] keep" (35). Lying wounded after carrying out his attack, he regards the western landscape: "The pleasure and pride of humanity are best enjoyed against the heedlessness, the slumbering power of the Earth. . . . To isolate oneself too much from it detracts from both our achievements and our failures" (48). Asked if his environmental activism is a "religious thing," Leishman replies, "I guess it is. . . . The Earth is my reward as well as my concern. . . . If we are as brutal to [commercial interests] as they are to the land, maybe then some of the exploiters will get the point, think twice" (65).

The same sentiments are voiced in the novel's concluding section, now narrated by Dennis. Although Smith declares in the above exchange that, if he weren't with the Children of Earth, he "would be throwing bombs with someone else" (66), by the time Smith meets Dennis in Part IV, his comments reflect Leishman's passionate commitment to the cause, if somewhat more pragmatically:

> I am a conservationist, an environmentalist, an ecological activist—whatever term is currently fashionable—because I am pro-land, not anti-city. . . . Being for the land does not mean being against the city. . . . When we blow up a dam or screw up a source of pollution, we are not telling them to turn off all the technology in the world. We are telling them to be more judicious in its disposition. (126–127)

Later, as Dennis approaches his examination by the aliens, still psychically touched by Leishman and Smith, he realizes that the attempt to return humanity to autonomy is inextricably bound up with preservation of the planet: "There rose in me the desire to do anything to preserve the ancient land and waters of my world. . . . We had had a rule of determinism forced upon us. Only by breaking it, somehow, could we save our home, our lives." (145). As previously noted, two of Zelazny's strongest characteristics were a passionate desire not to be ruled by outside forces combined with a fascination with structure, systems, and patterns. Small wonder, then, that he would be drawn to the themes and the rhetoric of environmental activism through his familiarity with the writings of naturalists such as Aldo Leopold and Joseph Wood Krutch[75] and, as he was writing *Bridge of Ashes* five years after the first Earth Day in 1970, the inescapable drumbeat of an increasingly activist U.S. environmental movement.

Indeed, the character of Roderick Leishman shows some similarities to the legendary writer and activist Edward Abbey (1927–1989), whose novel *The Monkey Wrench Gang*, published the year before *Bridge of Ashes*, became a bible for proponents of "direct action" environmentalism. Like Abbey, Leishman worked for the National Park Service (labeled the "Forest Service" in Zelazny's novel) whose tourist-centric policies concerning land informed his environmental radicalism; like Zelazny, Abbey lived in New Mexico. Although there is no way to confirm whether Zelazny had read *The Monkey Wrench Gang* before completing *Bridge*, it is reasonable to assume, given Zelazny's omnivorous reading and particular interest in nature writing, that he would have been familiar with Abbey's other famous book, *Desert Solitaire* (1968), in which the author expresses both his devotion to the land of the U.S. Southwest and his rage at its commercial exploitation.

In short, *Bridge* was, like *Today*, another case of Zelazny's continuing his experiments with narrative form, delving into deeper real-world issues, and paying homage to the science-fictional traditions of his youth. As was the case with the earlier novel, these ambitions did not prevent the critical attention it received from being mixed at best, with most critics finding both the characters and the ideas underdeveloped, and reviewers in *Thrust: SF in Review* and *SF Booklog* finding it Zelazny's worst novel.[76] Kovacs declared it "one of the least successful or popular of Zelazny's novels," with only *Italbar* "less well received."[77] In an introduction to a later paperback edition of the novel, Zelazny acknowledged that it "was a very difficult book for [him] to write" and that "of all [his] works it is the one on which [he had] had the least feedback." If *Bridge* was a learning experience for its author, it was, unlike *Italbar*, a positive one. Zelazny remarked: "This is one of the five key books from which I learned things that have borne me through 30 or so others. For this reason it would be special to me."[78] Although the novel is admittedly underdeveloped, it is, especially in the larger context of Zelazny's work, more substantial than *Italbar*, less convoluted than *Today*, and, arguably, more interesting than either.

Samuel R. Delany has more than once referred to *Bridge of Ashes* as a superior Zelazny novel, along with the other sf novel Zelazny published in 1976.[79] In the twenty-first-century setting of *Doorways in the Sand*, humanity, in the early stages of interstellar exploration, has made contact with extraterrestrials and been invited to join a community of many different alien civilizations. To this end, Earth is participating in a chain exchange of culturally significant objects, each participant passing on to another objects given to it by yet another, thus creating "a sense of mutual obligation and trust" (23)[80] among the participating civilizations. Earth's initial contribution has been to exchange the *Mona Lisa* and the Crown Jewels of England for the "Rhennius machine" (22), a device humans don't yet fully understand, and the "star stone," an object that is a mystery to both humans and aliens. This backstory is gradually revealed by Fred Cassidy, the novel's narrator, whose two most notable characteristics are a love of climbing—the novel opens with him perched contentedly on a rooftop—and a refusal to graduate from college. Having been granted a substantial income from a rich uncle for the duration of his undergraduate education, Cassidy maintains his inheritance by continually changing majors, remaining perpetually a few credits shy of graduation, and along the way receiving an unusually broad education. After thwarting an attempt by his increasingly hostile academic advisor to force his graduation, he discovers that his apartment has been broken into by one of his professors, Paul Byler, who attacks him and demands to know what Cassidy has done with a model of an alien artifact—the star stone that is part of the human-alien exchange.

Cassidy's escape from Byler begins what is, for most of the remainder of the novel, an almost uninterrupted chase as the narrator is pursued by and forced to deal with various parties trying to locate the star stone, including two hitmen employed by British zealots who want to steal the star stone in retaliation for Earth's surrender of the Crown Jewels and two alien policemen, Charv and Ragma, who have taken the Earth forms of a kangaroo and a wombat. Along the way, Cassidy periodically experiences episodes of synesthesia that contain scrambled messages from an unknown entity who at one point orders him to pass through the Rhennius machine, an experience that reverses both his physiology and his perceptions so that he experiences the world as if looking in a mirror. Having survived this cascade of events, Cassidy is recruited by the State Department to serve with a U.N. delegation tasked with finding the star stone. Eventually, Cassidy learns that the unknown entity who has been messaging him is, in fact, the star stone, an artificial intelligence that entered his body through a cut in his hand and whose mysterious instructions have been aimed at the goal of activating itself. The stone is extracted, but Cassidy obeys its final instruction by pursuing a black cat to the rooftops, only to discover that the cat is yet another alien, part of an even larger conspiracy of civilizations that opposes admission of new members to the intergalactic community. The chase concludes with the alien falling to its death, and the novel concludes with Fred's agreeing to resume being a host for the star stone, both cultural ambassador and recording observer, as more and more worlds become part of the chain of interstellar civilizations.

As with *Today* and *Bridge*, Zelazny cannot resist tinkering with *Doorways'* chronology, beginning each chapter after the second with a brief flashback. Fred Cassidy's voice, like the voices of many in Zelazny's most famous works, is sharp, cynical, and on occasion learnedly allusive: Early in the novel, Cassidy compares the intergalactic system of chain giving to the *"kula* chain" of the indigenous peoples of New Guinea, as observed by the twentieth-century anthropologist Branislaw Malinowski (23);[81] later, a moment of introspection is triggered by a quotation from the twentieth-century American poet John Berryman (107). Cassidy also has his own poetic moments, from quickly sketched personified landscapes ("I watched the day drive west. The man in the moon was standing on his head" [33]) to an actual poem written during Cassidy's time as a math major in praise of the nineteenth-century geometer Nikolai Lobachevsky (40).[82] And his descriptions of receiving messages from the star stone return to the lyricism that entranced Zelazny's early readers:

> Some upwelling in the dark fishbowl atop the spine later splashed dreams, patterns memory-resistant as a swirl of noctilucae, across consciousness' thin, transparent rim, save for the kinesthetic/synesthetic DO YOU FEEL ME LED? which must have lasted a timeless time longer than the rest, for later, much later, morning's third coffee touched it to a penny's worth of spin, of color. (26)

These devices recall Zelazny's early work, but the uses to which he puts them reflect his by-now extensive experience as a novelist. Unlike the shifting narrative grounds of *Faces* and *Ashes*, the flashbacks of *Doorways* are precisely and consistently deployed to maintain reader suspense without slowing the story's forward momentum. Cassidy's wide range of reference is perfectly appropriate to a man who has spent almost a decade and a half taking courses in every subject his university offers—as Zelazny acknowledged, an undeniable nod to the author's own eccentric curricular path through college and graduate school.[83] All of this is in service to an sf adventure story whose outrageous aliens, breathless chases, and Perils of Pauline cliffhangers would not have been out of place in the pulp magazines of Zelazny's childhood, a story that, for all its frantic action and casual violence, is much lighter in tone than its predecessors. If "He Who Shapes" was Zelazny's attempt at writing a literary tragedy, *Doorways in the Sand* marks his first major attempt to write a literary comedy.

All of the novel's carefully deployed devices are put to use for the character of Fred Cassidy, who is a different person at the end of the story than he was at the beginning. In the book's early chapters, he is as moody, self-absorbed, and belligerently independent as many another Zelazny protagonist. Circumventing bureaucratic paperwork, he declares, "I have always been a firm believer in my right to do anything I cannot be stopped from doing" (29); when confronted later with his university's finally coming up with a way to graduate him, his response is sheer rage (87–91). But after he has survived his adventures he listens to and ultimately accepts his mentor Professor Dobson's advice not to turn his back on a cosmos in which humanity's existence is intertwined with that of other races: "I know we have something to contribute. It remains to be found, but it must be found. . . . Learn something from [your experiences]. Humility, if nothing else" (178–79). In allowing himself to be linked to the star stone and becoming an ambassador, Cassidy moves from a life of trying to simultaneously manipulate and hide from a larger system of relationships and obligations to a life of exploration and service within the largest system of all—the universe itself.[84]

In his review for *F&SF* Budrys noted this move toward greater awareness of the rest of the world, finding in the novel both "a return toward the power Zelazny once displayed" and "a maturation that runs deeper than witticism." Other reviews were mixed and, on occasion, contradictory, with one reviewer's "deft, delicious, and zany" being another's "competent, entertaining potboiler." Some, such as Susan Wood, thought the book was still not on a par with what the author was fully capable of but better than his other recent efforts, a sentiment shared at least in part by Budrys, who praised Cassidy's characterization because it was "rather more than a collection of tics."[85] But Zelazny's peers and fans found it deserving of more than faint praise, as *Doorways in the Sand* was a finalist for the Hugo and the Nebula Awards, the first of his novels to make both ballots since *Lord of Light. Doorways* was also included on the American Library Association's annual list of best books for young adults.[86]

If *Doorways* considers how someone might ultimately function within a system, the protagonist of *My Name Is Legion* (1976) is determined to hide from the system altogether. The book is comprised of three previously published novellas: "The Eve of RUMOKO" (1969), "'Kjwalll'kje'k'koothailll'kje'k'" (1973), and "Home Is the Hangman" (1975). All are standalone stories that do not connect to form a continuous novel, but all feature the same protagonist, have the same early twenty-first-century setting (the first story is set in 2007), and take place in chronological order.

The stories' narrator—a man whose real name, per the book's title, is never given—is a computer programmer who is deeply involved in a massive project to link the world's computer systems into a "Central Data Bank" (21),[87] enabling instant access to all information about anyone in the world at any time. At first he is enthusiastic about the project, believing it would "eliminate crime" and facilitate health care (22). He eventually realizes, however, that such a system would not only inevitably fail to account for deception, malice, and greed but was also potentially "a monster" whose surveillance might be "the ultimate invasion of human privacy" (24). He destroys all his personal data, opting completely out of the system and committing to a life of shifting, constructed identities, becoming "the man who did not exist" (39). Now perfectly positioned to perform tasks for people who want their activities to remain outside the system, he educates himself to the point of being "not an expert in anything" but "know[ing] a little bit about lots of esoteric things" (41) and forms a relationship with Don Walsh, the head of Walsh's Private Investigations, "the third-largest detective agency in the world" (44). Four times each year he makes himself available to Walsh for jobs that require both his special skills and carefully maintained anonymity, jobs for which he is paid, of course, only in cash.

Each of the novellas centers on one of the narrator's jobs for Walsh. In "The Eve of RUMOKO" he investigates attempts to sabotage the RUMOKO Project, an effort to ease population pressures by using controlled atomic blasts to create a new chain of volcanic islands in the Caribbean. The narrator uncovers and prevents the attack on the project, and RUMOKO goes off successfully. He regrets his actions, however, when he discovers that the would-be saboteurs were agents of New Salem, an underwater city whose protective dome was damaged during the explosions, causing fatalities. He is torn between pride in accomplishing his mission and guilt about the fact that doing so meant committing torture and murder; he is also distraught because Eve, a woman he had loved and lost, had lived in New Salem and, it is implied, was one of the casualties. With another such project, Baltimore II, scheduled, the narrator decides to end the program once and for all by sabotaging the next one himself in a way that will yield not a controlled explosion but "a Krakatoa, at least" (63). Resigned to inevitable casualties, he can only hope the disaster of New Salem will lead the residents of Baltimore II to evacuate before the next explosion.

"'Kjwalll'kje'k'koothailll'kje'k" (hereafter "K") returns to an ocean setting as the narrator conducts an undercover investigation of two recent murders at an undersea park near the Bahamian island of Andros. The park is maintained by Beltrane Processing, a high-tech enterprise that extracts uranium from seawater. The case is unusual in that the murders have been blamed on a deliberate attack by dolphins. The narrator takes the job in part because Andros is home to Martha Millay, an underwater photographer and author whose work he admires. Once in place at Beltrane's Station One, he gradually uncovers a complicated web of criminal activity centered around a diamond-smuggling operation. During his investigation the narrator visits Millay, the half-Japanese daughter of "a Hiroshima baby" who keeps her distance from the world because of "genetic damage" that has affected the lower half of her body (84) but who willingly engages the narrator in an extended philosophical discussion concerning the nature of dolphin society and the possibility of a religious impulse within that society. The narrator solves the case and exonerates the dolphins, but in so doing he discovers that there may be someone on the island who knows who he truly is—information that in the past he has "killed to protect" (103). A final meeting with Millay reveals that she is a telepath who can link with dolphins as well as humans. Though not directly responsible for any of the killings, she orchestrated the circumstances within which they occurred in order to protect the site of the diamond cache, which was also the home of the title character, a dolphin whose transcendent "dreamsong" (139) provides the religious experience Millay had implied in their earlier conversation. After forming a telepathic link with Millay that enables the narrator to experience the dreamsong, the two agree to keep each other's secrets, the narrator concluding that "the best words are often those left unsaid" (140).

The investigation in "Home Is the Hangman" looks not beneath the ocean but out into the solar system. A spacecraft containing the Hangman,[88] a remotely controlled robot designed for outer-space exploration, has returned to Earth unexpectedly, landing in the Gulf of Mexico. The robot is suspected of murdering Manny Burns, one of four experts who originally trained and controlled it. Another member of the group, the powerful U.S. senator Jesse Brockden, is convinced that the robot is after all of them, while the other two—David Fentris, a consulting engineer in Memphis, and Leila Thackery, a psychiatrist in St. Louis—believe that Brockden is paranoid and that the robot is not a threat. The narrator is reluctant to pursue the matter, in part because he recognizes Fentris as someone he worked with on the Central Data Bank and who, therefore, knows his true identity. But when he discovers that Brockden is a member of the Senate committee considering possible reform of the Central Data Bank, he takes the case.

After interviewing Thackery and Fentris, the latter of whom does not appear to recognize him, the narrator learns that someone else has confessed to Burns's murder; relieved, he is ready to abandon the case. But after a video message from Fentris revealing that he has been attacked, is near death, and did recognize his interviewer, the narrator rushes back to Thackery, only to discover that she has been murdered as well. The action then shifts to Brockden's cabin in Wisconsin, where, in a frozen winter landscape, the senator admits to the narrator his belief that the robot seeks vengeance for the group's using it, during a drunken celebration, to commit a prank that went wrong and killed a security guard. When the robot arrives in search of Brockden, it does not kill anyone but permits the narrator to communicate one-on-one via the remote controller's helmet that he recovered from Fentris' residence. The narrator learns that the team members' deaths were caused not by the robot but by a web of human actions and that the robot simply sought "to say good-bye to [its] parents" (211). The robot returns to its exploration of space, leaving the narrator feeling a "kinship" with the Hangman "for the things [they] had in common, those ways [they] dwelled apart" (212). But when the narrator wonders "under what peculiar skies and in what strange lands [he] might one day be remembered," he concludes that "this thought should have made [him] happier than it did" (213).

The novellas of *My Name Is Legion* obviously function as science fiction mysteries, a longstanding subgenre examples of which range from Isaac Asimov's "robot detective" novels, begun with *The Caves of Steel* (1953), to China Mieville's *The City and the City* (2009) and Martha Wells's Murderbot series, begun in 2017. In the debut issue of *Isaac Asimov's Science Fiction Magazine* Charles N. Brown explicitly categorized *Legion* as an sf mystery, pairing it with another tryptic of novellas about a future detective, Larry Niven's *The Long Arm of Gil Hamilton* (1976). In his review Brown concludes that Niven "is a better whodunit writer" and Zelazny "falls more into the hardboiled school." Although the latter categorization is no surprise to anyone familiar with Zelazny's previous work, his "nameless, wise-cracking private eye" is his most overt nod to crime fiction in general and the *noir* tradition in particular.[89] Zelazny cited his own nameless investigator's predecessors in Dashiell Hammett's Continental Op and Walter Gibson's Shadow and considered the character a "tribute" to John D. MacDonald's Travis McGee, another detective who lived as much as possible off the grid while serving as "a last resort" for his clients—and who, like the narrator of "Hangman," resides on a boat.[90]

But also in the tradition of Hammett and MacDonald, not to mention Raymond Chandler, Zelazny crafted crime stories that are about much more than the crime. Indeed, in the *Legion* novellas the mystery itself is secondary to larger concerns: in "RUMOKO," the willfully ignored environmental consequences of high-tech interventions; in "K," the nature of the religious impulse in humans and nonhumans; in "Hangman," the problems inherent in the attempt to create artificial intelligence and, more deeply, the burdens of human responsibility and guilt. Behind all of these concerns lie the core issues of personal identity and the struggle to live a responsible but also autonomous and private life in a world of centralized databases and panoptic surveillance—a world inspired by Zelazny's experiences within the Social Security Administration[91] and, it seems almost redundant to note, a world quite similar to our own.[92] It may be equally redundant to note how fully *Legion*'s narrator fits the profile of many other Zelazny protagonists given his canonically inflected humor (his assumed names include John Donne and Stephen Foster), his occasionally lyrical descriptions ("and then the sun returned to dry the decks and warm the just-rinsed world" [85]), his wide knowledge of many subjects and deep philosophical interest in some, his obsession with avoiding control, and his willingness to engage in political violence. At the same time, he maintains a sincere concern for the stewardship of the natural world, a profound sense of guilt about his violent actions, and, as articulated in the conclusion of "Hangman," a nascent uncertainty as to the value of his much-defended autonomy if that autonomy leaves him as isolated from humanity as a spacefaring robot. Like Corwin by the end of the Amber series or Fred Cassidy at the end of *Doorways in the Sand*, Zelazny's nameless detective concludes his adventures facing the possibility that one's own way, in both the having and the going, may not be all there is to life.

If *My Name Is Legion* connects with the themes and concerns of Zelazny's earlier work, it also stands apart from that work, beyond its status as a science fiction mystery. Of all Zelazny's standalone sf books, it is the closest to "hard" science fiction, stories that describe a world that operates according to the principles of science and foregrounds those principles and the technologies that might emerge from them. In contrast to the far-future adventure of *This Immortal*, the "science fantasy" of *Lord of Light* and *Jack of Shadows*, and the painted-with-broad-strokes futures of his other novels of the 1970s, the novellas included in *Legion* do not hesitate to pause and explicate both concepts and hardware—the geology of the earth's crust in "RUMOKO," the biology of dolphins and the physics of scuba diving in "K," and computer science, engineering, and artificial intelligence theory in "Hangman," which first appeared in the most science-centric of the sf magazines, *Analog Science Fiction/Science Fact*.

The stories suggest that Zelazny's wide reading included works of science and technology as well as books about literature, history, and mythology and that he could apply the former kinds of knowledge to his fiction as readily as he could the latter. In correspondence with Carl Yoke, Zelazny discussed in detail the differing evaluations of the costs and benefits of technology offered by John McHale's *Future of the Future* (1969) and Eugene S. Schwartz's *Overskill* (1971), suggesting that in "RUMOKO" the "concern for possible disasters by the misuse of technology" anticipated Schwartz's arguments "quite nicely."[93] Within the narrator and Millay's discussion of the nature of dolphin thought and culture, "K" references by name, and at some length, Johan Huizinga's

Homo Ludens: A Study of the Play-Element in Culture (1938). And "Hangman" demonstrates sharp awareness of scientific and philosophical theories of the nature of intelligence.

The *Legion* novellas also show Zelazny's increasing maturity in terms of his presentation of female characters. "RUMOKO," published in 1969, harks back to the younger writer in that its protagonist is motivated in part by the loss of a true love; the female character actually on stage, security officer Carol Deith, is a strong and capable individual, but her interactions with the narrator are still largely defined by speculation as to whether she has fallen in love with him. In "K," however, Martha Millay is presented fully on her own terms, successfully enacts her own agenda, and is uninterested in any romantic entanglements. Although the narrator finds her "exceedingly attractive" (89), when he asks to see her again, she declines, and he does not pursue the matter. And in "Hangman," published six years after "RUMOKO," Leila Thackery is simply part of the team that designed the robot, presented on a matter-of-factly equal professional and intellectual footing with her male colleagues.[94]

In short, *My Name Is Legion* is one of Zelazny's most interesting and artistically successful books. Such an assessment was not reflected in the reviews of the day, which tended to see the book as formulaic even as they disagreed about the all-important narrator, with one reviewer put off by the character's "callousness," another claiming that his "ruthlessness" is "never adequately justified," and still another acknowledging the narrator's remorse for many of his actions.[95] The last of these, by Susan Wood, also praised "Hangman" in particular as equal to Zelazny's work of the 1960s, signaling what is as close to a universal consensus as may be found in the response of contemporary reviewers and later scholars: that "Hangman" is superior to the other two novellas.[96]

It is hard to argue with this appraisal. "RUMOKO" and "K" are most engaging when laying out the narrator's backstory and the larger issues at stake and much less so when advancing the mystery plot (with "K" carrying the added burden of being a novella with a novel's worth of characters). In contrast, "Hangman" is a perfectly paced story in which the mystery and the sf elements are effectively interwoven. The often expository dialogue propels rather than drags, and the author's more literary sensibilities are deeply and usefully embedded in the story. In particular, few if any Zelazny stories establish and elaborate a single literary allusion as does "Hangman" with Mary Shelley's *Frankenstein*, from Senator Brockden's early reference to the robot as "Frankenstein's monster" (158) to the story's opening and concluding with the narrator having a final confrontation with the escaped artificial being in the frozen North. Most of all, the narrator moves toward a greater awareness of the magnitude of the issues that confront him, even if none of those issues is close to being resolved. "Hangman" arguably answers in the affirmative the question Joanna Russ asked almost a decade earlier in her review of *Lord of Light*: "Will Zelazny ever write the inside stories of his stories?" The story won both the Hugo and the Nebula Awards for Best Novella, the only Zelazny work published in the 1970s to win either award, and, almost startlingly, the only one ever to win both.

On more than one occasion Zelazny indicated his fondness for *Legion*'s narrator and his interest in writing more stories about him.[97] Unfortunately, he never did, focusing instead on the novels with which he was supporting himself and his family and, especially with the Amber series, continuing to expand his popularity. Zelazny's last novel of the 1970s was *Roadmarks* (1979); like *Jack of Shadows*, it may be seen as a transitional work, looking back to earlier concerns and techniques while signaling what lay ahead in the next phase of Zelazny's career.

The central conceit of *Roadmarks* is "the Road," a construct that embodies the fundamental nature of time: "Time is a superhighway with many exits and entrances, main routes and secondary roads . . . the maps keep changing . . . only a few know how to find the access ramps" (45).[98] As with the actual U.S. interstate highway system, a vast support network of fueling stations, restaurants, overnight accommodations, and so on exists to support the few who can both access and navigate the road, individuals who identify themselves by century (e.g., "C Eighteen") and have developed a "foretalk lingo" (28) to bridge communication gaps both cultural and chronological. The novel's central character, Red Dorakeen, one of the few, is traveling the Road in search of a barely remembered destination that he thinks lies beyond one of the constantly shifting off-ramps. While on his journey, assisted by an AI in the form of a volume of Charles Baudelaire's *Flowers of Evil*, Red is subjected to repeated assassination attempts by agents of Chadwick, a former business partner who has declared a "black decade": a sanctioned series of murder attempts that, if not succeeding after ten tries, must be called off. Red's journey is presented in a continuous narrative in chapters titled "One." These alternate with more wide-ranging chapters, all titled "Two," that offer backstories for several of the assassins as well as a secondary narrative of Randy, a man of the present day who discovers that a copy of Walt Whitman's *Leaves of Grass* that belonged to his father, who disappeared long ago, is in fact a "microdot computer array" (83) that grants him access to the Road. In the novel's final chapters, the storylines come together as Red, finally encountering Chadwick, discovers that both the journey he was compelled to make and the black decade he tried to avoid were set in motion so that Chadwick might return to his, and Red's, original form: one of the "dragons of Bel'kwinith," powerful aliens who caused the Road to come into being. After Chadwick's transformation, Red, whose "time is not yet come," must continue on his journey (180). The novel concludes with Randy, contentedly spending his time in "C Eleven Abyssinia" (183), reunited with his father—who is, of course, Red.

Zelazny's claim that *Roadmarks* "was harder to write than to read"[99] is understandable given that the novel is one of his most conceptually audacious and perhaps his most formally experimental work since *Creatures of Light and Darkness*. Beyond simply alternating parallel storylines, one linear and one not, Zelazny claimed that he took the "Two" chapters and "shuffled them before reinserting them between the Ones."[100] Zelazny's editor asked that the "Two" chapters be rearranged yet again to reduce confusion.[101] Even with this accommodation, and despite Zelazny's claim above, the result is a book that, as it immerses the reader in near-constant motion and events, also demands the reader's patience and faith that all the moving parts will eventually form a coherent whole. For the most part, they do. The deeper background of the Road remains sketchy—the black decade is subject to regulation by a "Games Board" that is never really explained beyond its name, and the fantastic qualities of the Road are described primarily in terms of the impossibility of describing them. As the *Leaves of Grass* AI attempts to explain to Randy, "Only certain people or machines can find [the Road] and travel it. I do not know why. The Road is an organic thing. This is a part of its nature" (131). But by story's end, the far-flung cast of characters all manage to connect, more or less plausibly, and their stories resolve, more or less satisfactorily.

Along the way are many recognizable elements and callbacks to earlier stories: the mandatory martial arts set piece, in this case two assassins vying for the chance to dispatch Red; the semi-amnesiac protagonist capable of self-regeneration;[102] the blameless individual triggered by outside sources to recover his violent nature (the monk Timyin Tin; compare *Creatures of Light and Darkness*); the shifting of prose style to indicate different levels of reality—the latter emerging in the "Two" section describing Randy's life in the present day, written in the understated declarative sentences of many a work of late twentieth-century American literary fiction. Randy gains the ability to access the Road in a transitional journey from the real to the fantastic that recalls Corwin's first journey from Earth to Amber. The novel is also, at points, overtly comic, with a Marquis de Sade pressed into service as an instructor in a writer's workshop and the Flowers of Evil AI, who identifies as female[103] and has a sexual relationship with Mondamay, an alien killing machine whose deficient programming has left him an ineffective assassin who would much rather be a potter. As Krulik notes, although *Roadmarks* does not offer the consistent comedy of *Doorways in the Sand*, it is still an often whimsical novel whose "view of life . . . is certainly tongue in cheek."[104]

As indicated by the presence of de Sade (and, more briefly, Adolf Hitler and Jack the Ripper), Zelazny does not hesitate to bring historical figures into the mix, as he did in *Bridge of Ashes*. He also presents as characters more specifically literary figures, including the author Antoine de St. Exupéry and the pulp hero Doc Savage, and grounds the novel in prior works of the fantastic, including his own. The author acknowledged the book's overall debt to Philip José Farmer's Riverworld series, substituting a superhighway for a super-river, and suggested that Timyin Tin drew on another character of religious conviction, Sugata in *Lord of Light*.[105] In short, *Roadmarks* has something for almost everyone in Zelazny's audience.

There are also things the book does not have. Unlike *Lord of Light* or *Creatures of Light and Darkness*, which had the standing structures (however freely applied) of the Hindu and Egyptian pantheons to give shape to Zelazny's outbursts of language and imagination, *Roadmarks* offers the superficial conceit of the Road; unlike the Amber novels or *My Name Is Legion*, it does not have a charismatic narrator; unlike *Legion* or *Doorways in the Sand*, the linear narrative is interrupted not by carefully controlled flashbacks but by randomized sidebars; unlike even Zelazny's less well-regarded novels, there are no lyrical pauses, only exposition and dialogue and moving on down the Road. The protagonists learn important things about their place in the universe, but there is little sense of their having changed in a meaningful way that will lead to different subsequent behavior. Indeed, *subsequent* cannot have any meaning in the world of the novel, where time sprawls in all directions along an ever-shifting road and the journey of the hero is a journey toward youth: "Before those of my blood can reach maturity," he says, "we must be set upon the Road to grow young" (157). Perhaps most fundamentally, Zelazny's determination not to overexplain to the reader yields the same mixed results as in *Today We Choose Faces* and *Bridge of Ashes*, novels that leave the reader wanting more—not yearning for a continuation of an immersive narrative but yearning for more development of what is already there. Reviewing the novel in *Locus*, Charles N. Brown complained that it seemed more an "outline" than a "completed book."[106]

Zelazny himself seemed more interested in the journey than the destination, declaring that he "wouldn't have had the guts" to randomize the "Two" sections of *Roadmarks* "without [his] experience with [his] other experimental books and the faith it had given [him]e in the feelings [he'd] developed toward narrative."[107] If Zelazny began his career as a full-time writer terrified he would not be prolific enough to make a living, by the end of his first full decade of self-employment, it was clear that he need not have worried. He was also confident enough in his abilities not only to continue experimentation for its own sake but also to be satisfied with his efforts when critics and readers were not. Toward the end of the decade, acknowledging the mounting negative criticism of his more recent books, he insisted that he regarded those books not as "a let-down" but as "a series of different endeavors," remarking, "I never had the intention of writing the same sort of material *ad nauseum* [*sic*]. . . . I have been doing a variety of things during the past four years, just as I intend to do other sorts of things in the future."[108] More often than not, the author seemed satisfied with simply having tried something challenging. This was one of the many contradictions in Zelazny's character and career: the determined, calculating professional perfectly willing, even eager, to write to the market, but also determined to satisfy, at least occasionally, his own "feelings . . . towards narrative." That he interrupted the writing of *Roadmarks* to complete the fifth Amber novel[109] suggests which impulse ultimately took precedence. As Zelazny entered his second decade of full-time writing, his output would make his priorities still clearer.

NOTHING ON SPEC BUT STILL SOME JOY
1980–1995

On July 31, 1980, Roger Zelazny incorporated himself as The Amber Corporation.[1] Self-incorporation was not unusual for a successful writer—sf figures from Edgar Rice Burroughs to Isaac Asimov, Harlan Ellison, and Robert Silverberg had all done so. Zelazny's decision demonstrates both his careful attention to the finances of his writing career and the material success that career had brought him; his choice of corporate name signals his awareness of the main source of that success.

As Zelazny maintained that success in the 1980s and the early 1990s, his ever-expanding bibliography could be considered to support the belief that he had largely abandoned the artistic ambitions of his earlier career. From 1980 to 1995 he published twenty-three books. Of these, only two, *Eye of Cat* (1982) and *A Night in the Lonesome October* (1993), were standalone solo adult novels. The rest were installments in fantasy series (including five more volumes of the Amber series), collaborative novels, short fiction collections, or edited anthologies, as well as one novel for younger readers. During this period he actually produced more short fiction than he had in the previous decade, publishing approximately thirty stories.

It is difficult to argue that much of this prodigious output can be ranked with the best of his work from the 1960s and 1970s. Even so prominent an acolyte as Neil Gaiman felt that by the early 1980s Zelazny had "lost his inspiration, lost his joy[;] . . . [it] felt sometimes, terribly, as if he was going through the motions."[2] In a 1983 book review column Norman Spinrad summed up the situation in language that echoed the diagnoses of Sidney Coleman and Richard Cowper: "Today the general critical wisdom within the genre is that Zelazny has become a writer who somehow has failed to live up to his extraordinary promise, and one who is no longer considered to have 'serious literary ambition' by those who consider such things at all."[3] This evaluation was particularly damning coming from Spinrad, a well-known sf novelist and direct contemporary of Zelazny's who had also been strongly associated with the New Wave.

"General critical wisdom" notwithstanding, Zelazny the author proceeded apace through this period as a powerful commercial and popular force, moving from one contracted novel to the next: "I will not write a book on spec," he declared in 1987.[4] This is not to say that he did not derive personal satisfaction from his various projects or had completely abandoned artistic standards concerning them. He chafed at the extensive publisher-imposed restrictions on his one attempt at a young adult novel, A Dark Traveling (1987), and bemoaned the rushed revision process that left intact a brief passage of what he considered to be unnecessarily repetitive description.[5] He enjoyed collaborating with his friend and fellow New Mexico transplant Fred Saberhagen on the novels Coils and The Black Throne, and he was sufficiently taken with the material of Wilderness, a historical novel written with Gerald Housman, that he violated his own rule and worked on the book "as a hobby," without a contract.[6]

On the other hand, Zelazny wrote the fantasy novel Madwand when his agent offered increased royalties for a sequel to Changeling, and his collaborations with Thomas T. Thomas, The Mask of Loki and Flare, were, respectively, Thomas's novel from Zelazny's outline and Thomas's novel with Zelazny's editorial comments.[7] Perhaps most tellingly, Zelazny admitted in correspondence that his motivation for writing the Dilvish the Damned series—his most straightforward sword-and-sorcery fiction, consisting of a 1981 novel, *The Changing Land*, and eleven works of short fiction published from 1964 to 1981 and collected in 1982 as *Dilvish the Damned*—was that of the pragmatic professional: "To tell the truth," he wrote Joseph Sanders, "I invented the series because I find that sort of thing very easy to write, and I thought it would be useful to have such a thing going for those occasions when I might need a story in a hurry."[8] It is reasonable to think that Zelazny saw all of this as part and parcel of being a productive professional. But it is also understandable that admirers such as Spinrad and Gaiman would see such output as a betrayal of early promise or, at best, going through the motions.

Of the series and collaborative work that Zelazny produced in the final decade and a half of his career, the most significant by far was the second series of Amber novels, beginning with *Trumps of Doom* (1985). Kovacs describes Zelazny's continuation of the chronicles of Amber as a combination of "requests by fans, pressure from publishers, and ideas for new stories," and Zelazny stated on more than one occasion that he did in fact have more Amber stories that he wanted to tell.[9] One may assume, however, that the offer by Avon Books of a six-figure advance for three more Amber books—"a huge advance in those days," according to Zelazny's editor David G. Hartwell—was also a deciding factor. As Hartwell noted, "He was a commercial writer and went with the biggest money first."[10]

Trumps of Doom opens with the narrator, Merle Corey, a San Francisco computer programmer, warily noting the current date of April 30, the date on which someone has tried to kill him for seven consecutive years. In short order, Merle is revealed to be Corwin of Amber's son Merlin, and an escalating series of violent encounters reveals that there are people on Earth who know of Amber and of Merlin's connection to it. During a visit to Bill Roth, his father's attorney from his days on Earth, Merlin demonstrates his access not only to the powers of the Trumps but also to the Logrus, through which, as the son of Dara of Chaos as well as Corwin of Amber, he can channel the powers of the Courts of Chaos. His conversations with Roth also reveal that Corwin's whereabouts have remained a mystery and confirm the existence of Ghostwheel, a computer program that Merlin has designed to function outside of the norms of shadow Earth.

Inevitably, Merlin returns to Amber, where his uncle Caine has been murdered. Funeral preparations are under way, and Merlin reunites with several of the surviving royals of Amber who populated the first series: his uncles Gerard, Julian, and Random, his aunts Flora and Fiona, and his cousin Martin. During a quick return to shadow Earth, Merlin learns that it was a college friend, Luke Reynard, who has tried to kill him every April 30. Back in Amber after Caine's funeral, Merlin admits to Random, who still reigns as king, that Ghostwheel draws on the powers of the Pattern of Amber. Fearing that Ghostwheel could be weaponized, Random orders Merlin to travel to the shadow world to shut his creation down. Merlin grudgingly agrees, but various forces impede him in his journey, including Ghostwheel itself, which appears to be self-aware and does not want to be shut off. By the end of the novel Merlin find himself imprisoned, like his namesake, in a crystal cave by Luke, who is actually Rinaldo, son of Brand, Merlin's uncle, who attempted to seize power in Amber, engaged in prolonged battle with Corwin, and was finally killed by Caine. It was Luke who killed Caine and has tried to kill Corwin's son each year on the anniversary of the day Luke learned of his own father's death.

As in the original series, the books advance the narrative almost without interruption, each picking up where the previous one left off; the next volume, *Blood of Amber* (1986), begins with Merlin's escaping the cave. After reestablishing contact with his family, he continues his quest to determine the whys and wherefores of his situation, with the added imperative of finding Luke and preventing more violence against himself and his family. As the story unfolds through this and the remaining three novels in the series—*Sign of Chaos* (1987), *Knight of Shadows* (1989), and *Prince of Chaos* (1991)—Merlin essentially abandons shadow Earth while sinking deeper into the worlds of his origin, Amber and Chaos, and points in between. Corwin's siblings fade into the background as Merlin has to deal with a new array of relatives and interested parties, all of whom are either immediate or potential threats. Throughout, Merlin remains almost constantly in motion and conflict. In both transporting and defending himself he continually draws on not only the teleportation function of the Trumps and the energy of the Pattern (which, in *Blood of Amber*, he walks successfully) but also the powers of Chaos as channeled through the Logrus and the periodic help of his own creation, Ghostwheel (which, as the series progresses, becomes an incarnate, though not embodied, intelligence, often troublesome but frequently useful, who calls Merlin "Dad"). In his most prolonged and difficult journey, which takes up much of *Knight of Shadows*, he struggles to navigate a silent, photo-negative landscape in which he is sequentially confronted by creatures including ghosts of dead relatives who try to steer him toward a path he does not want to take and choices he does not want to make.

In the final two volumes of the series the core dilemma of choice versus destiny comes to the fore as Merlin learns that there are larger issues at stake than the palace intrigues of Amber. Both Pattern and Logrus have, in effect, become sentient forces, intractably opposed. Each demands that Merlin—a son of Amber and Chaos whose father's construction of an alternate Pattern disrupted the balance of power—choose sides. Complicating matters is Merlin's discovery that he stands third in line for the throne of Chaos, that his mother Dara and stepbrother Mandor are eager for him to assume power, and that his very conception was a strategic act in which the Logrus selected Corwin so that Dara would produce "an ideal Lord of Chaos . . . fit to rule" (1182).[11] After numerous battles with Pattern-generated ghosts of both the living and the dead and a reunion with his father, who has been held prisoner in Chaos the entire time, Merlin agrees to take the throne of Chaos, but only after a sorcery-laden battle at the end of which he has subdued his mother and stepbrother, ensuring that his rule in Chaos will be on no one's terms but his own.

More than any of Zelazny's books, the novels of the second Amber series exemplify popularity and commercial success at odds with critical regard. His publisher extended what had been a large advance for three novels into a five-book deal for, presumably, even more money.[12] Although ignored by the Hugo and Nebula voters, the first three volumes of the new series placed, respectively, first, second, and third in the *Locus* magazine annual readers' polls for best fantasy novel,[13] as the readership for the Amber novels evolved into its own subfandom.

Reviewers were less enthusiastic. Martin Morse Wooster, writing in the *Washington Post Book World*, praised *Trumps of Doom*'s "cool tone, Chandleresque in its wry depictions of contemporary Albuquerque," but regretted that the novel seemed simply a setup for subsequent volumes, suggesting that in an earlier era the entire book "would have been the first three chapters of a novel." Both the *Post* and the *New York Times*, reviewing *Blood of Amber*, found the novel a lesser display of Zelazny's abilities. The *Post*'s Gregory Feeley noted that the author's "range has narrowed considerably over the past dozen years," while the *Times*'s Gerald Jonas suggested that Zelazny "whittled down his narrative to two kinds of scenes: scenes of action . . . and scenes of reflection." Whereas Feeley still found value in the "force of his slangy, off-hand lyricism," Jonas condemned not just the novel but the entire Amber series as "full of ambiguities of a particularly perverse kind, since the rules that govern this universe can be understood only by the author, who made them up in the first place."[14] The entire second series was all but ignored by reviewers in the major science fiction magazines of the day.

It is hard to argue that Merlin's story carries the thrill of discovery of Corwin's narrative, the sense of encountering a new approach to an old story. As the second series progresses, Merlin commands multiple magics—the Pattern, the Logrus, Ghostwheel, a semi-sentient strangling cord named Frakir that leaps into action as needed—that can do everything from teleporting him away from a charging opponent to fetching him a beer. As a result, he seems, at any given moment, under significantly less threat than his father ever was. The apparatus of serialization that increasingly undercut the first five volumes becomes even more unwieldy in the second series, as the author must continually remind the readers—and, via the increasingly expository dialogue, the characters must remind themselves—of what has come before. In his review of *Blood of Amber*, and in a curious echo of at least one of the readings of *Lord of Light* discussed in Chapter 2, Jonas went so far as to suggest the novel's prologue "reads like a parody of the entire sword and sorcery genre."[15] As both the *Times* and the *Post* noted, for all its complex action and cast of characters, there is almost a sense of constriction within the second series, as any given scene is either one of action, in which anything can happen, or one of dialogue, in which the characters are so thoroughly misleading one another that often it is difficult to maintain interest in any of them. It is understandable that, as Kovacs notes, many found Merlin's adventures "more like a haphazard series of episodes, lacking a coherent story."[16]

Still, there is much in the second Amber series that is relevant to Zelazny's work as a whole. Merlin is a charming, articulate, clever fellow who can hold his own in a fight and win the loyalty of those around him; he is also wounded, suspicious, and uncertain of his place in the world. In short, he is very much his father's son and fully within the tradition of the Zelazny hero. Merlin demonstrates the same eclectic cultural literacy as do his predecessors, from offhandedly referencing a lesser-known Robert Browning poem to name-checking contemporary jazz musicians. As always, Zelazny cannot resist sharing an occasional joke with the reader, be it absurd (the bridge between *Blood of Amber* and *Sign of Chaos* is a psychedelic hallucination featuring characters from *Alice's Adventures in Wonderland*; when Luke's mother Jasra is put under a spell that leaves her frozen like a statue, she is occasionally used as a coat rack) or crude (the court jester of Amber is named Droppa MaPantz; Merlin's initial discovery of the Keep of Four Worlds evokes a famously obscene limerick when he encounters an old hermit named Dave). From the first volume on, there are enough one-on-one combat sequences, with and without swords, to reassure any Zelazny devotee that the author has maintained his expertise in fencing and martial arts.

There are also aspects of the second series that show Zelazny the writer keeping up with the times while returning to his interest in combining science fiction and fantasy and never completely abandoning his interest in experimenting with the technical aspects of narrative. As *Nine Princes in Amber* is a product of its time, more than a decade later *Trumps of Doom* opens the second series with yet more direct markers of time and place. If Corwin, created in the 1960s, was a popular songwriter on shadow Earth, then Merlin, created in the early 1980s, is a computer programmer; *Princes* opens in a vaguely sketched-in upstate New York, while the opening chapters of *Trumps* are specifically set in San Francisco and Zelazny's adopted town of Santa Fe. A minor character wears a Pink Floyd tee shirt, and Random's son Martin sports a mohawk. In addition, Merlin's creation Ghostwheel is introduced in at least a somewhat science-fictional manner, as Merlin attempts to deflect Luke's initial inquiries by asserting that the device is "only [amenable] to a mathematical explanation" and cannot work on Earth because of "theoretical crap involving space and time and some guys named Everett and Wheeler" (627).[17] The physicists Hugh Everett and John Wheeler were famously associated with the "many worlds" interpretation of quantum mechanics, a reference that was certainly apt for the Amber series. A reader encountering the novel on its publication in 1985 might well wonder whether Zelazny was making a move back to the mashup of science fiction and fantasy that marked his early work. And there is at least a glimpse of Zelazny the technician of narrative when, in the final chapters of *Knight of Shadows*, Merlin discovers a mysterious ring in Brand's apartment in Castle Amber and puts it on. In one of the most subtle stylistic moves in any Zelazny work, for the remainder of the novel Merlin's narration quietly but discernibly takes on a more distant, imperial, and quietly threatening tone, advancing plot through style by signaling that the act of putting on the ring has somehow changed him.

Perhaps the most notable progression in the second Amber series is in its female characters. As Lindskold and Khanna have noted, the women in the second series are more prominently featured and operate with significantly more agency than do those in the first series, and, as Khanna notes, Merlin seems to spend more time with his aunts than with his uncles.[18] Aunts Flora, Fiona, and Vialle are continually involved in the story, with Vialle, Random's wife and Queen of Amber, much more of a royal power than in the first series: She actively directs Merlin's actions and at a crucial moment puts Luke under her protection. Nadya and Coral, sisters from a neighboring kingdom, pursue their own political agendas beyond their increasingly personal engagement with Merlin and, eventually, Luke, and Jasra, although primarily an oppositional force, is nonetheless a strongly individuated one. For that matter, the two nonhuman forces tasked with protecting Merlin, the Farkir and the "ty'iga," a demon compelled by Dara to protect him that does so by serially possessing various people in his life, are both identified as female.[19] Although, as Khanna observes, the increased presence of women diminishes as the series progresses, with the various female characters (Dara notably excepted) becoming more and more reactive,[20] on the whole, women are more actively and independently present in Merlin's life than in Corwin's.

Of all the female characters, it is Merlin's mother Dara who has the greatest impact on him. As Feeley observed in his review of *Blood of Amber*, many of Zelazny's stories involve fathers and sons. This is certainly true of the Amber chronicles: In the first series, almost everything Corwin does is touched by the absence or the presence of Oberon, patriarch of the royal house of Amber; in the second, in addition to Merlin's search for Corwin, Oberon continues to cast a long shadow because the majority of Merlin's allies and enemies are, thanks to his grandfather's near-endless series of sexual liaisons, blood relations. At the same time, Merlin is both demoralized and personally hurt by the revelation that his very existence is a product not of love but of political calculation; he is angered by what he sees as his mother's heavy-handed interference in his life by the intervention of the ty'iga. His resentments come to the fore in Chapter 6 of *Prince of Chaos*, when, summoned to dine with his mother, Merlin lays out his complaints, only to have Dara coldly dismiss them: "'I am my own law, Merlin'" (1183). He elicits a passionate response only when he presses her about Corwin's fate: "'Wretched child! . . . You're just like him'" (1185). This confrontation is, along with the depiction in *Princes* of Corwin's imprisonment, the most emotionally honest and resonant scene in the series.

Perhaps most significant is the degree to which Merlin both continues and complicates the tradition of the Zelazny hero. As we have seen, through the 1970s the protagonists showed a gradual but discernible move away from reflexive rebellion and willful isolation toward a greater awareness of the consequences of their actions and their place in a society beyond themselves. Merlin tries to have it both ways. When, unlike his father, he accepts the crown offered him, he acknowledges his place and his responsibilities within his family and society. He does so, however, after not only dealing with the various outside forces that threaten him and his family but also crushing the efforts within his family to control him and set the agenda of his rule. The series ends, in the grand tradition of the classic European literature the author so loved, with a capable ruler filling a power vacuum and therefore stabilizing the kingdom. At the same time, the new king's victory is also a victory for the autonomy of the exceptional man who is beholden to no one. Such conflicting elements are perhaps appropriate to a work that, in the end, lies somewhere between the artistic ambitions of Zelazny's standalone work and the commercial imperatives of his adventure stories.

If critics largely refused to acknowledge any artistic ambitions that Zelazny may have brought to the saga, readers more than fulfilled its commercial imperatives. Even before the new series appeared, Zelazny was becoming increasingly identified with Amber, especially after the Science Fiction Book Club's 1979 reprinting of the first five novels in *The Chronicles of Amber*, a two-volume set offered to new club members for a nominal cost or for free.[21] As the volumes of the new series appeared, Amber generated a subfandom of its own, acolytes who might or might not be deeply familiar with the author's other work. There were series fanzines, increased fan mail, and conventions that welcomed not only Amber masquerades but, on occasion, hosted "Amber-themed weddings."[22] Zelazny had for many years been a celebrity within the sf community; with the rise of the series, his status at conventions rose to another level, with some fans appearing to conflate Zelazny the writer with Corwin the character.[23] The writer Mary Turzillo remembers that "teen girls hung on him as if he were some sort of *noir* rock star," and at least one of the author's convention appearances was, at his request, contingent on hotel staff's escorting him via alternate routes "to protect him from throngs of fans."[24] Meanwhile, the Amber universe expanded to include a role-playing board game, a computer game, Amber Tarot cards, art portfolios, and reference books.[25] The one thing fans did not have was authorized stories by other writers set in the Amber universe, which, with a couple of exceptions (two children's choose-your-own-adventure books and a zine featuring fan fiction derived from the role-playing games), Zelazny never permitted.[26]

Fame, fortune, and merchandising notwithstanding, Zelazny continued to write. But as he concentrated on his more commercial work, ambitious fiction never disappeared altogether. Although his book-length works were often disregarded, he added to his Hugo Award collection with the novelettes "Unicorn Variation" (1981), a lightly comic tale in which the author, always up for a challenge, proved that one can combine a barroom story, a chess puzzle story, and a unicorn story in a single narrative, and "Permafrost" (1986), an sf story whose interplanetary setting, conflicts between human and computer intelligence, and deft allusions (the opening paragraph rewrites the opening of Ernest Hemingway's "Snows of Kilimanjaro" and several section headings describe parts of Salvador Dali's most famous painting, *The Persistence of Memory*) recalls the breakthrough novelettes of the 1960s. Zelazny's major achievements in the later years of his career were two novels and a novella that proved he was still capable of more than going through the motions and still possessed the "feelings . . . toward narrative" that characterized his finest work.

Set in the early twenty-second century, *Eye of Cat* (1982) tells the story of William Blackhorse Singer, a Navajo renowned as a hunter of alien species, "an expert on the pursuit and capture of exotic lifeforms" who "practically stocked the Interstellar Life Institute single-handed" (23).[27] One factor in Singer's near-legendary status is his longevity; he is 170 years old, his life extended by cryogenic freezing and the time-dilating effects of space travel. Weary of hunting and still mourning the loss of his wife Dora in a mountain-climbing accident, Singer has retired to his native region, the traditional Navajo territory of Dinetah, in the northern border area of Arizona and New Mexico. There he lives simply and comfortably but broods about his cultural identity, or lack of it, as the last of his clan, all too aware that "a Navajo alone . . . is said to be no longer a Navajo" (12). Called out of retirement to track and stop a member of the alien race of Stregeans from assassinating the secretary-general of the United Nations, Singer revisits one of his most memorable captures: Cat, a shapeshifting alien who is, Singer discovers, not only sentient but telepathic, biding his time until he can take revenge on Singer. Cat refuses Singer's apologies and offer of immediate freedom, but finally they strike a bargain. Cat will help Singer hunt and capture the Stregean assassin, and then he will have a chance to kill Singer. After Cat quickly locates and kills the alien assassin, Singer offers up his life to Cat, but the latter counters that if Singer can elude him for a week, he will spare the human's life.

During Cat's planet-wide pursuit of Singer, the latter falls deeper and deeper into a more traditional mindset, experiencing numerous visions and what seem to be supernatural interventions that force him to confront the darkness within himself. Meanwhile, a group of human telepaths, assembled by the U.N. to monitor the situation and operating as a kind of gestalt entity, follow the hunt and try to help Singer survive, but he consistently rejects their aid. When one of their own dies after a devastating telepathic encounter with Cat, the group decides to abandon their efforts. One member of the group, however, James MacKenzie Ironbear, of Sioux ancestry, feels a strong kinship with Singer and makes the physical journey to Dinetah to assist him. Ironbear is wounded by Cat during the pursuit, Singer finally kills Cat on his own, and the telepaths gratefully turn to other matters. But when Singer encounters what seems to be a still-living Cat, he realizes that he has one more confrontation, that with his own shadow self. The battle becomes a transcendent merger, and Ironbear finally locates Singer in the ruins of what appears to have been a violent confrontation. It is unclear whether Singer lives, but he has drawn a smiley face on the wall. Whatever his immediate fate, Singer has met and absorbed his shadow self and is whole.

With a protagonist whose extended life sets him apart from the world that surrounds him, a prolonged chase facilitated in part by human-alien telepathic communication, and a deeply researched application of the mythology of a non-European culture, *Eye of Cat* revisits so much familiar Zelazny territory that the knowledgeable reader might well conclude that the author is not revisiting or rethinking the materials of his earlier stories but simply recycling them, down to the specifics of plot (the Stregean storyline conflates similar material from both *Doorways in the Sand* and *Bridge of Ashes*). In a 1984 magazine article titled "Constructing a Science Fiction Novel," an unusually detailed account of his process in conceptualizing, researching, and writing *Eye of Cat*, Zelazny acknowledges, "I was, at one level, still plagiarizing my earlier self," but immediately adds, "Nothing wrong with that, if some growth has occurred in the meantime."[28] It is fair to say that some growth had occurred, and *Eye of Cat* stands out from Zelazny's other novels of the 1980s in several respects.

On a purely formal level, it is one of Zelazny's most ambitious novels. In addition to telling its story with numerous jump cuts and flashbacks presented with little or no warning to the reader, *Eye of Cat* represents Zelazny's most overt use of the modernist playbook as he presents the novel's background in "Disks," sections of documentary collage that recall the "Newsreel" sections of John Dos Passos's U.S.A. Trilogy (1930s) (and, inevitably, Zelazny contemporary John Brunner's use of the same device in his 1968 Hugo-winning novel *Stand on Zanzibar*). Zelazny presents several of his protagonist's deepest emotional responses in stream-of-consciousness prose modeled on James Joyce's *Finnegans Wake* and Anthony Burgess's *Joysprick* and the backstories of the human telepaths in free-verse poetry that the author thought "Whitmanesque"[29] but that also recalls Edgar Lee Masters's *Spoon River Anthology*. Zelazny's structural and stylistic adventurousness is such that one imagines a reader familiar only with Zelazny's recent fantasy fiction struggling to recognize it as written by the author of the stories of Amber or Dilvish the Damned.

One established Zelazny device that is largely absent from the novel is the kind of lyric outburst that often punctuates even his most straightforward adventure narratives. Instead, he devotes a significant amount of the novel to poetry.[30] In addition to presenting character exposition as free verse, Zelazny also places throughout the novel the songs and chants of William Blackhorse Singer—who is trained as a shaman within Navajo tradition—modeled on and, on occasion, paraphrased from "actual Navajo material."[31] Zelazny even reinforced the poetic aspects of the novel with its print design. In its original hardcover editions, the right-hand margins of the text are unjustified, yielding what the author considered a "rough-hewn, shaggy look . . . appropriate for mythic materials"[32] but also the appearance of the poetic line rather than the prose paragraph.

That Zelazny wished to foreground his use of "mythic materials" in the physical appearance of the text reminds us of the issue of how a white author chooses to represent nonwhite characters and culture—an issue, as discussed earlier, also relevant to *Lord of Light* and *Creatures of Light and Darkness*. There is no denying that there are moments in the novel that are, and should be, jarring to a twenty-first-century audience: one of the telepaths notes that Singer's "mind is running everything through a filter of primitive symbolism" (123), and another character refers to Singer as a "crazy Indian" (124). But it may also be argued that, the author's poetic improvisations notwithstanding, the presentation of Native American culture in *Eye of Cat* is more precise, more accurate, and more deeply rooted in actual tradition and practice than the presentation of Hinduism in *Lord of Light* or Egyptian mythology in *Creatures*. The depth of this correspondence stems in part, perhaps, from Zelazny's preparations for writing his story, which incorporated actual field research, visiting and photographing the locations where much of the novel takes place, on at least one occasion led by a Navajo guide.[33] The result is a novel that is more specifically grounded in the American Southwest than is *Bridge of Ashes* or the second Amber series (a map of the novel is also an accurate map of the northern border area of Arizona and New Mexico) and more attentive to both the facts and the nuances of the culture it references (Zelazny is careful, for example, to make distinctions between Navajo traditions and those of other tribes).

Such respectful research is admirable, but what matters in the end is what's on the page. And what occupies the pages of *Eye of Cat* is, above all else, the character of Singer. In "Constructing a Science Fiction Novel" Zelazny asserts that the work is "a novel of character . . . a consideration of change and adjustment, of growth," and that the complexity of the novel's presentation reflects the complexity of Singer's character and the issues that surround him.[34] If Singer is not the most fully developed or vividly realized of Zelazny's protagonists, he is the most carefully considered. If he is, yet again, a long-lived adventurer of poetic inclination uncertain of his place in the universe,[35] Singer feels his estrangement in terms not just temporal and existential, but social. The passing of his clan and the loss of his wife mean an absence not only of companionship but of community.

In addition, to be a Navajo is to be continually adaptable. Unlike earlier Zelazny protagonists, Singer does not stand in defiance of the world; he wants to be a part of it, and when he believes he cannot, he risks succumbing to a death wish. Significantly, he does not. Although the novel's conclusion begs the question of Singer's physical survival, it is clear that he has confronted his own darkness, become whole with it, and moved on. To the extent that they reflect the degree to which Singer, on his journey to wholeness, is in danger of being torn apart by the conflicting pulls of the ancient and the contemporary, the challenging narrative and stylistic choices on display in *Eye of Cat* well represent its protagonist. To the extent that he is aware throughout of his status as a member of a larger community, Singer marks another stage in the growth of awareness that began to emerge in Corwin of Amber and continued with Fred Cassidy of *Doorways in the Sand* and the nameless narrator of *My Name Is Legion*. William Blackhorse Singer is Zelazny's most emotionally mature protagonist, and *Eye of Cat* may be his most mature novel.

Zelazny was well aware that the novel marked a break from his more commercial fiction, requiring much more research than he could afford to give his "straight adventure books" and offering the chance for him to "use all the tricks [he'd] learned plus a few new ones to tell the tale to maximum effect."[36] One might expect readers and critics who had found his recent books wanting to greet the product of such labor with rejoicing. The actual response was more muted. In the same review cited at the beginning of the present chapter, Norman Spinrad thought that the novel "reads like three discontinuous novellas" but also demonstrates Zelazny's desire to "get back to his roots." Gerald Jonas of the *New York Times* admired the author's working with a mythology he had not previously explored and found the book "genuinely moving." *Kirkus*, however, labeled the book "a poetic drama that fizzles . . . Zelazny at his most fractured, slight, and lackadaisical."[37] *Eye of Cat* did not make the final ballots for the Hugo or Nebula Award, but it placed fifteenth in that year's *Locus* poll for best sf novel.

Three years later Zelazny produced another significant work that was more than a straight adventure, and the response was far different. Set at the turn of the twenty-first century, the novella "24 Views of Mt. Fuji, by Hokusai" is narrated by Mari, a Japanese woman who, after many years of living in the United States and dealing with the effects of multiple sclerosis, has returned to her native country. Carrying a book of Japanese woodblock art titled *Hokusai's Views of Mt. Fuji*, she methodically visits the sites represented in the book, all of which offer varying perspectives on Japan's highest mountain. While on her pilgrimage she has encounters with "epigons," visual manifestations linked to sites of electronic/computer activity. She is also being monitored and followed by humans, including a Russian operative named Boris; her confrontation with him reveals that she is a former covert operative.

As Mari continues her pilgrimage, the reader learns that her journey is a mission to confront and stop her husband Kit, a computer programmer who died after excessive time spent working with his "nervous system coupled to the data net" (402)[38] only to have his consciousness "translated" (401) to the net. In his desperate desire for Mari to join him on the other side, the disembodied Kit contacts her via any and all modes of electronic communication, which rapidly escalates into stalking and harassment. At the same time, both the epigons and her human pursuers continue to intervene in her life. Mari is worried not only for her own safety but for that of her and Kit's daughter, born after his physical death and unknown to him, whom she has hidden away in a remote community without the sort of electronic portals through which Kit could find her. Moreover, Kit is beginning to use his near-transcendental abilities to meddle in world affairs. After tracking down Kit's primary location, a mainframe in a temple where he is worshipped by monks who believe him to be "the new bodhisattva" (426), Mari is almost defeated in combat with the monks but triumphs when Boris reappears and comes to her aid at the cost of his life. The story concludes with Mari's agreeing to join Kit in cyberspace but, at the last second, disabling the terminal, permanently sealing Kit behind a virtual wall and ending her own life in an act of *jigai*, female ritual suicide.[39]

This story once again revisits many elements of earlier Zelazny works. It is carefully laid out in twenty-four sections, each subtitled with the name of one of Hokusai's prints and beginning with Mari's description of and response to the artwork. Mari is in many ways a classic Zelazny protagonist: world-weary, extremely well-read, skilled in martial arts, at once in hot pursuit and continually pursued, and immersed in non-Western culture—in this case, the art, literature, and mythology of Japan. Indeed, "24 Views" is perhaps Zelazny's most erudite and allusive work since "He Who Shapes" / *The Dream Master*. Mari seems almost incapable of encountering either a landscape or an antagonist without framing the experience with multiple cross-cultural allusions. Her response to the thirteenth view, "Mt. Fuji from Koishikawa in Edo," for example, cites Yasunari Kawabata's 1937 novel *Snow Country*, the traditional folk ballad "The Twa Corbies," and the poetry of Wallace Stevens and Ted Hughes (397), while her memory of Kit's initial interest in the concept of "translation" is framed by evocations of Cervantes, Dostoevsky, Ortega y Gasset, and the films of Akira Kurosawa (402). And although he is not explicitly referenced in the story, "24 Views" as a whole is subtly but unmistakably informed by Matsu Bashō's *Narrow Road to the Deep North* (1694), a travel memoir in prose and poetry that, in recounting the author's journey across Japan, frequently conveys his responses to his country's landscape through the lens of classic Japanese and Chinese literature.

With its foregrounding of computers, data nets, and especially the projection of a human consciousness into virtual landscapes, "24 Views" inevitably connects with the "cyberpunk" movement, which was approaching the height of its influence when Zelazny's story appeared (a year after the publication of William Gibson's landmark novel *Neuromancer*) in the July 1985 issue of *Isaac Asimov's Science Fiction Magazine*—the magazine which, along with *Omni*, provided readers with many of the key works of 1980s cyberpunk sf (including the serialization of Gibson's second novel, *Count Zero*). As a veteran of the New Wave controversies of the 1960s, Zelazny likely recognized a similar impulse in cyberpunk's most ardent devotees. Writing in publications such as *Cheap Truth* and *Science Fiction Eye*, cyberpunk's advocates energetically denounced what they saw as the shortcomings of recent science fiction, which they viewed for the most part as squishy and boring, and argued for a return to rigorous technological extrapolation with special attention to the emerging computer revolution but with a streetwise sensibility—*Blade Runner* as opposed to *E.T.* As a prominent writer and a popular figure within the sf community, Zelazny was aware of, and affected by, the tidal forces at work in his field; a few months after the publication of "24 Views," Zelazny wrote to a correspondent that a contemporary photograph of Hong Kong made him "think of a William Gibson story."[40]

Zelazny was not, however, merely jumping on a literary bandwagon with "24 Views." A number of his previous science fiction stories dealt with computer technology and artificial intelligence, virtual landscapes, electronic data nets, and the interface between machine and human: "He Who Shapes," "For a Breath I Tarry," *Creatures of Light and Darkness*, "The Force That Through the Circuit Drives the Current," "Halfjack," and the *My Name Is Legion* novellas. Lindskold references *Creatures*, "Halfjack," and the 1982 novel *Coils* (written with Fred Saberhagen) as evidence that "Zelazny had been fascinated by human/computer interaction long before cyberpunk arrived and made such fashionable," and a 2012 article suggests that *Lord of Light* "anticipated many of cyberpunk's thematic concerns" with its portrayal of "mind uploading" and "putting technology back into the hands of the people."[41] If Mari is indeed a recognizable Zelazny protagonist, the story itself also falls within the territory of Zelazny's ongoing fictional concerns.

There is, of course, one way in which Mari is an atypical Zelazny protagonist: she is female. This was not an arbitrary choice. In a 1989 letter to Lindskold, Zelazny stated that he gave the story a female lead as a direct response to criticism that the main characters of his longer works were always men.[42] The result is a character who is every bit as erudite, contemplative, driven, and—as needed—ruthless as any of Zelazny's men. Admittedly, the twenty-first-century reader may find the author's portrayal of Mari more conventional than did the author or his readers at the time. Her actions are driven to a significant degree by her relationships with men and, in sharp contrast to Zelazny's male protagonists, she does not survive.

This last decision was also a response to a challenge regarding the fact that, as Zelazny acknowledged, "I so seldom killed off my characters."[43] In this, as in writing Mari's story in the first place, he was always ready, even eager, to try something he had never tried before. Whatever the motivation, devoting a substantial novella to a woman's story was a notable step for him to take, and it supports Lindskold's assertion that the later works "mostly left behind" superficial presentations of women: "Many of the female characters in the latter Zelazny stories seem quite capable of seizing the day for themselves."[44]

In foregrounding the elements that had originally made Zelazny's reputation along with the concerns of its day—the evolution of both computer technology and representations of women—"24 Views," perhaps more than any of Zelazny's other post-1980 works, had as much to offer to new readers as it did to early fans. It earned the author his twelfth Nebula nomination and, at the 1986 Worldcon in Atlanta, Georgia, won him his fifth Hugo Award.

If the most distinctive element of "24 Views" is that it is a story in which the "Zelazny protagonist" is female, perhaps the most distinctive element of the author's final standalone novel is that it lacks a Zelazny protagonist. The idea of writing a story about Jack the Ripper's dog had come to the author as early as 1979, as had the idea of the story's being illustrated by the legendary cartoonist Gahan Wilson. On learning that Wilson was unavailable for the project, Zelazny put the idea aside. A dozen years later, hearing that his agent Kirby McCauley was going to have dinner with Wilson, Zelazny recovered his story notes and, unable to get the idea out of his mind, wrote *A Night in the Lonesome October* (once again breaking his rule against writing a book without a contract in hand), finishing the draft in March 1992. When McCauley learned this, he secured Wilson to do the illustrations, and the book was published in 1993.[45]

Presented in thirty-two chapters—a brief prologue followed by one chapter for every day of the month of October—each containing a single full-page illustration by Wilson, *Lonesome October* is narrated by Snuff, a "watchdog" who lives "outside of London" with his master Jack, the latter of whom labors "under a curse from long ago and must do much of his work at night to keep worse things from happening" (1).[46] Thus the reader knows from the opening paragraph that the story is narrated by a dog and likely soon realizes, between the London setting and Snuff's reference in the third paragraph to Jack's "big knife" (2), that Snuff's master is none other than the Ripper. Everything else in the story, however, is doled out gradually. Snuff and Jack are participants in a game with numerous other characters, several identified only by occupation and almost all of whom also have companion animals such as Jill the Witch and her cat Greymalk, Rastov and the snake Quicklime, "the Count" and his bat Needle, "the Good Doctor" and Bubo the rat, and "the Great Detective" and his human companion. By the time we meet Larry Talbot, who seems to prefer exotic plants to animals, it is clear that Zelazny is populating his story with characters from history and literature, some obvious (the Count is Dracula, the Good Doctor is Victor Frankenstein, the Great Detective is Sherlock Holmes, and Larry Talbot is the name of the Wolf Man in the 1941 film), others less so (Greymalkin was the familiar of one of the witches in Shakespeare's *Macbeth*; Morris and McCab likely correspond to the historical nineteenth-century body snatchers Burke and Hare).[47]

For the bulk of the novel these characters interact in various meetings and rendezvous, public and private, each trying to figure out where the other stands in the game, or, in some cases, whether they are involved at all. But the main focus is on the animals, in continual negotiation on behalf of their masters but themselves fully invested in the outcome of events. In particular, Snuff and Greymalk, who form an unlikely but close friendship, move events forward, with Snuff acting as a "calculator," continually measuring lines of connection between various locations in an attempt to figure out the central point around which the game will eventually play out.

Attentive readers familiar with Zelazny's sources will probably not have much trouble figuring out the basic situation as the characters' investigations center on determining who among the players are "openers" and who are "closers" and as the story increasingly makes direct references to the work of H. P. Lovecraft. At one point Greymalk complains about "Nyarlathotep, Cthulhu, and all the rest of the unpronounceables" (152), while the Vicar Roberts is shown relatively early on to be not simply a caricature of a nineteenth-century divine but a malevolent figure conducting dark rituals that evoke other gods and lands from Lovecraft's stories. And when, on October 22, Snuff follows Greymalk on a visit to her "dreamworld," the landscape described is taken directly, and in some detail, from Lovecraft's *Dream-Quest of Unknown Kadath* (1927). It is not until the chapter for October 28, however, that Zelazny reveals exactly what the game is:

> A number of the proper people are attracted to the proper place in the proper year on a night in the lonesome October when the moon shines full on Halloween and the way may be opened for the return of the Elder Gods to Earth. . . . Some of these people would assist in the opening of the way for them while others

would strive to keep the way closed. For ages, the closers have won—often just barely. (236)

Thus "the game" is in fact a regularly scheduled existential struggle to keep the Elder Gods, the ghastly entities who lie behind Lovecraft's stories of the Cthulhu mythos, from breaking through a cosmic barrier and overwhelming Earth. By October 31 the ranks of the "closers" have been reduced to Jack, Snuff, and the Count, and the openers are poised to win for the first time. But by means of a plot reversal involving Bubo the rat, who has not been a player but wants to be part of the game, the closers are once again triumphant. Despite each pair's having played on opposite sides, Jack and Snuff exit the game in the company of their friends Jill and Greymalk.

A Night in the Lonesome October is, in the Zelazny tradition, a smorgasbord of references to both high and popular culture from the title, which quotes Edgar Allan Poe's poem "Ulalume," to the final sentence, which rewrites a famous nursery rhyme.[48] The voice of Snuff, on the whole more straight-forwardly declarative than that of some Zelazny narrators, still periodically modulates between lyric and slang. When, for instance, a bolt of lightning strikes above the Good Doctor's house, "a triple-pronged piece of brightness fell from overhead to dance among the rods on the old building's roof" (55), but when Snuff has to negotiate an encounter with Larry Talbot in wolf form, he quickly reviews his "knowledge of the submissive postures these guys are into" (93). The gradual reveal of the elaborate backstory returns to the narrative strategy of *Lord of Light* and *Creatures of Light and Darkness*, while the bickering gamesmanship of the characters—not to mention that the story's central problem can be solved only by the navigation of an elabo-rate pattern—is an intriguing echo of the Amber series. And, of course, the sprawling cast of characters places front and center the author's devotion to the stories he loves; the chapter of October 17, in which several of the players, ransacking a graveyard in search of "ingredients," toss body parts back and forth to one another, recalls nothing so much as a 1950s EC horror comic. The overall effect is of the Universal movie studio of the 1930s and the Ham-mer movie studio of the 1950s co-producing a live-action role-playing game whose gamemaster is—as was Zelazny in real life—adept at string magic and elaborate cat's cradles.[49]

Indeed, one of the main ways in which *Lonesome October* stands apart from the rest of Zelazny's later standalone works is its playfulness. Zelazny's propensity for the nod and the wink is unapologetically foregrounded here. Despite its dark subject matter—in addition to the presence of Jack the Ripper, it is a story of human sacrifice, malevolent gods, and overall bloody occult doings—it is arguably Zelazny's most cheerful novel. It is a horror story but also a horror carnival,[50] an approach strongly supported, as Lindskold notes, by Wilson's "sinuous, grotesque black and white line drawings" that "capture the tone of whimsical horror that dominates Zelazny's text."[51]

As regards the novel's lack of a Zelazny protagonist, one might imagine a version focused on Jack the Ripper, Larry Talbot, or even Victor Frankenstein in which the story's events emerge from the viewpoint of a disaffected, erudite loner who often does terrible things but has his reasons and whose mission is to save the world and recover his autonomous place within it. But Jack does not tell the story and is not really even one of the main characters. The story truly belongs to the familiars. These animals' desire to preserve the world and themselves does not exceed their desire to serve and protect their masters, even as they acknowledge to one another that their masters are imperfect creatures who engage in unfortunate behavior. Early on, when Snuff advises Cheeter the squirrel to avoid Quicklime the snake because "his master is mad," Cheeter replies, "Aren't they all?" (17). They understand each other ("We chuckled") but such understanding does not keep Snuff from later acknowledging, as Jack gathers obscure materials for the forthcoming Halloween confrontation, that "Jack was happy, so I was, too" (31). And what is perhaps the book's most engaging element, the bantering friendship between Snuff and Greymalk, is a coming together of antagonists—dog and cat, closer and opener—for a greater purpose and in service to others. The royals of Amber sought to master the Pattern by themselves, either to acquire individual power or to keep it from others (although Corwin, eventually, learned better); Snuff and his fellow familiars and their masters must finally cooperate in order to figure out the patterns and save the world. *A Night in the Lonesome October* completes the movement in most of Zelazny's later standalone novels from the uncertain and often violent hero who struggles to protect his own space to the more thoughtful protagonist whose goal is not isolation but connection and community. In writing what proved to be his most distinct move away from the often near-anarchic individualism of his early fiction and his final novel, Zelazny returned to one of the oldest forms of story we have, the beast fable, and one of the oldest characters, the wise servant. In doing so, he affirmed his lifelong devotion to the classic mainstream of world literature, and clearly demonstrated that what he wanted to say in this particular book, however cleverly constructed, needed to be grounded in the deepest of storytelling traditions.

Perhaps as a sign of Zelazny's declining critical reputation at the time, *Lonesome October* was not noticed by the reviewers of the major sf magazines or major U.S. newspapers. *Kirkus Reviews*, however, hailed the novel as "sparkling, witty, delightful: Zelazny's best for ages, perhaps his best ever."[52] Although it did not make the Hugo ballot, it earned Zelazny his fourth Nebula nomination for best novel, his first since *Doorways in the Sand* in 1976 and his last nomination for either award. And perhaps more than any of his novels, its popularity has increased in the decades since its first publication. It is a favorite of some of the author's most famous fans (Neil Gaiman found it a "pure delight," and George R. R. Martin regards it as Zelazny's "last great novel").[53] For some, it has become close to a cult classic. In 2018 the sf journal *io9* declared it "the best Halloween book you've never heard of," and another commentator noted the phenomenon of fans' rereading the book every October, one chapter per day.[54]

Zelazny's final novel supports Neil Gaiman's declaration that, after "going through the motions" for too long, "in the late eighties and early nineties he got his joy back."[55] But it should be noted that, since moving to Santa Fe in 1975, Zelazny had been leading what was, by all appearances, a prosperous and comfortable life with his wife and children, seemingly untouched by any lost critical accolades. He and his family traveled widely in the United States and abroad, often in his role as convention guest but also on vacations; from the late 1970s through the mid-1990s Zelazny and his family visited, among other locations, Australia, Ireland, the Soviet Union, China, Hong Kong, and Paris.[56]

At home in Santa Fe, Zelazny was an enthusiastic supporter of the arts, regularly attending concerts and theater performances.[57] The latter, recalling the pleasures of his graduate studies in Elizabethan and Jacobean drama, was a particular passion. He remarked, "I love the theater so much that I could see a fresh play every night for a year and not get tired of them."[58] He studied a variety of martial arts, earned a black belt in aikido and, after his teacher's death, taught the class.[59] Judy Zelazny earned a law degree at the University of New Mexico, working thereafter at the New Mexico Court of Appeals and the state Supreme Court.[60] Perhaps most important in terms of Zelazny's writing, apart from the continuing influence of the New Mexico landscape, was his forming personal and professional relationships with a new generation of writers—in particular, fellow New Mexico writers Melinda Snodgrass, Walter Jon Williams, Gerald Hausman, and Martin—and with editors such as Kristine Kathryn Rusch, Gardner Dozois (whom he had known from the Guilford Gafia days in Baltimore), and Ellen Datlow (who published Zelazny's short fiction, including "Permafrost," in *Omni*, the highest-profile outlet for sf short fiction in the 1980s). Moreover, whether from a lifetime of market research or an abiding love of the literature of the fantastic, "he never stopped reading the newer writers."[61]

But there is no such thing as an uncomplicated life. After a sequence of traumas and life changes in the early 1960s, Zelazny had led an uneventful life in Baltimore and then in Santa Fe. Then, in 1994, within the space of a few months, Zelazny underwent a second such sequence of trauma and life change. He separated from Judy, his wife of twenty-eight years, and moved in with Jane Lindskold, a writer and academic. Apparently, neither event was precipitous. Citing testimony from Zelazny's friends and family, Kovacs reports that after Judy received her law degree, "the couple's careers took them in divergent directions professionally and socially," and Zelazny claimed that his wife never read his work and was unimpressed by sf and fantasy literature and by Zelazny's friends in the field.[62]

Meanwhile, Zelazny had been corresponding with Lindskold since 1988, when she had written him asking for permission to write her own Amber novel. Zelazny declined, but the exchange of letters continued. After the two met at a 1989 sf convention, the letters grew into a voluminous, best-friends-type correspondence, he sending her packages of books and jazz recordings, she sending him David Bowie albums.[63] A fiction writer herself, Lindskold also held a PhD in English; in 1990, with Zelazny's cooperation, she began writing a study of his work. The study appeared in 1993 as *Roger Zelazny*, a volume in Twayne Publishers' venerable United States Authors series. When in 1993 she notified Zelazny that her own marriage had ended, he asked her to move to Santa Fe. She agreed, and the two moved in together in June 1994.[64]

The delay in Lindskold's arrival was due to devastating news that Zelazny had received. A medical checkup prompted by his "experiencing low energy for some months"[65] revealed that he had inoperable colorectal cancer. After experiencing improvement following chemotherapy, Zelazny began his new life with Lindskold, who had refused his offer to cancel their plans after receiving his diagnosis.[66]

Those who knew Zelazny during his final year report that he was happy in his relationship with Lindskold and remained active professionally and socially. He was introduced to role-playing games, which he greatly enjoyed.[67] He resumed his normal writing schedule. He and Lindskold took a trip to New Zealand followed by domestic travel that, as Zelazny wrote to Joseph L. Sanders, paled in comparison: "New Zealand was beautiful, Des Moines wasn't."[68] Although at least one friend noted that, by 1994, "Roger had finally aged,"[69] none of his friends and acquaintances were aware of how seriously ill he was. Characteristically, Zelazny shared his health status with almost no one, reportedly going so far as to receive blood transfusions before public appearances.[70]

The illness, however, could not be overcome. In early June 1995, according to Walter Jon Williams, Zelazny had acted disoriented at a game session. He collapsed forty-eight hours later and died the next day, June 14, 1995. His ashes were scattered along the Sangre de Christo mountain range near Santa Fe. Fred Saberhagen and his spouse Joan hosted a memorial service at their New Mexico home, where attendees included George R. R. Martin and Neil Gaiman.[71]

As discussed in the introduction to this book, the science fiction and fantasy community reacted to the news of Zelazny's death with shock and sorrow. Apart from the grief of Zelazny's friends and colleagues, his readers also took the loss personally, as reported by Gaiman, who wrote, "Lots of people who had never met Roger were broken up on a level I've only seen when rock stars died."[72]

At the time of Zelazny's death a number of his works awaited publication. Appearing in 1995 were *A Farce to Be Reckoned With*, the final volume of his collaborative comic fantasy trilogy with Robert Sheckley; two edited anthologies, *Wheel of Fortune* and *Warrior of Blood and Dream*, each containing an introduction by Zelazny; *Forever After*, a "shared world" anthology of stories by other authors based on Zelazny's concept and surrounded by interstitial stories ("Preludes") by Zelazny; two new short stories set in the Amber universe, "Blue Horse, Dancing Mountains" and "Hall of Mirrors"; and a new standalone sf story, "The Three Descents of Jeremy Baker." The last was published in *VB Tech Journal*, immediately reprinted in *F&SF*, later reprinted in David G. Hartwell's *Year's Best SF* anthology, and ranked #5 for Best Short Story in that year's *Locus* poll. A collaborative novel, three editorial projects, two minor additions to the Amber universe, and a well-received short story: the bibliography for the year of Zelazny's death clearly indicates both his unflagging work ethic and the late arc of his writing career.

As indicated in the Zelazny bibliography at the end of this book, the second half of the 1990s saw several other posthumous publications; since 2000 there have been numerous reprints and reissues of Zelazny's work, as well as a smaller number of posthumous volumes. Of these, the most significant are the reissue of all ten Amber novels in a one-volume edition, *The Great Book of Amber* (1999), and the 2009 publication by the New England Science Fiction Association Press of the annotated six-volume *Collected Stories of Roger Zelazny*, containing an extended critical biography, "'. . . And Call Me Roger': The Literary Life of Roger Zelazny," by co-editor Christopher S. Kovacs, serialized through the six volumes.

I have suggested ways of looking at Zelazny's work beyond either the crucial but incomplete framework of mythology and prose style or the equally incomplete narrative of the writer who abandoned artistic ambition for commercial success. But there is no denying that both of these perceptions have continued to dominate, if not determine, Zelazny scholarship since the 1990s. As previously noted, Kovacs's discussion is the only extended consideration of Zelazny to appear between Lindskold's 1993 study and this book; the flood of scholarship and appraisal anticipated in the *Locus* tributes never occurred. The invaluable *New York Review of Science Fiction* has published a number of critical works about Zelazny since his death; tor.com, the online component of Tor Books, has provided a platform for much useful Zelazny material, including Rajan Khanna's comprehensive summaries and discussion of the Amber series and outtakes from the extended interviews that formed the basis of Theodore Krulik's *Roger Zelazny*. But the level of academic analysis and widespread awareness within a broader range of literary communities that has come to the work of such Zelazny contemporaries as Delany, Russ, and Le Guin never fully came to Zelazny's work in his lifetime and has been elusive since his death. Seeking an ultimate cause for this—be it the reductive narrative of Zelazny's career, the shifting sands of literary criticism, or the continued issue of academic attitudes toward genre writers who have not established some degree of reputation outside their chosen genres—can end only in speculation.

Where Zelazny's work endures most strongly is, of course, with its readers, those who remember it well and those who encounter it for the first time. *Lord of Light* and *The Great Book of Amber* are mainstays of bookstore science fiction and fantasy departments, with the latter an upper-tier seller on Amazon.com;[1] as noted in Chapter 5, many fans of *A Night in the Lonesome October* continue to reread it every year. But perhaps most significant, Zelazny remains a remarkably strong influence on other writers. We have already seen the degree to which science fiction and fantasy writers were mesmerized by his early work and how strongly the generations that followed were imprinted by both the work and the man.

Less well documented, but equally important, is the degree to which writers of the present day—writers who did not know Zelazny personally, whose careers were not fully under way until after his death, and whose works spans multiple genres—are equally indebted to him. We have already noted Jo Walton's call-out to Zelazny in her award-winning 2011 novel *Among Others* and novelist Rajan Khanna's contribution to Zelazny criticism. The fantasy novelist Max Gladstone writes of Zelazny's influence, "I was inspired by the hard-liquor intensity of his writing and the scope of his vision. . . . I can't think of anyone who I more aspired to become, back when I was still aspiring to be other people. . . . For most of my childhood, Zelazny was THE science fiction writer. I'd still be writing if I'd never read his work, but I don't know what shape my writing would have taken." The sf novelist Elizabeth Bear cites Zelazny as "probably the biggest single influence on my career, frankly. I love his work; I grew up reading it; and found myself deeply captivated by his noir voice, breakneck plotting, sharply honed characters, and the elegance with which he uses an extensive bag of stunt-writing tricks without it ever seeming pretentious." And horror and crime writer Laird Barron attests, "Roger Zelazny meant a lot to me in my youth; and still does. He taught me to fight the good fight and to appreciate nobility in defeat. I miss him. I wish I'd met him."[2]

Beyond the phenomenon of long-term influence, as of this writing, if there has not yet been a full-fledged Zelazny revival, a number of recent publications suggest a new level of interest in his work. In 2017 the specialty press Positronic Publishing released a new tribute anthology, *Shadows and Reflections: Stories from the Worlds of Roger Zelazny*, edited by Warren Lapine and Trent Zelazny. The following year, the same publisher issued *The Magic (October 1961–October 1967): Ten Tales by Roger Zelazny*, which collects all the major early novelettes and novellas (including "He Who Shapes" under its original title "The Ides of Octember") as selected and introduced by Samuel R. Delany. As we have seen, Delany was not only Zelazny's colleague but also one of his earliest and most passionate advocates. His introduction to *The Magic* makes it clear that, more than a half-century after his essay "Faust and Archimedes"—still the single best critical assessment of the early work—his regard for Zelazny is undiminished, concluding, after a detailed and admiring discussion of the stories he chose for the book, "one should continue to read him."[3] Zelazny's *Seven Tales in Amber*, a compilation of short stories set in Amber but not used in the series, appeared in 2019. Outside the confines of sf specialty publishers, Chicago Review Press issued new editions of *A Night in the Lonesome October* (2014) and *Jack of Shadows* (2016), while the prestigious Library of America included . . . *And Call Me Conrad* in *American Science Fiction: Eight Classic Novels of the 1960s* (2019), alongside Daniel Keyes's *Flowers for Algernon* and Delany's *Nova*.

Ironically, the most intriguing prospects for greater awareness of Zelazny's work may lie in film and television adaptations, an arena from which he was largely absent during his lifetime. The 2012 release of *Argo*, a film about the 1980 rescue of American hostages in Iran, brought renewed attention to an aspect of the mission not revealed until a 1999 memoir by CIA operative Antonio J. Mendez. At the core of the rescuers' cover story—that they were in Iran to shoot a science fiction movie—was an actual unproduced screenplay of *Lord of Light*, which had been optioned in 1979.[4] Although neither the novel nor its author is mentioned by name in the film, *Argo*'s high profile (it was directed by and starred Ben Affleck) and major success (winning the Academy Award for Best Picture) all but guaranteed at least some level of publicity for the Zelazny connection.[5] In July 2016 the *Hollywood Reporter* announced that Robert Kirkman, creator of the graphic novel series *The Walking Dead* and producer of its long-running television adaptation, had partnered with Skybound Entertainment to adapt the Amber series for television. The story cited the series as "one of the main inspirations" for George R. R. Martin's *Game of Thrones* and quoted Skybound CEO David Alpert's claim that the Amber series "is one of [his] favorite book series of all time, and one of [his] main inspirations for working in film and television."[6] And in November 2018, *Variety* reported that Martin's shared-world anthology series *Wild Cards* would be developed for television by the subscription streaming service Hulu. Zelazny contributed four novelettes to the anthologies; as of March 2019, plans were in place to include the Zelazny protagonist Croyd Crenson in episodes of the series.[7] Although one can never be certain of the outcome of any given film or television project (witness the fate of the *Lord of Light* screenplay) there is no question that Zelazny's work is receiving renewed attention, not only within the science fiction community but also in the larger world of entertainment media.

In his introduction to *The Magic* Delany refers to "the conflict that is what must rumble about in the socio-aesthetic landscape for a century or so after the death of the author before any reputation can begin to settle."[8] Although it has already been a quarter-century since Roger Zelazny's untimely death, it may still be too soon to settle his ultimate reputation. As we have seen, a common wisdom has grown up around Zelazny's work, and aspects of that common wisdom are valid. One cannot deny the impact and innovation of the stories and novels that made his reputation in the 1960s or do other than marvel at the sustained, brilliant burst of sheer creative energy, shaped by a near-obsessive devotion to improving his craft and a shrewd awareness of both the market and the times, that produced those stories and novels. And it is difficult not to regret the degree to which, over time, market awareness so often overtook brilliance, and perhaps long for a world in which another "Home Is the Hangman," "24 Views of Mt. Fuji" or *Lonesome October* might have been as remunerative as another Amber novel.

But it is both possible and necessary to challenge any common wisdom that finds Zelazny's work simply a dazzle of language and repurposed myth, that bows to the brilliant early work and dismisses the rest. The twin threads that run unbroken through Zelazny's art are a determination to do things exactly his own way and to learn as much as possible while doing so. In the editorial in which he declared many of Zelazny's novels "frustratingly incomplete," Charles N. Brown acknowledged that this was a response the author did not share: "they [the novels] had ended for *him*."[9] It would be yet another oversimplification to say that Zelazny always knew exactly what he was doing. But he almost always knew exactly what he wanted to do, and saw each new story as an opportunity to learn how to do it better.

In a fascinating essay published less than a year after Zelazny's death, Robert Silverberg contrasted the passing of Zelazny with that of John Brunner, who died of a massive stroke less than two months after Zelazny lost his battle with cancer. Silverberg argued that Brunner's death was a genuine tragedy in the classic literary sense of a great man falling to ruin: At the time of his death, Brunner's personal and professional life were both in a precipitous decline. In contrast, Zelazny was "a man successful virtually from the start in all that he attempted and greatly beloved by all who knew him, and at a particularly joyous time of his life was cruelly picked off . . . the happy man who led the happy life." Accordingly, his death, although "a sad thing, a great loss, a cause for lamentation," was not a tragedy but, rather, "a damned shame."[10]

There is, of course, no way to know, on the outside looking in, whether any other person is truly happy. But it would appear that, to the end, Zelazny was satisfied with what he had done as a writer and possessed of the confidence that comes with such satisfaction. In the early 1990s he told his friend and colleague Walter Jon Williams that he wanted to find some time to work on half a dozen novellas he was interested in writing and declared that four of the six would be Hugo winners.[11] Many years later, in her afterword to *Shadows and Reflections*, Zelazny's daughter Shannon recalled a childhood incident in which her father came out of his office after a session of writing and announced, "God *damn* I'm good at what I do." When she accused him of being conceited, he replied, "It's not conceited if it's true."[12]

What is true is that, as far as anyone knows, Zelazny never wrote those potentially award-winning novellas. But his declaration to his daughter was also true, more often than not. Perhaps it is appropriate that it takes more than one truth to stand in summation of Roger Zelazny's extraordinary career.

Conducted by Jeffrey D. Smith and Richard E. Geis and reprinted from *The Alien Critic: An Informal Science Fiction and Fantasy Journal*, vol. 2, no. 4 (Whole Number Seven), November, 1973, pp. 35–40, as "Up Against the Wall, Roger Zelazny: An Interview." Originally published in *Phantasmicom,* November 1972. The interview as published in *The Alien Critic* adds questions by Geis.

PHANTASMICOM: When you began writing, you wrote stories the best you could and hoped they would sell. Now, everything you write is already under contract, with an almost-guaranteed acceptance.

How does this fact affect you?

Do you think that perhaps it allows you to sleep a little, to relax and not worry about rewriting that slightly off chapter, to submit a novel that is just "good enough"?

Do you then have a sense of cheating your readers, by publishing a lesser work under your quality name? Or does *Jack of Shadows* have the same amount of work in it that *This Immortal* did?

ZELAZNY: The main effect of having contracts in advance of writing something is that I have perforce shifted almost exclusively to the writing of novels in recent years. This is something I both desired and required, in order to reach a point of freedom necessary for many things I wished to do. Short stories were, and still are, my first love in sf. I will eventually get back to them. In the meantime, however, there are quite a few things I want to learn about writing which I can only learn from the novel.

In every book that I have written to date, I have attempted something different—a structural effect, a particular characterization, a narrative or stylistic method—which I have not used previously. It always involves what I consider my weak points as a writer, rather than my strong points.

These efforts are for purposes of improving my skills and abilities.

Let x represent a book I am writing, and y the elements with which I am experimenting. Then x–y is what I know I can do well. I count on my x–y for sufficiency in carrying the entire book, regardless of how y is received. I could not attempt such experiments in a short story. Too tight a format.

The sum of all my y's since I began writing is the quantity which interests me most, for it is out of this I hope to enlarge my x–y ability.

In any given experiment, the balance of these factors is a difficult thing to predetermine. For example, increasing the value of y to the extent that I did in, say, *Creatures of Light and Darkness*, cut the force of x–y down near the break-even point. I probably learned more from writing this book than I have from any other, though.

What I am trying to say is that I operate under a continuing need to experiment, and the nature of the experimenting requires that at least part of the time I write from weakness. It would be easy to write a[n] (I think) very good book by not purposely introducing the y-element, by consciously avoiding it, by writing around and slicking over my deficiencies.

If I were to do this though, and do it repeatedly, I would have strong books for a while—and then someone would notice that they were sounding more and more alike. I might as well be stamping them out with a cookie-cutter. I would start to shrivel up as a writer.

The nature of my book contracts has very little, if anything, to do with the substance of the books themselves. To date, I have found myself possessed of as much freedom as I ever had with respect to what I say or do not say. And what I say, or do not say, is governed by my continuing consideration of y.

The work involved in *Jack of Shadows*, for example, as compared with that in *This Immortal*, was work of a very different sort because of the value I had assigned to y—but sweat-wise they were about equal.

If a lesser work should appear under my name, it will not be because I did not try, but rather that y proved too potent a value or x–y insufficient for its assigned function. Such is the number of the beast.

GEIS: What specifically do you consider your strengths as a writer? Which weaknesses do you feel you have strengthened, which remain?

What are your favorite themes or plots? Do you have to resist the temptation to use them too much?

ZELAZNY: As I see them, my strengths as a writer tend to lie in and about the creation of one solid character per tale, in descriptions of settings and occasionally in dialogue. Basic things I have recently tried to improve, with—I think—some success, are stronger characterizations for secondary characters and a general tightening of plot. Right now, I am much concerned with the structure of the novel itself—pacing, accent, temporal sequence.

I don't really have any favorite themes or plots. Consciously, that is. If the same thing crops up over and over until I finally become aware of its too frequent appearance my most recent reaction has been to suppress it rather than exploit it again.

Not that I would *not* do another book involving mythological themes and the experiences of, say, an immortal or long-lived individual. I would find it easier than lots of other things because I have had some practice at that sort of business. I could even do a number of quick books of that ilk if all that I wanted to do was a number of quick books.

However, I do not want to get into a rut. My feelings now are that I will use such devices again only if I come up with a variation that makes it seem worth doing—in terms of my own interest in the themes and the opportunities there for experimentation—with what looks like a possibility for producing a good book bobbing ahead on the end of the stick. To answer the other part more directly: Do I or have I resisted the temptation to use these and other familiars too much?—Yes, I have resisted, several times, recently even.

PHANTASMICOM: What is the difference between a struggling young writer and a multiple-award-winning author admired as one of the best in the field?

ZELAZNY: The struggling is shifted from break-into-the-field-and-consolidate-your-position level to a situation where you are competing with the person you were when you broke into the field and consolidated your position.

GEIS: Do you worry about competition from other established writers?

ZELAZNY: No. There is room in the world for a helluva lot of books and their authors. So long as I can make a living at it, I cannot consider it competitive in the only objective sense that matters.

Subjectively, if someone else writes a really fine book, the whole area is actually enriched by it, since it spreads its man[n]a over more of sf than itself. My best wishes to the next guy doing it.

GEIS: Do you consider your success mostly due to your talent—or skill?

ZELAZNY: You left out genius, but that's okay. Also, luck. Some days I feel talented, other times skillful. Occasionally, stupid and lucky. Then again, brilliant but tired. The worst days are the ones when I feel tired and stupid both. I really don't know how it all averages out. Somewhere in the middle, I guess. How all this hooks up with success is a deep metaphysical problem which I am content to leave with my elders until I can pass it on to my juniors.

PHANTASMICOM: What kinds of satisfaction do you get out of your writing—in the actual process of writing? C. S. Lewis said (somewhat simplified) that before you can approach the criticism of literature you have to realize that people read for different reasons—and with different consciousnesses, in a sense—and that perhaps the more qualitative ways you can read a book, the better it is. It could be the same with writing: the more satisfaction one seeks to effect in his writing, the richer his writing will be.

ZELAZNY: Kinds of satisfaction? Many. I would have to get quite autobiographical in order to answer this question in more than a general way.

— Emotional satisfaction, for one. My own, plus analogues of the characters' feelings. My own mainly being release, relief and a kind of high followed by a pleasant fatigue, in that order.

— Intellectual, for another. From the pleasure of contemplating an intentional or unintentional symmetry, balance, contrast—pattern—as it emerges and works through to some sort of completion. Something akin to listening to a piece of music I enjoy. I give everything I am at the moment to what I write and I enjoy it in the same capacity. It is a funny feedback sensation that I do not fully understand, but then I do not wish to understand it fully.

PHANTASMICOM: In keeping with the fact that much of your writing is subconscious, if you come up with any last doubts about what you've written and some apparently reasonable alternatives for certain sections arise, do you tend to (perhaps superstitiously) regard your initial intuitions as more correct and truer?

ZELAZNY: Always.

GEIS: If your writing is intuitive to a large degree, how does this square with your conscious striving to strengthen your weaknesses? Do you feel a risk in "tampering" with your subconscious?

ZELAZNY: Since my subconscious has survived all of my conscious intentions for this long and still comes across when I need it, I tend to trust its viability, malleability and low animal cunning.

It does seem to operate on an inertia principle, though. That is, it is not self-critical and it does not seem to go looking for new problems just for the fun of solving them.

However, it also seems to behave in an acceptable Kraft-Ebbings [*sic*] fashion, in that once I lay some restrictions on it and kick it into performing under new rules we achieve a kind of sadist-masochist relationship, with me holding the whip during waking hours. With this understanding, once things start clicking properly joy prevails all over the place.

I can write the other way, too: plot everything meticulously and then just sit down and hit keys. But I like to leave dark areas, just to see what will come to fill them. That is one of the chief pleasures I get out of writing. The other way, hitting keys[,] gets boring and I start feeling like an extension of the machine, rather than vice-versa. *Lord of Light* was full of dark areas when I began work on it. *Jack of Shadows*, on the other hand, was only about 20% shaded. Thus does it shift, vary and waver.

GEIS: Who do you consider the finest sf and/or fantasy writers alive and working today? Why?

ZELAZNY: Hard to say. My tastes vary and so does any writer's output. This in mind, the best? In no particular order, then: Clarke, Le Guin, Dick, Tolkien, Heinlein, Niven, to name the first half-dozen fine ones who come to mind.

Why? De gustibus, is all.

GEIS: Who are the worst? Why?

ZELAZNY: The worst? A low opinion is a delicate and exotic thing. If I have one too often their potency may decline. Then, when there is someone I really dislike, disapprove of and snap my fingers at, I will be lacking in the wherewithal to smite him properly. Excalibur will have been dulled. I will have been too free with my kisses of death and no one will respect me any more. Ergo, I have no answer for this question at this time.

GEIS: That's the prettiest "no comment" I've read in years.

PHANTASMICOM: What major works did you use for research in your major mythological works *Lord of Light* and *Creatures of Light and Darkness*? Did *This Immortal* involve any similar research?

ZELAZNY: I already knew something of the subject area before I began work on *Lord of Light*, but I read the following:

The Wonder That Was India by A. L. Basham;
The Upanishads by Nikhilinada;
Indian Philosophy: A Critical Survey by Chandradhar Sharma;
The Ramayana;
Traditional India, ed. by O. L. Chavarria-Aguilar;
Gone Away by Dom Moraes;
Light of Asia by Edwin Arnold;
Philosophy of the Buddha by A. J. Bahm;
Shilappadikaram by Prince Ilango Adigal;
Buddhists Texts Through the Ages (I forget the editor's name);
Gods, Demons and Others by R. K. Narayan.

And around three dozen others—skim-wise—which now elude me.
For *Creatures of Light and Darkness*: Nothing.
For *This Immortal*: A roadmap of Athens.

PHANTASMICOM: In *F&SF* when the first portion of *Lord of Light* was published, the author's note said you were working on *Nine Princes in Amber* then, and were 40,000 words into it. Does this equate to the first half of the novel as published? Do the two halves of the novel strike you as being stylistically or thematically different?

ZELAZNY: I do not honestly remember the point at which this was said. The book was written very rapidly, so it is all of a close piece, time-wise. I do remember[,] though, that I did not think of it in first-half, second-half terms, but rather as part of a much longer story.

Now the second book—*The Guns of Avalon*—has a stylistic shift (I'll leave it to you to determine where) because of a long time lapse between the writing of one part and the rest. This was unintentional, however, and simply the effect of my writing style changing during the interval. I don't see the book as suffering for it, though—or if I did, I wouldn't admit it.

PHANTASMICOM: Is there any chance of your writing "purer" fantasy than *Jack of Shadows* and the *Amber* trilogy—i.e., world-creation à la Tolkien? Have we seen the last of the Dilvish series, or do you have further plans for it?

ZELAZNY: Yes, there is. In all likelihood, I will—eventually. I can't say when, though. Not in the immediate future. I do intend, also, to get back to Dilvish, but not before I get back to shorter pieces. I think I would like to put him in a novel one day, but I see him in a number of short pieces first.

PHANTASMICOM: Which of your works—long or short, whichever it may be— do you consider to be the most ambitious, and to have been the most difficult to execute? Is this one your favorite? Which piece of fiction do you get the most satisfaction from, and which do you find to be the most miserable failure?

ZELAZNY: *Lord of Light* was the most ambitious and the most difficult. It is a toss-up between this and *This Immortal* as my favorite and most satisfying longer work.

I favor "For a Breath I Tarry" and "This Moment of the Storm" among my novelettes, and "Love Is an Imaginary Number" among the shorts.

My worst? "Song of the Blue Baboon." I wrote it to go behind a cover for *If* or *Galaxy*. I had twisted, stretched, bent, folded, spindled and mutilated things to fit in the cover scene. I sort of looked upon the cover as the scaffolding that was holding up the building. Due to a complex mixup, the story did not get paired with the cover. Unfortunate. All the king's horses, and all the king's guys in armor . . . et cetera.

PHANTASMICOM: What sort of typewriter do you generally use? Can you work with an electric on a first draft?

ZELAZNY: First of all, I do not like to sit at a desk. I have never been able to do much in the classic *underwood observa* position. I write in a semi-reclined position with my feet elevated and the typewriter on my lap.

My favorite typewriter for this purpose is my Remington portable. If something should be wrong with it, my Smith-Corona Galaxie portable with a special snap-apart case is my backup machine.

Then I have a very light, very small Smith-Corona which I take with me when traveling but do not use at any other time. Too light for prolonged use, and I am not overly fond of the close grouping of the keys.

My electric is an Olivetti Underwood Praxis 48, on which I *can* compose—but of course this involves sitting at a desk. I save it for letters, pretty stuff, and very very fast stuff.

I also keep an old upright Royal around for sentimental purposes. It was my first typewriter. My father got it for me some 24 years ago, used, and it cost all of $5 then. It is still in great shape, but I seldom use it these days—both because it is not lap-able and because it has an Elite typeface.

The most satisfying typewriter I ever had was a Sears & Roebuck Tower portable, purchased in 1955. Unfortunately, it fell apart some years ago and I never could find another like it. The present Remington—which I've had a little over four years—is the closest thing to it that I have since come across.

PHANTASMICOM: How much time, relatively speaking, do you spend on—how conscious are you of—the prose, the sentences with which you phrase your answers to the sort of questions being asked here? (You've got to expect this sort of thing when you're a legitimate Lord of Sci-Fi.)

ZELAZNY: I don't really know. I pay very little attention to time when I am not writing and even less when I am writing.

But non-fiction does seem to come faster because I am not working with a plot. I am just translating my thoughts into word, and it works pretty much like a reflex. I am not constrained to juggle my words within the plot-sub-plot-situation nest of boxes and, flowing from the sessions of sweet silent thought, I can bash them and toss them—this way, that—with a pitiless irresponsibility, safe in the knowledge that the medium, like a padded cell, is stout enough to contain the sense.

PHANTASMICOM: Do you like the term Sci-Fi? Science Fiction? Speculative Fiction?

ZELAZNY: I prefer "science fiction" because it is the term I learned first. I never even heard "sci-fi" until the mid-sixties. "Speculative fiction" sounds a bit pretentious, and I learned it later, also. Maybe it wouldn't sound funny if I'd heard it first. Dunno. I'll stick with my habit, though . . . probably.

PHANTASMICOM: Do you find cat hairs a hazard, psychologically and/or physically?

ZELAZNY: Only when they are attached to a vicious and sadistic cat.

PHANTASMICOM: Have you anything to say in your own defense?

ZELAZNY: I am innocent, pure, noble and sweet, by reason of artistic license.

FICTION

Novels and Story Collections

The Dream Master. New York: Ace, 1966. Revised and expanded from "He Who Shapes" (*Amazing Stories*, January–February 1965).

This Immortal. New York: Ace, 1966. Revised and expanded from . . . *And Call Me Conrad* (*Magazine of Fantasy & Science Fiction,* October–November 1965).

Four for Tomorrow. New York: Ace, 1967. Collects "The Furies," "The Graveyard Heart," "The Doors of His Face, the Lamps of His Mouth," "A Rose for Ecclesiastes."

Lord of Light. New York: Doubleday, 1967.

Creatures of Light and Darkness. New York: Doubleday, 1969.

Damnation Alley. New York: Putnam, 1969. Revised and expanded from magazine publication (*Galaxy*, October 1967).

Isle of the Dead. New York: Ace, 1969.

Nine Princes in Amber. Amber series, #1. New York: Doubleday, 1970.

The Doors of His Face, The Lamps of His Mouth, and Other Stories. New York: Doubleday, 1971. Collects "The Doors of His Face, the Lamps of His Mouth," "The Keys to December," "Devil Car," "A Rose for Ecclesiastes," "The Monster and the Maiden," "Collector's Fever," "This Mortal Mountain," "This Moment of the Storm," "The Great Slow Kings," "A Museum Piece," "Divine Madness," "Corrida," "Love Is an Imaginary Number," "The Man Who Loved the Faioli," "Lucifer."

Jack of Shadows. Jack of Shadows series, #1. New York: Walker, 1971. Revised and expanded from magazine publication (*Magazine of Fantasy & Science Fiction*, July–August 1971.

The Guns of Avalon. Amber series, #2. New York: Doubleday, 1972.

Today We Choose Faces. New York: Signet, 1973.

To Die in Italbar. New York: Doubleday, 1973.

Sign of the Unicorn. Amber series, #3. New York: Doubleday, 1975.

Bridge of Ashes. New York: Signet, 1976.

Deus Irae [with Philip K. Dick]. New York: Doubleday, 1976.

Doorways in the Sand. New York: Harper & Row, 1976. Revised and expanded from magazine publication (*Analog Science Fiction/Science Fact,* June–August 1975).

The Hand of Oberon. Amber series, #4. New York: Doubleday, 1976. Revised and expanded from magazine publication (*Galaxy* May, July, September 1976).

My Name Is Legion. New York: Del Rey/Ballantine, 1976. Collects "The Eve of RUMOKO," "'Kjwalll'kje'k'koothailll'kje'k," "Home Is the Hangman."

The Courts of Chaos. Amber series, #5. New York: Doubleday, 1978. Revised and expanded from magazine publication (*Galaxy*, November–December 1977, January–February 1978).

The Illustrated Roger Zelazny. New York: Baronet, 1978. Collects "Shadowjack," "A Rose for Ecclesiastes," "The Furies," "The Doors of His Face, the Lamps of His Mouth," "Rock Collector."

Roadmarks. New York: Del Rey/Ballantine, 1979.

Changeling. Pol Detson series, #1. New York: Ace, 1980.

The Last Defender of Camelot. New York: Pocket Books, 1980; New York: Underwood-Miller, 1981. The Pocket Books edition collects "Passion Play," "Horseman!," "The Stainless Steel Leech," "A Thing of Terrible Beauty," "He Who Shapes," "Comes Now the Power," "Auto-Da-Fe," "Damnation Alley," "For a Breath I Tarry," "The Engine at Heartspring's Center," "The Game of Blood and Dust," "No Award," "Is There a Demon Lover in the House?" "The Last Defender of Camelot," "Stand Pat, Ruby Stone," "Halfjack." The Underwood-Miller edition collects all stories in the Pocket Books edition plus "Exeunt Omnes," "Fire and/or Ice," "A Very Good Year . . .," "Shadowjack."

The Changing Land. Dilvish series, #12. New York: Del Rey/Ballantine, 1981.

Madwand. Pol Detson series, #2. New York: Phantasia, 1981; New York: Ace, 1981.

Coils [with Fred Saberhagen]. New York: Wallaby, 1982.

Dilvish, the Damned. Dilvish series, #1–11. New York: Del Rey/Ballantine, 1982. Collects "Passage to Dilfar," "Thelinde's Song," "The Bells of Shoredan," "A Knight for Merytha," "The Places of Aache," "A City Divided," "The White Beast," "Tower of Ice," "Devil and the Dancer," "Garden of Blood," "Dilvish, the Damned."

Eye of Cat. New York: Underwood-Miller, 1982; Timescape/Simon & Schuster, 1982.

Unicorn Variations. New York: Timescape/Simon & Schuster, 1983. Collects "Unicorn Variation," "The Last of the Wild Ones," "Recital," "The Naked Matador," "The Parts That Are Only Glimpsed: Three Reflexes," "Dismal Light," "Go Starless in the Night," "But Not the Herald," "A Hand Across the Galaxy," "The Force That Through the Circuit Drives the Current," "Home Is the Hangman," "Fire and/or Ice," "Exeunt Omnes," "A Very Good Year . . .," "My Lady of the Diodes," "And I Only Am Escaped to Tell Thee," "The Horses of Lir," "The Night Has 999 Eyes," "Angel, Dark Angel," "Walpurgisnacht," "The George Business."

Trumps of Doom. Amber series, #6. New York: Arbor House, 1985.

Blood of Amber. Amber series, #7. New York: Arbor House, 1986.

A Dark Traveling. New York: Walker, 1987.

Sign of Chaos. Amber series, #8. New York: Arbor House, 1987.

Frost and Fire. New York: William Morrow, 1989. Collects "Permafrost," "LOKI 7281," "Dreadsong," "Itself Surprised," "Dayblood," "The Bands of Titan," "Mana from Heaven," "Night Kings," "Quest's End," "24 Views of Mt. Fuji, by Hokusai."

Knight of Shadows. Amber series, #9. New York: William Morrow, 1989.

The Black Throne [with Fred Saberhagen]. New York: Baen, 1990.

The Mask of Loki [with Thomas T. Thomas]. New York: Baen, 1990.

Bring Me the Head of Prince Charming [with Robert Sheckley]. Azzie Elbub series, #1. New York: Bantam Spectra, 1991.

Prince of Chaos. Amber series, #10. New York: William Morrow, 1991.

Flare [with Thomas T. Thomas]. New York: Baen, 1992.

Gone to Earth: Author's Choice Monthly Issue 27. Eugene, OR: Pulphouse, 1992. Collects "Deadboy Donner and the Filstone Cup," "Kalifriki of the Thread," "Devil Car," "The Last of the Wild Ones."

If At Faust You Don't Succeed [with Robert Sheckley]. Azzie Elbub series, #2. New York: Bantam Spectra, 1993.

A Night in the Lonesome October. New York: William Morrow, 1993.

Wilderness [with Gerard Hausman]. New York: Tor/Forge, 1994.

A Farce to Be Reckoned With [with Robert Sheckley]. Azzie Elbub series, #3. New York: Bantam Spectra, 1995.

Donnerjack [with Jane Lindskold]. New York: Avon, 1997.

Psychoshop [with Alfred Bester]. New York: Random House/Vintage Press, 1998.

Lord Demon [with Jane Lindskold]. New York: Avon Eos, 1999.

The Great Book of Amber: The Complete Amber Chronicles, 1–10. New York: Avon, 1999. Collects all 10 Amber novels.

The Last Defender of Camelot. New York: ibooks, 2002. Collects "Comes Now the Power," "For a Breath I Tarry," "The Engine at Heartspring's Center," "Halfjack," "Home Is the Hangman," "Permafrost," "LOKI 7281," "Mana from Heaven," "24 Views of Mt. Fuji, by Hokusai," "Come Back to the Killing Ground, Alice, My Love," "The Last Defender of Camelot."

Manna from Heaven. DNA Publications/Wildside Press, 2003. Collects "Godson," "Mana from Heaven," "Corrida," "Prince of the Powers of This World," "The Furies," "The Deadliest Game," "Kalifriki of the Thread," "Come Back to the Killing Ground, Alice, My Love," "Lady of Steel," "Come to Me Not in Winter's White," "The New Pleasure," "The House of the Hanged Man," "Epithalamium," "The Last Inn on the Road," "Stowaway," "Angel, Dark Angel," "Prologue from *The Trumps of Doom*," "Blue Horse," "Dancing Mountains," "The Salesman's Tale," "Coming to a Cord," "Hall of Mirrors," "The Shroudling and the Guisel."

The Collected Stories of Roger Zelazny, vol. 1, *Threshold*. Ed. David G. Grubbs, Christopher S. Kovacs, and Ann Crimmins. Framingham, MA: NESFA Press, 2009.

The Collected Stories of Roger Zelazny, vol. 2, *Power and Light*. Ed. David G. Grubbs, Christopher S. Kovacs, and Ann Crimmins. Framingham, MA: NESFA Press, 2009.

The Collected Stories of Roger Zelazny, vol. 3, *This Mortal Mountain*. Ed. David G. Grubbs, Christopher S. Kovacs, and Ann Crimmins. Framingham, MA: NESFA Press, 2009.

The Collected Stories of Roger Zelazny, vol. 4, *Last Exit to Babylon*. Ed. David G. Grubbs, Christopher S. Kovacs, and Ann Crimmins. Framingham, MA: NESFA Press, 2009.

The Collected Stories of Roger Zelazny, vol. 5, *Nine Black Doves*. Ed. David G. Grubbs, Christopher S. Kovacs, and Ann Crimmins. Framingham, MA: NESFA Press, 2009.

The Collected Stories of Roger Zelazny, vol. 6, *The Road to Amber*. Ed. David G. Grubbs, Christopher S. Kovacs, and Ann Crimmins. Framingham, MA: NESFA Press, 2009.

The Dead Man's Brother. 1971. New York: Hard Case Crime, 2009.

The Magic (October 1961–October 1967): Ten Tales by Roger Zelazny. Selected and introduced by Samuel R. Delany. Floyd, VA: Positronic, 2018. Collects "A Rose for Ecclesiastes," "The Graveyard Heart," "The Doors of His Face, the Lamps of His Mouth," "The Ides of Octember," "The Furies," "For a Breath I Tarry," "This Moment of the Storm," "The Keys to December," "This Mortal Mountain," "Damnation Alley."

Edited Anthologies

Nebula Award Stories Three. New York: Doubleday, 1968.
Forever After. New York: Baen, 1995.
Warriors of Blood and Dream [with Martin H. Greenberg]. New York: AvoNova, 1995.
Wheel of Fortune [with Martin H. Greenberg]. New York: AvoNova, 1995.
The Williamson Effect. New York: Tor, 1996.

Short Fiction

"Conditional Benefit (part 1)." *Thurban I*, #3, August–September 1953.
"And the Darkness Is Harsh." *Eucuyo*, 1954.
"Mr. Fuller's Revolt." *Eucuyo*, 1954.
"Youth Eternal." *Eucuyo*, 1955.
"The Outward Sign." *Skyline* #31, April 1958.
"Passion Play." *Amazing Stories*, August 1962.
"Horseman!" *Fantastic Stories of Imagination*, August 1962.
"The Teachers Rode a Wheel of Fire." *Fantastic Stories of Imagination*, October 1962.
"Moonless in Byzantium." *Amazing Stories*, December 1962.
"On the Road to Splenoba." *Fantastic Stories of Imagination*, January 1963.
"Final Dining." *Fantastic Stories of Imagination*, February 1963.
"The Borgia Hand." *Amazing Stories*, March 1963.
"Nine Starships Waiting." *Fantastic Stories of Imagination*, March 1963.
"The Malatesta Collection." *Fantastic Stories of Imagination*, April 1963.
"Circe Has Her Problems." *Amazing Stories*, April 1963.
"A Thing of Terrible Beauty" [as Harrison Denmark]. *Fantastic Stories of Imagination*, April 1963.
"The Stainless Steel Leech" [as Harrison Denmark]. *Amazing Stories*, April 1963.
"Threshold of the Prophet." *Fantastic Stories of Imagination*, May 1963.
"Monologue for Two" [as Harrison Denmark]. *Fantastic Stories of Imagination*, May 1963.
"A Museum Piece." *Fantastic Stories of Imagination*, June 1963.
"Mine Is the Kingdom" [as Harrison Denmark]. *Amazing Stories*, August 1963.
"King Solomon's Ring." *Fantastic Stories of Imagination*, October 1963.
"A Rose for Ecclesiastes." *The Magazine of Fantasy & Science Fiction*, November 1963.
"The Great Slow Kings." *Worlds of Tomorrow*, December 1963.
"The Graveyard Heart." *Fantastic Stories of Imagination*, March 1964.
"Collector's Fever." *Galaxy*, June 1964. Variant title: "Rock Collector" in *The Illustrated Roger Zelazny* (1978).
"Lucifer." *Worlds of Tomorrow*, June 1964.
"The Salvation of Faust." *The Magazine of Fantasy & Science Fiction*, July 1964.
"The New Pleasure." *Double:Bill* #10, August 1964.
"The Night Has 999 Eyes." *Double:Bill* #11, October–November 1964.
"The Monster and the Maiden." *Galaxy*, December 1964.
"The Injured." *Kronos* #2, 1965.
"He Who Shapes." *Amazing Stories*, January, February 1965. Variant title: "The Ides of October" in *The Magic (October 1961–October 1967): Ten Tales by Roger Zelazny* (2018).
"Passage to Dilfar." Dilvish series, #1. *Fantastic Stories of Imagination*, February 1965.

"The Doors of His Face, the Lamps of His Mouth." *The Magazine of Fantasy & Science Fiction*, March 1965.

"Devil Car." Jenny/Murdock series, #1. *Galaxy*, June 1965.

"The Furies." *Amazing Stories*, June 1965.

"Of Time and the Tan." *The Magazine of Fantasy & Science Fiction*, June 1965.

"Thelinde's Song." Dilvish series, #2. *Fantastic Stories of Imagination*, June 1965.

"The Drawing." *Algol* #10, September 1965.

"But Not the Herald." *Magazine of Horror* #12, Winter 1965–1966.

"Love Is an Imaginary Number." *New Worlds* #158, January 1966.

"The Bells of Shoredan." Dilvish series, #3. *Fantastic Stories of Imagination*, March 1966.

"For a Breath I Tarry." *New Worlds* #160, March 1966. Revised/corrected text *Fantastic Stories of Imagination*, September 1966.

"Late, Late Show." *Tightbeam* #37, May 1966.

"Divine Madness." *Magazine of Horror* #13, Summer 1966.

"This Moment of the Storm." *The Magazine of Fantasy & Science Fiction*, June 1966.

"The Keys to December." *New Worlds* #165, August 1966.

"The House of the Hanged Man." *Double:Bill* #15, September 1966.

"Comes Now the Power." *Magazine of Horror* #14, Winter 1966.

"Auto-da-Fe." *Dangerous Visions*, ed. Harlan Ellison. New York: Doubleday, 1967.

"This Mortal Mountain." *Worlds of If*, March 1967.

"Dawn." *The Magazine of Fantasy & Science Fiction*, April 1967. Excerpted from *Lord of Light* (1967).

"Death and the Executioner." *The Magazine of Fantasy & Science Fiction*, June 1967. Excerpted from *Lord of Light* (1967).

"The Man Who Loved the Faioli." *Galaxy*, June 1967.

"In the House of the Dead." *New Worlds* #173, July 1967. Incorporated into *Creatures of Light and Darkness* (1969).

"Angel, Dark Angel." *Galaxy*, August 1967.

"A Knight for Derytha." Dilvish series, #4. *Kallikanzaros* #2, September 1967.

"Damnation Alley." *Galaxy*, October 1967. Revised and expanded in *Damnation Alley* (1969).

"The Last Inn on the Road" [with Dannie Plachta]. *New Worlds* #176, October 1967.

"A Hand Across the Galaxy." *Arioch!* #1, November 1967.

"The Princes." *Kallikanzaros* #3, December 1967. Incorporated into *Nine Princes in Amber* (1970).

"Corrida." *Anubis*, vol. 1, no. 3, [Spring] 1968.

"Heritage." *Nozdrovia* #1, 1968.

"He That Moves." *Worlds of If*, January 1968.

"Dismal Light." Francis Sandow series, #1. *Worlds of If*, May 1968.

"Stowaway." *Odd Magazine* #19, Summer 1968.

"Song of the Blue Baboon." *Worlds of If*, August 1968.

"Creatures of Light." *Worlds of If*, November 1968. Incorporated into *Creatures of Light and Darkness* (1969).

"The Eve of RUMOKO." *My Name Is Legion*/Nemo series, #1. *Three for Tomorrow*, ed. Robert Silverberg. New York: Meredith, 1969.

"The Steel General." *Worlds of If*, January 1969. Excerpted from *Creatures of Light and Darkness* (1969).

"Creatures of Darkness." *Worlds of If*, March 1969. Excerpted from *Creatures of Light and Darkness* (1969).

"Come to Me Not in Winter's White" [with Harlan Ellison]. *The Magazine of Fantasy & Science Fiction*, October 1969.

"The Year of the Good Seed" [with Dannie Plachta]. *Galaxy*, December 1969.

"The Man at the Corner of Now and Forever." *Exile* #7, 1970.

"My Lady of the Diodes." *Granfaloon*, January 1970.

"Alas! Alas! This Woeful Fate." *Unofficial Organ of the Church of Starry Wisdom* #1, 1971.

"Add Infinite Item." *The Dipple Chronicle* #2, April–June 1971.

"Sun's Trophy Stirring." *The Dipple Chronicle* #2, April–June 1971.

"'Kjwalll'kje'k'koothailll'kje'k." *My Name Is Legion* / Nemo series, #2. *An Exaltation of Stars*, ed. Terry Carr. New York: Simon & Schuster, 1973.

"The Engine at Heartspring's Center." *Analog*, July 1974.

"The Game of Blood and Dust." *Galaxy*, April 1975.

"Home Is the Hangman." *My Name Is Legion* / Nemo series, #3. *Analog*, November 1975.

"The Force That Through the Circuit Drives the Current." *Science Fiction Discoveries*, ed. Fred and Carol Pohl. New York: Bantam, 1976.

"No Award." *Saturday Evening Post*, January–February 1977.

"Is There a Demon Lover in the House?," *Heavy Metal*, September 1977.

"Shadowjack." Jack of Shadows series, #2. *The Illustrated Roger Zelazny*. New York: Baronet, 1978. Revised and expanded in *The Last Defender of Camelot*, 1981.

"Stand Pat, Ruby Stone." *Destinies*, November–December 1978.

"The Places of Aache." Dilvish series, #5. *Other Worlds 2*, ed. Roy Torgeson. New York: Zebra, 1979.

"Halfjack." *Omni*, June 1979.

"Garden of Blood." Dilvish series, #10. *Scorcerer's Apprentice* #3, Summer 1979.

"The Last Defender of Camelot." *Asimov's SF Adventure Magazine* #3, Summer 1979.

"The White Beast." Dilvish series, #7. *Whispers* #13–14, October 1979.

"Go Starless in the Night." *Destinies*, October–December 1979.

"A Very Good Year . . ." *Harvey*, December 1979.

"Exeunt Omnes." *After the Fall*, ed. Robert Sheckley. New York: Ace, 1980.

"Fire and/or Ice." *After the Fall*, ed. Robert Sheckley. New York: Ace, 1980.

"The George Business." *Dragons of Light*, ed. Orson Scott Card. New York: Ace, 1980.

"The Horses of Lir." *Whispers III*, ed. Stuart David Schiff. New York: Doubleday, 1981.

"Recital." *A Rhapsody in Amber*. New Castle, VA: Cheap Street, 1981.

"Tower of Ice." Dilvish series, #8. *Flashing Swords #5: Demons and Daggers*, ed. Lin Carter. New York: Dell, 1981.

"Walpurgisnacht." *A Rhapsody in Amber*. New Castle, VA: Cheap Street, 1981.

"The Last of the Wild Ones." Jenny/Murdock series, #2. *Omni*, March 1981.

"Unicorn Variation." *Isaac Asimov's Science Fiction Magazine*, April 1981.

"And I Only Am Escaped to Tell Thee." *Twilight Zone* #2, May 1981. Variant title: "And I Alone Am Escaped to Tell Thee," *100 Great Fantasy Short Stories*. New York: Avon Books, 1984.

"The Naked Matador." *Amazing Stories*, July 1981.

"Madwand." *Amazing Stories*, September 1981. Excerpted from *Madwand*, 1981.

"A City Divided." Dilvish series, #6. *Dilvish, the Damned*. New York: Del Rey/Ballantine, 1982.

"Devil and the Dancer." Dilvish series, #9. *Dilvish, the Damned*. New York: Del Rey/Ballantine, 1982.

"Dilvish, the Damned." Dilvish series, #11. *Dilvish, the Damned*. New York: Del Rey/Ballantine, 1982.

"Eye of Cat." *Science Fiction Digest*, September–October 1982. Excerpted from *Eye of Cat* (1982).

"Mana from Heaven." *Satellite Orbit: The Magazine of Satellite Entertainment and Electronics*, September, October 1983. Larry Niven's The Magic Goes Away series.

"LOKI 7281." *R-A-M: Random Access Messages of the Computer Age*, ed. Thomas F. Monteleone. Hasbrouck Heights, NJ: Hayden, 1984.

"Itself Surprised." *Omni*, August 1984. Saberhagen Berserker series.

"Dreadsong." *The Planets*, ed. Byron Preiss. New York: Bantam, 1985.

"Dayblood." *Twilight Zone*, June 1985.

"24 Views of Mt. Fuji, by Hokusai." *Isaac Asimov's Science Fiction Magazine*, July 1985.

"The Bands of Titan." *Per Ardua Ad Astra*. Toronto: Ad Astra Convention, 1986. Collects *The Bands of Titan* (Zelazny), *A Freas Sampler* (by Kelly Freas), *and A Dream of Passion* (by Steven Brust).

"Permafrost." *Omni*, April 1986.

"Night Kings." *Worlds of If*, September–November 1986.

"The Sleeper." Croyd Crenson series, #1. *Wild Cards*, ed. George R. R. Martin. New York: Bantam, 1987.

"Ashes to Ashes." Croyd Crenson series, #2. *Wild Cards II: Aces High*, ed. George R. R. Martin. New York: Bantam, 1987.

"Quest's End." *Omni*, June 1987.

"Concert for Siren and Serotonin." Croyd Crenson series, #3. *Wild Cards V: Down and Dirty*, ed. George R. R. Martin. New York: Bantam, 1988.

"Deadboy Donner and the Filstone Cup." *Terry's Universe*, ed. Beth Meacham. New York: Tor, 1988.

"Kalifriki of the Thread." Kalifriki series, #1. *Hidden Turnings*, ed. Diana Wynne Jones. York, UK: Methuen, 1989.

"The Deadliest Game." *Drabble II: Double Century*, ed. Rob Meades and David B. Wake. Essex, UK: Beccon, 1990.

"Bring Me the Head of Prince Charming." Azzie Elbub series, #1. *ConNotations*, Fall 1992. Excerpted from *Bring Me the Head of Prince Charming* (1991, with Robert Sheckley).

"Here There Be Dragons." *Here There Be Dragons/Way Up High*. Hampton Falls, NH: Donald M. Grant, 1992.

"Way Up High." *Here There Be Dragons/Way Up High*. Hampton Falls, NH: Donald M. Grant, 1992.

"Come Back to the Killing Ground, Alice, My Love." Kalifriki series, #2. *Amazing Stories*, August 1992.

"Looking Forward: Excerpt from *Flare*." *Amazing Stories*, August 1992. Excerpted from *Flare* (1992).

"The Long Sleep." Croyd Crenson series, #4. *Wild Cards XIII: Card Sharks*, ed. George R. R. Martin. New York: Baen, 1993.

"Prince of the Powers of This World." *Christmas Forever*, ed. David Hartwell. New York: Tor, 1993.

"Godson." *Black Thorn, White Rose*, ed. Ellen Datlow and Terri Windling. New York: AvoNova/Eos, 1994.

"The Salesman's Tale." Amber Short Story series, #1. *Amberzine #6*, February 1994.

"Tunnel Vision." *Galaxy #3*, May–June 1994.

"The Shroudling and the Guisel." Amber Short Story series, #3. *Realms of Fantasy*, October 1994.

"Blue Horse, Dancing Mountains." Amber Short Story series, #2. *Wheel of Fortune*, ed. Roger Zelazny and Martin H. Greenberg. New York: AvoNova, 1995.

"Epithalamium." *Fantastic Alice*, ed. Margaret Weis and Martin H. Greenberg. New York: Ace, 1995.

"Forever After: Preludes and Postlude." *Forever After*, ed. Roger Zelazny. New York: Baen, 1995.

"Lady of Steel." *Chicks in Chainmail*, ed. Esther Friesner. New York: Baen, 1995.

"The Long Crawl of Hugh Glass." *Superheroes*, ed. John Varley and Ricia Mainhardt. New York: Ace, 1995. Excerpted from *Wilderness* (1994).

"Postlude." *Forever After*, ed. Roger Zelazny. New York: Baen, 1995.

"Prelude the First." *Forever After*, ed. Roger Zelazny. New York: Baen, 1995.

"Prelude the Fourth." *Forever After*, ed. Roger Zelazny. New York: Baen, 1995.

"Prelude the Second." *Forever After*, ed. Roger Zelazny. New York: Baen, 1995.

"Prelude the Third." *Forever After*, ed. Roger Zelazny. New York: Baen, 1995.

"Coming to a Cord." Amber Short Story series, #4. *Pirate Writings*, June 1995.

"The Three Descents of Jeremy Baker." *VB Tech Journal*, June 1995; *The Magazine of Fantasy & Science Fiction*, July 1995.

"Hall of Mirrors." Amber Short Story series, #5. *Castle Fantastic*, ed. John DeChancie. New York: DAW, 1996.

"A Secret of Amber" (with Ed Greenwood). Amberzine #12–15, March 2005.

"Studies in Saviory." 1965. Zlaz and Yok series. *Collected Stories* 1, 2009.

"Hand of the Master." Early 1960s, unfinished. *Collected Stories* 1, 2009.

"The Juan's Thousandth." 1965–1968. *Collected Stories* 2, 2009.

"There Shall Be No Moon!" 1965–1968. *Collected Stories* 2, 2009.

"Through a Glass, Greenly." 1965–1968. *Collected Stories* 2, 2009.

"Time of Night in the 7th Room." 1965–1968. *Collected Stories* 2, 2009.

"The Window Washer." 1965–1968. *Collected Stories* 3, 2009.

"The Hounds of Sorrow." 1967. *Collected Stories* 3, 2009.

"The Insider" [as Philip H. Sexart]. 1967. *Collected Stories* 3, 2009.

"Head Count." 1980s. *Collected Stories* 5, 2009.

"Godson: A Play in Three Acts." 1994–1995. *Collected Stories* 6, 2009.

POETRY COLLECTIONS

Poems. Discon II, 1974.

When Pussywillows Last in the Catyard Bloomed. Carlton, Australia: Norstrilia, 1980.

To Spin Is Miracle Cat. San Francisco: Underwood-Miller, 1981.

Hymn to the Sun: An Imitation. Brightwaters, NY: DNA Publications, 1996.

SELECTED NONFICTION

Two Traditions and Cyril Tourneur: An Examination of Morality and Humor Comedy in The Revenger's Tragedy. M.A. thesis, Columbia University, 1962.

"Sundry Notes on Dybology and Suchlike." *Science Fiction Parade*, September 1964.

"The Search for the Historical L. Sprague de Camp, or, The Compleat Dragon-Catcher." *Tricon Progress Report* #1, 1966.

"Afterword to 'Auto-da-Fe.'" *Dangerous Visions*. Ed Harlan Ellison. New York: Doubleday, 1967.

"Guest of Honor Speech, Ozarkcon 2." *Sirruish* #5, 1967.

"In Praise of His Spirits, Noble and Otherwise." Introduction to *From the Land of Fear* by Harlan Ellison. New York: Belmont Tower Books, 1967.

"De Gustibus." *Nyarlathotep* #5, May 1967.

"On Writing and Stories." *Science Fiction Times* #446, September 1967.

"Sorry, Folks, I Never Could Think up Imaginative Titles." *Hugin & Munin* #3, October 1967.

"Shadows." *Kallikanzaros* #3, December 1967.

"Afterword." *Nebula Award Stories Three*. New York: Doubleday, 1968.

"Re: A Rose for Ecclesiastes." *No-Eyed Monster Summer* #14, 1968.

"Secretary-Treasurer's Handbook." [Enfield, CT]: Science Fiction Writers of America, 1968.

"Cordwainer Smith." *Riverside Quarterly*, August 1968.

"Daniel F. Galouye: An Appreciation." *Nolazine* #7, second annual Deep South Con issue, August 1968.

"Lester del Rey: Toward a Sufficient Demonalatry." Marcon VI program booklet, 1971.

"Science Fiction and How It Got That Way." *The Writer*, May 1971.

"sLegislations." *Science Fiction Writers of America Bulletin* #40, 1972.

"The Genre: A Geological Survey." *Baltimore Sun*, June 24, 1973.

"A Sense of Wonder." *Baltimore Sun*, September 2, 1973.

"Appreciation of J. R. R. Tolkein." *Locus* #149, September 14, 1973.

"Who Done It? And Why? *The Times of London Anthology of Detective Stories*." *Baltimore Sun*, October 14, 1973.

"Roger Zelazny Interviews Frederik Pohl." *Thrust*, April 1974.

"Three Newspaper Pieces." *Phantasmicom* #11, May 1974. Collects "The Genre: A Geological Survey," "A Sense of Wonder," and "Who Done It? And Why?"

"Some Science Fiction Parameters: A Biased View." *Galaxy*, July 1975.

"Ideas, Digressions, and Daydreams: The Amazing Science Fiction Machine." *Insight* (Case Western Reserve University alumni periodical), Summer 1976.

"Musings on *Lord of Light*." *Niekas* #21, 1977.

"Introduction to 'A Passion Play.'" *Unearth: The Magazine of Science Fiction Discoveries*, Winter 1977, 111–113.

"An Amber Tapestry." *The Illustrated Roger Zelazny*. New York: Baronet, 1978.

"Foreword." *Other Worlds*, ed. Floyd Collins. n.p.: Void, 1978.

"Foreword." *Rooms of Paradise*, ed. Lee Harding. Melbourne, Australia: Quartet, 1978.

"Zelazny Speaks." *The Illustrated Roger Zelazny*. New York: Baronet, 1978.

"A Zelazny Tapestry." *The Illustrated Roger Zelazny*. New York: Baronet, 1978.

"The Great Amber Questionnaire." *Hellride* #3, January 28, 1978.

"The Parts That Are Only Glimpsed: Three Reflexes." *Science Fiction Writers of America Bulletin* #67, Summer 1978.

"A Burnt-Out Case?" *SF Commentary* #54, November 1978.

"Brief Comment (Response to Query)." *Science Fiction and Fantasy Literature: A Checklist, 1700–1974, with Contemporary Science Fiction Authors II*, ed. R. Reginald. Detroit: Gale Research, 1979.

"Jack Williamson." Program book for Williamson lecture series, 1979.

"The Guest of Honor: Philip Jose Farmer." Norwescon 2 program booklet, 1979.

"Review of 'Sword of the Demon' by Richard Lupoff." *Starlog's Science Fiction Yearbook* 1, Starlog Press, 1979.

"Future Crime." *Future Life* #10, May 1979.

"Afterword to 'He Who Shapes.'" *Science Fiction Origins*, ed. William F. Nolan and Martin H. Greenberg. New York: Fawcett Popular Library, 1980.

"Foreword." *When Pussywillows Last in the Catyard Bloomed*. Carlton, Australia: Norstrilia, 1980.

"The Road to Amber." *Kolvir* heroic fiction issue, 1980.

"Brief Comment." *Twentieth Century Science Fiction Writers*, ed. Curtis Smith. New York: MacMillan, 1981.

"Comment on Black Swan (Cygnus atratus)." *Finder's Guide to Australterrestrials*, ed. Jan Howard Finder. Latham, NY: Wombat Enterprises, 1981.

"Foreword." *Jack of Shadows*. New York: Signet, 1981. Rprt., New York: Signet, 1989.

"10 Favorite Mysteries." *The Illustrated Book of Science Fiction Lists*, ed. Mike Ashley. London: Virgin, 1982.

"Philip K. Dick: An Appreciation." *Locus* #256, May 1982.

"Caught in the Movement of a Hand-Wound Universe." *Philip K. Dick: In His Own Words*, ed. Gregg Rickman. Long Beach, CA: Fragments West, 1984.

"Constructing a Science Fiction Novel." *The Writer*, October 1984. In *Frost and Fire*, 117–124.

"Foreword." *To Reign in Hell*, ed. Stephen Brust. Minneapolis, MN: SteelDragon, 1984.

"'I remember tea rooms, small shops, ruined Muckross Abbey': A Writer's Guide to Getting Away from It All in Ireland." *Writer's Yearbook* 1984.

"The Process of Composing." *Science Fiction Source Book*, ed. David Wingrove. New York: Van Nostrand, 1984.

"The Balance Between Art and Commerce." *SFWA Bulletin* #90, Winter 1985.

"The Writer's Life and Uniqueness." *L. Ron Hubbard Presents Writers of the Future*, ed. Algis Budrys. Los Angeles: Bridge, 1985.

"Memoir." *Worlds of If: A Retrospective Anthology*, ed. Frederik Pohl, Martin H. Greenberg, and Joseph D. Olander. New York: Bluejay, 1986.

"10 Favorite Biographies." *Future Focus Book of Lists II: The Sequel*, ed. Roger Reynolds. Findlay, OH: Future Focus, 1987.

"The Dark Traveling and the Burning Tree; or, It's All Done with Mirrors and Lights Except for the Part I Don't Understand." *Basics of Writing for Children*, ed. William Brohaugh. [Cincinnati, OH]: Writer's Digest Books, 1987.

"Fantasy and Science Fiction: A Writer's View." *Intersections: Fantasy and Science Fiction*, ed. George E. Slusser and Eric S. Rabkin. Carbondale: Southern Illinois University Press, 1987.

"A Sketch of Their Father." *Portraits of His Children* by George R. R. Martin. Arlington Heights, IL: Dark Harvest, 1987.

"Top Ten Favorite SF Novels and Stories." *How to Write Tales of Horror Fantasy and Science Fiction*, ed. J. N. Williamson. [Cincinnati, OH]: Writer's Digest, 1987.

"Beyond the Idea." *The Writer*, October 1988.

"Musings from Melbourne." *PKDS Newsletter* #16, January 1988. Abbreviated version of "A Burnt-Out Case."

"An Exorcism, of Sorts." *Frost and Fire*, 1989.

"Foreword to 'He Who Shapes.'" *The Best of the Nebulas*, ed. Ben Bova. New York: Tor, 1989.

"Foreword to 'The Doors of His Face, the Lamps of His Mouth.'" *The Best of the Nebulas*, ed. Ben Bova. Tor, 1989.

"Generational Saga." *New York Review of Science Fiction* #12, August 1989.

"Read This: Recently Read and Recommended." *New York Review of Science Fiction* #22, June 1990.

"On Writing Horror After Reading Clive Barker." *The Stephen King Companion: Grimoire*, ed. George Beahm. London: Macdonald, 1990.

"Science Fiction Writing at Length." *The Writer*, November 1991.

"How I Spent My Last 30 Years." *Amazing Stories*, August 1992.

"About Fred Saberhagen." Philcon 93 Program Book, 1993.

"Fredburgers." *The Galactegg Gourmet: A Culinary Tour Through Fandom*, ed. Thea and Hawk. Starling Designs and Random Productions, 1993.

"Art of Fantasy." *Science Fiction Age*, January 1994.

"'When It Comes It's Wonderful': Art Versus Craft in Writing." *Deep Thoughts: Proceedings of Life, the Universe and Everything XII, February 16–19, 1994*, ed. Steve Setzer and Marny K. Parkin. Life, the Universe, and Everything, 1995.

"Self-Interview." 1972. *Collected Stories 3*, 2009.

"Tomorrow Stuff." 1968. *Collected Stories 3*, 2009.

"Black Is the Color and None Is the Number." 1976. *Collected Stories 4*, 2009.

SELECTED INTERVIEWS

"On Roger Zelazny." By Gil Lamont. *Tightbeam* #37, 1966.

"Fantastic Convention." By Olivia Skinner. *St. Louis Post-Dispatch*, August 8, 1967.

"After the Fanfare Dies." By Norman E. Masters. *No-Eyed Monster* #13, Winter 1967–1968.

"Authorgraphs—An Interview with Roger Zelazny." *Worlds of If*, January 1969.

"An Interview with Roger Zelazny." By Ulf Westblom. *Mentat* #11, May 1969.

"How About This? Roger Zelazny." By Patrick Kelly. *Phantasmicom* #2, Winter 1970; #5, Winter 1971. Transcripts of two separate radio interviews.

"A Brief Interview with Roger Zelazny." By Jim Rehak. *Nova* #1, June 1972.

"The Universe: R. Zelazny, Owner." By Stephen Hunter. *[Baltimore] Sun Magazine*, July 9, 1972. Revised and expanded *Phantasmicom* #10, November 1972.

"Up Against the Wall: Roger Zelazny." By Jeffrey D. Smith. *Phantasmicom* #10, November 1972.

"Zelazny at Marcon '72." By Bill Conner. *Cozine* #3, March 30, 1972.

"An Interview with Roger Zelazny." By Paul Walker. *Luna Monthly* #43, December 1972. Excerpted from "Self-Interview."

"Interview with Poul Anderson and Roger Zelazny." By D. Douglas Fratz. *Thrust*, April 1973.

"Up Against the Wall: Roger Zelazny." By Jeffrey D. Smith and Richard E. Geis. *Alien Critic* #7, November 1973.

"Author's Choice." By Paul Walker. *Vector* #65, May–June 1973. Revised and expanded *Alien Critic* #7, November 1973.

"Roger Zelazny Speaks at the University of Maryland, Fall 1973." *Counter Thrust* #1, February 1976.

"Tangent Interviews Roger Zelazny." By Paul McGuire and David A. Truesdale. *Tangent* #4, February 1976.

"Roger Zelazny Answers Questions." By Darrell Schweitzer. *Procrastination* #13, November 1977.

"Close Adventures of the Conventional Kind: Downtown with the Zelazny[s]." By Michael O'Brien. *Anzapa* #61, 1978.

"A Conversation with Roger Zelazny." By Terry Dowling and Keith Curtis. *Science Fiction (Australian)*, June 1978.

"Roger Zelazny." By D. Scott Apel and Kevin C. Briggs. *Approaching Science Fiction Writers*, ed. D. Scott Apel and Kevin C Briggs. Privately bound thesis, 1980.

"Roger Zelazny." By Neal Wilgus. *Science Fiction Review* #36, August 1980. Revised and expanded in "Roger Zelazny: Lord of Shadows, Jack of Light." *Seven by Seven: Interviews with American Science Fiction Writers of the West and Southwest*, ed. Neal Wilgus. San Bernardino, CA: Borgo Press, 1996.

"Interview: Roger Zelazny." By W. B. Thompson. *Future Life* #25, March 1981.

"An Interview with Roger Zelazny." By Matthew Berger. *Alternities* #6, Summer 1981.

"Sky's the Limit for Roger Zelazny." By Rusty Cawley. *Brian–College Station Eagle*, April 10, 1982.

"An Interview with Roger Zelazny." By Michael Vance and Bill Eads. *Fantasy Newsletter* #55, January 1983.

"Roger Zelazny: From Myth to Science Fiction." By Darrell Schweitzer. *Amazing Stories*, July 1984.

"Roger Zelazny: The New Wave King of Science Fiction." By Michael Vance and Bill Eads. *Media Sight* 3(1): 1984.

"Theater of the Subconscious." By Peter Heck. *Xignals*, February–March 1986.

"Roger Zelazny: Out of This World." *Pasatiempo, The Santa Fe New Mexican*, June 9, 1989.

"Interview with Roger Zelazny." *Albuquerque Journal*, 31 December 1989.

"Building a Universe." By Andrew Campbell. *Reserve* [Case Western Reserve University Magazine Supplement], August 1990.

"Interview with Roger Zelazny." By Elton Elliott. *Science Fiction Review*, Summer 1990.

"Roger Zelazny Interview." By Ian Murphy. *Imagination* #9, August–September 1991.

"Roger Zelazny: Forever Amber." By Charles N. Brown. *Locus* #369, October 1991.

"Science Fiction Fantasy Come True." By Janelle Biddinger. *Standard-Examiner* (Ogden, UT), May 10, 1992.

"Roger Zelazny." By Dannette L. Giron. *ConNotations*, Fall 1992.

"The Song Beneath the Skin: Roger Zelazny Interviewed." By Steve Sneyd. *Critical Wave Magazine* #33, November 1993.

"An Interview with Roger Zelazny." By Garner Johnson. *Parallel Universe Parking* #1, March 1994.

"Staying Power: An Interview with Roger Zelazny." By J. C. Shannon. *Leading Edge* #29, August 1994.

"An Interview with Roger Zelazny." By Warren Lapine. *Absolute Magnitude*, Fall–Winter 1994.

"An Interview with Roger Zelazny." By Alex J. Heatley. *Phlogiston* #44, 1995.

"Bring Me the Mind of Roger Zelazny." By Ken Rand. *Beyond Fantasy and Science Fiction* #3, September–October 1995.

"An Interview with Roger Zelazny." By John Nizalowski. *New York Review of Science Fiction* #211, March 2006. Interview conducted in 1989.

ABBREVIATIONS

CS	*The Collected Stories of Roger Zelazny*, eds. Grubb, Kovacs, and Crimmins
ZP Baltimore	Papers of Roger Zelazny, University of Maryland, Baltimore County, Alban O. Kuhn Library and Gallery
ZP Syracuse	Roger Zelazny Papers, Syracuse University Libraries Special Collections Center

INTRODUCTION

1. Silverberg, "Zelazny Appreciation," 42; "Roger Zelazny, 1937–1995," 7; Bishop, "Roger Zelazny: An Appreciation," 39; Spinrad, [Appreciation], 39; Martin, "The Lord of Light," 40; Williams, "My Three Rogers," 41.

2. Brown, "Editorial Matters," 63; Silverberg, "Zelazny Appreciation," 42; "Roger Zelazny, 1937–1995," 63; Bryant, "Roger Zelazny: A Remembrance," 43.

3. Brown, "Editorial Matters," 63.

4. In researching this book I spoke with a number of writers who knew Zelazny, and they also remember him, without exception, as a man who, while keeping some degree of distance between himself and the world, was a friendly and welcoming figure.

5. "All-Time Novel Results 2012." https://locusmag.com/2012/12/all-time-novel-results-2012/, December 22, 2012; "All-Time Short Fiction Results 2012," https://locusmag.com/2012/12/all-time-short-fiction- results-2012/, December 30, 2012.

6. Silverberg, "Out of Nowhere," 1:11.

7. Pringle, "Obituary: Roger Zelazny."

8. Le Guin, quoted in Attebery, *Fantasy Tradition*, 162.

9. Coleman, review of *To Die in Italbar*, 55.

10. Cowper, "A Rose Is a Rose Is a Rose," 145–147.

11. Krulik, *Roger Zelazny*, ix.

12. "Roger Zelazny, 1937–1995," 63. A subject search of "Roger Zelazny" in the *MLA International Bibliography* (accessed June 10, 2019) yielded sixteen entries since the year of his death, 1995. In contrast, searches for the same time period yielded the following results for his best-known American peers: Samuel R. Delany, 27; Ursula K. Le Guin, 49; and Joanna Russ, 66.

13. Zelazny, quoted in Lindskold, *Roger Zelazny*, 68.

14. Crane, "A Letter to Harriet Monroe," 165.

15. Kovacs, "Literary Life, Part Three," 504.

16. Roger Zelazny to Damon Knight, July 10, 1965, Roger Zelazny Papers, Syracuse University Libraries Special Collections Center (hereafter ZP Syracuse).

17. Krulik, *Roger Zelazny*, 23–24.

18. Aldiss, *Trillion Year Spree*, 294.

19. Delany, "Zelazny/Varley/Gibson—and Quality," 286.

20. Zelazny, "Introduction," *Warriors of Blood and Dream*, 8.

21. Ibid., 3, 8; Kovacs, "Literary Life, Part 2," 2:543–544; Kovacs, "Literary Life, Part 3," 3:515 (see also the author interview in this book); Zelazny to "Jim," October 9, 1971, Papers of Roger Zelazny, University of Maryland, Baltimore County, Alban O. Kuhn Library and Gallery (hereafter ZP Baltimore).

22. Lindskold, *Roger Zelazny*, 16–17.

23. Silverberg, "Reflections," 10.

CHAPTER 1. OUT OF NOWHERE

1. Lindskold, *Roger Zelazny*, 1.

2. Kovacs, "Literary Life, Part 1," 1:496.

3. Lindskold, *Roger Zelazny*, 1.

4. Zelazny, quoted in Lindskold, *Roger Zelazny*, 1.

5. Kovacs, "Literary Life, Part 1," 1:499.

6. Lindskold, *Roger Zelazny*, 2; Kovacs, "Literary Life, Part 1," 1:499–501.

7. Kovacs, "Literary Life, Part 1," 1:504, 506.

8. Zelazny, quoted in Lindskold, *Roger Zelazny*, 68.

9. Kovacs, "Literary Life, Part 1," 1:505.

10. Collister Hutchison to Mrs. Klotman dated "Spring '59," Syracuse University Libraries Special Collections Research Center (hereafter ZP Syracuse).

11. Kovacs, "Literary Life, Part 1," 1:505.

12. As its title indicates, this play, first performed in 1606, is an example of Jacobean revenge tragedy. The scholarship of Zelazny's day attributed the play to Cyril Tourneur; more recent scholarship credits the play to Thomas Middleton.

13. Yoke, quoted in Kovacs, "Literary Life, Part 1," 1:506.

14. Lindskold, *RZ*, 3; Kovacs, "Literary Life, Part 1," 1:507.

15. Zelazny, quoted in Lindskold, *Roger Zelazny*, 68.

16. Kovacs, "Literary Life, Part 1," 1:503, 506.

17. Ibid., 507. Although never as famous as her contemporaries Joan Baez and Judy Collins, West became a respected and influential figure in folk music, recording two albums for Vanguard Records and performing with Pete Seeger; the English musician A. L. Lloyd called her "far and away the best of American girl singers" of the folk revival. She lived in England and Germany, recorded several more albums for independent labels, eventually settled in the northeastern United States, married twice, had a daughter with her second husband, and died of cancer in 2005 at the age of sixty-seven. See Schofield, "Hedy West"; "Hedy West" (Wikipedia).

18. Kovacs, "Raw Emotion," 21.

19. Zelazny, quoted in Lindskold, *Roger Zelazny*, 69.

20. Zelazny, "A Rose for Ecclesiastes," in Grubb, Kovacs, and Crimmins, eds., *Collected Stories* (hereafter *CS*), 1:62. All additional citations in the text are to this edition.

21. Zelazny, quoted in Kovacs, "Literary Life, Part 1," 1:64.

22. Friend, quoted in Lindskold, *Roger Zelazny*, 124; Huntington, *Rationalizing Genius*, 108–109.

23. Kovacs, "A Word from Zelazny," *CS*, 1:64.

24. Lindskold, *Roger Zelazny*, 3–4.

25. Ibid., 4. Zelazny did briefly teach English part-time at Fenn College, now Cleveland State, but gave it up when he saw that it would take too much time from both his full-time job and his writing—plus, "he discovered to his surprise that he disliked teaching anyway" (Kovacs, "Literary Life, Part 1," 1:513).

26. Zelazny, quoted in Kovacs, "Literary Life, Part 1," 1:509.

27. Zelazny, "Passion Play," *CS*, 1:85. All additional citations in the text to this story and to "Horseman!" are to this edition.

28. Silverberg, quoted in Kovacs, "A Word from Zelazny," *CS*, 1:156. For additional discussion of the degree to which Zelazny's early stories set out his basic themes, see Krulik, *Roger Zelazny*, 27–29.

29. Zelazny, quoted in Kovacs, "A Word from Zelazny," *CS*, 1:228.

30. Zelazny, "Introduction," *Unearth*, 111–112.

31. Quoted in Kovacs, "Literary Life, Part 1," 1:511.

32. Ibid.

33. Ibid.

34. Davidson to Zelazny, July 7, 1962, ZP Syracuse.

35. Kovacs, "Literary Life, Part 1," 1:513.

36. Ibid.; Lindskold, *Roger Zelazny*, 4–5.

37. Kovacs, "Literary Life, Part 1," 1:514.

38. Lindskold, *Roger Zelazny*, 5.

CHAPTER 2. EVERYBODY LOVES A WINNER

1. Zelazny, quoted in Kovacs, "Literary Life, Part 1," 1:517.

2. Zelazny, "The Graveyard Heart," *CS*, 1:96. All citations in the text are to this edition.

3. Lindskold, *Roger Zelazny*, 79.

4. Ibid.

5. Zelazny, "The Furies," *CS*, 2:28. All citations in the text are to this edition.

6. Kovacs, "A Word from Zelazny," *CS*, 2:59.

7. Delany, *In Search of Silence*, 449; Delany, "Zelazny!" 14. Delany's story is perhaps better known under the title used in his 1971 collection *Driftglass*: "We, in Some Strange Power's Employ, Move on a Rigorous Line."

8. Sturgeon, "Introduction," 11; Pohl, quoted in *CS*, 2:59.

9. Kovacs dates the composition of "Rose" to October 1961 and that of "Doors" to January 1963. See *CS*, 1:64, 286.

10. Krulik, *Roger Zelazny*, 19.

11. Zelazny, quoted in ibid., 19–20.

12. Zelazny, "The Doors of His Face, the Lamps of His Mouth," *CS*, 258. All citations in the text are to this edition.

13. Delany, "Zelazny / Varley / Gibson—and Quality," 284.

14. Lindskold, *Roger Zelazny*, 124–128.

15. Krulik, *Roger Zelazny*, 47.

16. Zelazny, quoted in ibid., 57.

17. Krulik, *Roger Zelazny*, 49–50; see also Delany, "Faust and Archimedes," 50–51.

18. Lindskold, *Roger Zelazny*, 133–134.

19. Zelazny, "He Who Shapes," *CS*, 1:425. All other citations in the text are to this edition.

20. The car crash was also the core of Zelazny's first professionally published sf story, "Passion Play," and was an image he would return to in several other works, including the novels *Damnation Alley* and *Nine Princes in Amber*. Kovacs finds autobiographical resonance with the actual collision in which Zelazny's fiancée Sharon Stebrel was seriously injured, as does Thomas F. Monteleone. Given that the real-life crash occurred only four months before "He Who Shapes" appeared in *Amazing Stories*, however, it is likely that Zelazny had finished the story before the accident. See Kovacs, "Literary Life, Part 1," 1:514; Lindskold, *Roger Zelazny*, 5.

21. For a detailed annotation of the story, see *CS*, 1:477–485.

22. Lindskold, *Roger Zelazny*, 26; Sturgeon, "Introduction," 9.

23. Smith, *M Train*, 68.

24. Zelazny, *. . . And Call Me Conrad*, *CS*, 2:372. All citations in the text are to this edition.

25. Aldiss, *Trillion Year Spree*, 294.

26. Lindskold, *Roger Zelazny*, 87.

27. Ibid., 105. Kovacs cites the mention of "immortal Penelope" (2:445) as a reference to Pan's mother and specifically not to Odysseus's wife, but given the parallels between Conrad and Odysseus noted above, it is reasonable to assume that the name has more than one referent. See *CS*, 2:505.

28. Zelazny, quoted in *CS*, 2:430.

29. Kovacs, "Literary Life, Part 1," 1:519–521; "Literary Life, Part 2," 2:531–534. In keeping with the often fraught textual history of many classic science fiction stories, whereas *The Dream Master* was in fact expanded from the novella "He Who Shapes," as serialized in *Amazing*, *This Immortal* was not a rewrite of the story serialized in *F&SF* but, rather, the original version of the novel that had been cut for magazine publication. Complicating things further, the Ace edition still omitted some material from Zelazny's original text, material that was not restored until a Science Fiction Book Club edition appeared more than two decades later (Kovacs, "Literary Life, Part 1," 1:520).

30. Zelazny, introduction to "He Who Shapes," in *The Last Defender of Camelot*, 22; Delany, "Faust and Archimedes," 54.

31. Sturgeon, "Introduction," 12.

32. Budrys, "Galaxy Bookshelf," 131. See J. Sanders, *Primary and Secondary Bibliography*, for the reviews by Merril (46), *TLS*, (51), and the *London Tribune* (49). Sanders also cites more extended considerations by sf fan critics Banks Mebane and Sandra Miesel, as well as the initial publication of Delany's "Faust and Archimedes"—a level of commentary well beyond what might be expected concerning a still relatively new voice. See J. Sanders, *Primary and Secondary Bibliography*, 53–54, 58.

33. Zelazny's "Devil Car" (*Galaxy*, June 1965), another story involving a high-tech car, was also a Nebula finalist for best short story.

34. Delany, "Zelazny / Varley / Gibson—and Quality," 274.

35. Ibid., emphasis in original.

36. Wolfe, "Literary Movements," 62.

37. Moorcock, quoted in ibid.

38. Ballard, quoted in Greenland, *Entropy Exhibition*, 50.

39. Mebane, "Mebane's Magazine Mortuary," 4, ZP Syracuse.

40. Aldiss, "Brian W. Aldiss," 279, 281–282.

41. Delany, "Sex, Race, and Science Fiction," 225.

42. Ellison, "Introduction: Thirty-Two Soothsayers," xx; Ellison, "Introduction: The Waves in Rio," 4. See also Ellen Weil and Gary K. Wolfe, *Harlan Ellison*, 131.

43. Zelazny, quoted in Kovacs, "Literary Life, Part 2," 2:543. Compare Delany's reference, in a 1967 letter to Zelazny, to "that critical fannish blather in which we are always turning up in the same paragraph." See Delany, *In Search of Silence*, 449.

44. Zelazny, quoted in Kovacs, "Literary Life, Part 2," 2:542.

45. Zelazny to Ms. Barraford, September 11, 1975, ZP Baltimore.

46. Zelazny, quoted in Lindskold, *Roger Zelazny*, 6.

47. Kovacs, "Literary Life, Part 2," 2:534.

48. Ibid.

49. Zelazny consistently kept his private life private. In contrast to his friends Delany and Ellison, both of whom published significant autobiographical writing, Zelazny's nonfiction contains next to no discussion of his family or other aspects of his life apart from his writing career.

50. Zelazny, "This Moment of the Storm," *CS*, 2:196. All other citations in the text are to this edition.

51. Zelazny, "The Keys to December," *CS*, 2:257. All other citations in the text are to this edition.

52. "For a Breath I Tarry" originally appeared in the March 1966 issue of *New Worlds* but with a corrupted text; the *Fantastic* publication stands as the corrected text.

53. Zelazny, "For a Breath I Tarry," *CS*, 2:86. All other citations in the text are to this edition.

54. Zelazny, "This Mortal Mountain," *CS*, 3:22. All other citations in the text are to this edition.

55. Kovacs, *CS*, 2:219.

56. Kovacs, *CS*, 3:58. See also Delany, "Zelazny!" 20.

57. Lindskold, *Roger Zelazny*, 147.

58. For the story's connection to the Faust legend, see Kovacs, *CS*, 2:116, and Lindskold, *Roger Zelazny*, 93.

59. Lindskold, *Roger Zelazny*, 18.

60. Ibid., 5.

61. "Marcon 2 Presents Roger Zelazny," publicity flyer; Skinner, "Fantastic Convention," ZP Syracuse.

62. One of the most striking aspects of Zelazny's relationship with his readers was his diligence in acknowledging correspondence. The collections of Zelazny's papers at Syracuse University and at the University of Maryland, Baltimore County, contain numerous examples of his not only replying, but often replying at length, to fan letters requesting information about his work, about science fiction, or about the business of writing.

63. Krulik, *Roger Zelazny*, 80; Kovacs, "Literary Life, Part 2," 2:536.

64. Zelazny, "Musings on *Lord of Light*," *CS*, 3:499.

65. Kovacs, "Literary Life, Part 2," 2:536.

66. Zelazny, quoted in ibid., 2:538. Compare Zelazny's similar remarks concerning . . . *And Call Me Conrad*.

67. Zelazny, *Lord of Light*, 156. All other references in the text are to this edition.

68. Yoke, *Roger Zelazny*, 20.

69. Krulik, *Roger Zelazny*, 75–76.

70. Rottensteiner, quoted in J. Sanders, introduction to *Primary and Secondary Bibliography*, xvii; Blish, *More Issues at Hand*, 137.

71. Any discussion of the death and rebirth of gods inevitably evokes Joseph Campbell's *Hero of a Thousand Faces* (1946). Lindskold asserts, however, that Zelazny did not read Campbell until the 1980s. See Lindskold, *Roger Zelazny*, 26.

72. Zelazny, "Guest of Honor Speech, Ozarkcon 2," *CS*, 2:514–515. All additional citations in the text are to this edition.

73. J. Sanders, introduction to *Primary and Secondary Bibliography*, vxii–xviii.

74. Zelazny, quoted in Kovacs, "Literary Life, Part 2," 2:538. Zelazny exhaustively researched both Hinduism and Buddhism for *Lord of Light*, but it is safe to assume that his "interpretations" of these texts were derived from English translations.

75. Delany, "Zelazny/Varley/Gibson—and Quality," 286.

76. "One of": Khanna, "Revolutions in Fantasy," n.p.; "took freely," "crossed the line," and "honored": all in Khanna, "Taking from the World Tree," n.p.; Walton, "Fantasy Disguised as Science Fiction." For additional discussion of these issues see Jemisin, "Appropriateness of Appropriation"; Shawl, "Appropriate Cultural Appropriation."

77. All quoted in J. Sanders, *Primary and Secondary Bibliography*, 52, 54, 55.

78. Russ, review of *Lord of Light*, 37–38.

79. Walton, "Fantasy Disguised as Science Fiction."

80. Zelazny, letter to Damon Knight, July 19, 1965, ZP Syracuse.

81. Zelazny, introduction to "Damnation Alley," in *The Last Defender of Camelot*, 125.

82. Zelazny, "Damnation Alley," *CS*, 3:126. All other citations in the text are to this edition.

83. Zelazny, quoted in *CS*, 3:187.

84. Knight, letter to Zelazny, March 1, 1967, ZP Syracuse.

85. Krulik, *Roger Zelazny*, 52; Lindskold, *Roger Zelazny*, 112.

86. O'Connor, "A Good Man Is Hard to Find," 132, 133.

87. Kovacs, "Literary Life, Part 2," 2:543–544.

88. Ibid., 2:544, 556.

89. Zelazny, introductions to "The Cloud-Sculptors of Coral D" and "Mirror of Ice," *Nebula Award Stories Three*, 1, 39.

90. Ballard, postcard to Zelazny, n.d., ZP Syracuse. Ballard's comments are ironic given that, as noted in Chapter 1, Zelazny considered the story to which Ballard was apparently referring, "Nine Starships Waiting" (*Fantastic*, March 1963), to be one of his weakest. See *CS*, 1:228.

91. Letters to Zelazny from Moorcock, September 3, 1965; Merril, May 30, 1965; Sallis, October 1965, June 1966; Bloch, December 28, 1966; Dick, December 2, 1967; Ellison, June 3, 1967, ZP Syracuse.

92. Letters to Zelazny from Ashmead, January 5, 1968; Morrison, January 10, 1968, ZP Syracuse.

93. Kovacs, "Literary Life, Part 2," 2:544–545.

CHAPTER 3. DO QUIT YOUR DAY JOB

1. The story "Dismal Light" (*If*, May 1968), which included *Isle*'s protagonist, Francis Sandow, as a character, appeared before the novel. Nothing in the story made its way into the novel, however, so the story remains more an outtake than an excerpt. See *CS*, 3:241.

2. Zelazny, introduction to "Damnation Alley," *Last Defender of Camelot*, 125; Lindskold, *Roger Zelazny*, 111.

3. Krulik, *Roger Zelazny*, 61; Zelazny, introduction to "Damnation Alley," *Last Defender of Camelot*, 125. Compare "He Who Shapes," which Zelazny also preferred to its novel version, *The Dream Master*.

4. Kovacs, "Literary Life, Part 2," 2:546.

5. Ellison, "Introduction to Ozymandias," *Again, Dangerous Visions*, 794.

6. Gustafson, Nicholls, and Langford, "Dillon, Diane and Leo," *Science Fiction Encyclopedia*, n.p.

7. Ellison, "Introduction to Ozymandias," *Again, Dangerous Visions*, 794.

8. Edwards and Clute, "Carr, Terry," *Science Fiction Encyclopedia*, n.p.

9. Zelazny, *Isle of the Dead*, 12. All references in the text are to this edition.

10. Kovacs, "Literary Life, Part 2," 2:563.

11. Delany, "Faust and Archimedes," 62–63.

12. Kovacs, "Literary Life, Part 6," 6:500. Intriguing evidence of Zelazny's political coyness may be found in the competing petitions, published in the June 1968 issue of *Galaxy*, wherein SFWA members declared either their support for or opposition to the Vietnam War. Zelazny's name does not appear on either petition. http://www .scottedelman.com/wordpress/wp-content/uploads/2014/02/SFWAVietNam.jpg

13. Delany, "Faust and Archimedes," 53.

14. Zelazny, "Introduction," *Warriors of Blood and Dream*, 8.

15. Compare William Sanders's account of meeting Zelazny in the mid-1960s, which included a waitress's comment that Zelazny "tipped well." W. Sanders, "Afterword," *Lord of the Fantastic*, 252.

16. "Mélange of irrelevant": R. G. Meadley, quoted in J. Sanders, *Primary and Secondary Bibliography*, 65; "wholly new": Ted White, quoted in ibid., 61; "finest work": Alexis Gilliland, quoted in ibid., 60; "amateur detective": John Bangsund, quoted in ibid., 57; "Travis McGee": White, quoted in ibid., 61. Thus Sandow also prefigures later narrators such as the anonymous investigator of *My Name Is Legion* and the private detective in *The Dead Man's Brother*.

17. Kovacs, "Literary Life, Part 2," 2:549; Krulik, *Roger Zelazny*, 73; Lindskold, *Roger Zelazny*, 81.

18. Krulik, *Roger Zelazny*, 73.

19. Zelazny, *Creatures of Light and Darkness*, 5. All references in the text are to this edition.

20. Loeffelholz, "Introduction: American Literature 1914–1945," 14.

21. See Krulik, *Roger Zelazny*, 74–75, for additional point-by-point contrasts between the two novels.

22. Ibid.

23. In the course of its defeat, The Thing That Cries in the Night "becomes an old man with a long beard" (166), and Set later brags to Marak, "I have defeated God in battle" (177). Compare *Lord of Light*'s representative of Christianity, Captain Olvegg, the chaplain aboard the *Star of India*.

24. "Bizarre coagulation": anonymous UK review, quoted in J. Sanders, *Primary and Secondary Bibliography*, 62; "could empathize": *Luna* review, ibid., 63; "uneasy in tone": *Renaissance* review, ibid., 67; "curious hollowness": *Science Fiction Review*, ibid., 68; "best novel": *Phantasmicon* review, ibid., 64; "flat failure": Blish, ibid., 63; "full of adventure": Budrys, ibid., 67.

25. Zelazny, quoted in Kovacs, "Literary Life, Part 2," 2:557, 549.

26. Ibid., 2:557.

27. Carr, letter to Zelazny, March 21, 1967, ZP Syracuse.

28. Kovacs, "Literary Life, Part 2," 2:557, 549.

29. Ibid., 2:545, 559.

30. Ibid., 2:559.

31. Zelazny, *Nine Princes in Amber*, in *The Great Book of Amber*, 19. All references in the text to this and all other books in the Amber series are to this all-in-one edition.

32. Krulik, *Roger Zelazny*, 89.

33. Zelazny, quoted in Kovacs, "Literary Life, Part 2," 2:547.

34. Lindskold, *Roger Zelazny*, 28.

35. Zelazny, quoted in ibid., 30.

36. Kovacs, "Literary Life, Part 2," 2:546.

37. Le Guin, quoted in Attebery, *Fantasy Tradition*, 162.

38. Blish, review of *Nine Princes in Amber*, "Books," 39.

39. Ibid.

40. That Corwin is, like several other characters in Zelazny's works, a poet, but in this case one who applies his art to a popular and commercial form—a bard in Amber, a songwriter on Earth—not only doubles down on his dual identity but perhaps comments on Zelazny's move, in *Princes*, to a more "popular" form.

41. Blish's praise for *Princes* notwithstanding, this judgment was not universally shared by contemporary reviewers. *Publisher's Weekly* dismissed the novel as a "little-league version of Conan" (J. Sanders, *Primary and Secondary Bibliography*, 62); Darrell Schweitzer, writing in the fanzine *Renaissance*, found the novel wanting because of "superficial characterization" (ibid., 67).

42. Kovacs, "Literary Life, Part 3," 3:509.

43. Zelazny, *Jack of Shadows*, 52. All references in the text are to this edition.

44. Kovacs, "Literary Life, Part 3," 3:509.

45. Zelazny, "Foreword," *Jack of Shadows* (1989), 6. For a more complete comparison and contrast of the two novels, see Krulik, *Roger Zelazny*, 108–118.

46. Lindskold, *Roger Zelazny*, 108.

47. Blish, review of *Jack of Shadows*, 103–104.

48. Jack's actions arguably provide a further link to Jack Vance, who was not above employing extreme violence in his own work. Compare Quazer's fate with that of the

Deodand in Vance's *The Dying Earth* (1950): suspended in the air by the magician Mazirian and rotated at greater and greater speed until centrifugal forces tear its body to pieces. For additional comparison with Vance's novel, see J. Sanders, *Primary and Secondary Bibliography*, 81.

49. Lindskold, *Roger Zelazny*, 110.

50. Carter, quoted in J. Sanders, *Primary and Secondary Bibliography*, 71; Clark, quoted in ibid., 72; Gillespie, quoted in ibid., 73.

51. Zelazny, quoted in Kovacs, "Literary Life, Part 3," 3:510.

52. Zelazny, "Foreword," *Jack of Shadows* (1989), 7.

CHAPTER 4. A SERIES OF DIFFERENT ENDEAVORS

1. Lindskold, *Roger Zelazny*, 9.

2. Zelazny, letter to Henry Morrison, April 15, 1972, ZP Baltimore.

3. Zelazny, introduction to *Last Defender of Camelot*, 1.

4. Zelazny, quoted in Kovacs, "Literary Life, Part 3," 3:503.

5. Zelazny, letter to Henry Morrison, May 7, 1973, ZP Baltimore.

6. Kovacs, "Literary Life, Part 3," 3:519.

7. Zelazny, letter to Rich Benyo, June 20, 1971, ZP Baltimore.

8. J. Sanders, *Primary and Secondary Bibliography*, 4–27.

9. The collection contained many but not all: "The Furies" and "The Graveyard Heart," included in *Four for Tomorrow*, and "He Who Shapes," expanded into *The Dream Master*, were excluded, presumably because of length and prior publication. "For a Breath I Tarry" is also missing, because Zelazny did not have a copy of the story on hand when he was assembling the collection. See Zelazny, story note to "For a Breath I Tarry," *Last Defender of Camelot*, 209.

10. Quoted in J. Sanders, *Primary and Secondary Bibliography*, 68.

11. This is a punning reference to the legendary Milford sf workshops, begun in the 1950s, whose members were sometimes referred to as the "Milford Mafia." "Gafia," an sf fan term, is an acronym for "getting away from it all."

12. Kovacs, "Literary Life, Part 3," 3:526.

13. Dann, quoted in ibid., 3:526–527.

14. Ibid., 3:537.

15. Zelazny, quoted in Kovacs, "Literary Life, Part 4," 4:522.

16. Zelazny, quoted in Krulik, *Roger Zelazny*, 2.

17. Quoted in Walker, "Roger Zelazny," 83.

18. Lindskold, *Roger Zelazny*, 10.

19. Krulik, *Roger Zelazny*, 2.

20. The sum was $50,000, approximately $289,000 in 2020 dollars. See Kovacs, "Literary Life, Part 4," 4:534.

21. Letter to Zelazny from Henry Morrison, October 7, 1971, ZP Baltimore.

22. Kovacs, "Literary Life, Part 3," 3:508.

23. Ibid., 3:534.

24. Zelazny, quoted in ibid., 3:188.

25. See Kovacs, "Literary Life, Part 4," 4:558–559.

26. Yoke, *Roger Zelazny*, 105; Lindskold, *Roger Zelazny*, 9; Kovacs, "Literary Life, Part 3," 3:505. Yoke presumably refers to the events of 1964–1965 described in Chapter 1 of this book.

27. Yoke, *Roger Zelazny*, 105.

28. Krulik, *Roger Zelazny*, 37.

29. Zelazny, *To Die in Italbar*, 23. All other citations in the text are to this edition.

30. For an extended discussion of this commonality among the three novels, see Krulik, *Roger Zelazny*, 31–46.

31. *Kirkus Reviews*, quoted in J. Sanders, *Primary and Secondary Bibliography*, 75; P. Schuyler Miller, quoted in ibid., 77.

32. Coleman, review of *To Die in Italbar*, 53, 55.

33. Kovacs, "Literary Life, Part 3," 3:505.

34. Ibid., 3:505.

35. Letter to Henry Morrison, January 9, 1973, ZP Baltimore.

36. Kovacs, "Literary Life, Part 3," 3:515.

37. For a fuller discussion of the novel and its posthumous publication see Trent Zelazny, "*The Dead Man's Brother*: An Afterword," *Dead Man's Brother*, 253–256.

38. Letter to Zelazny from Philip K. Dick, December 2, 1967, ZP Syracuse.

39. Ibid.

40. Walker, "Roger Zelazny," 84; Kovacs, "Literary Life, Part 2," 2:561; Kovacs, "Literary Life, Part 4," 4:525; Zelazny, "Roger Zelazny: Forever Amber," 68.

41. Walker, "Roger Zelazny," 84; Kovacs, "Literary Life, Part 4," 4:525.

42. D'Ammassa, quoted in J. Sanders, *Primary and Secondary Bibliography*, 89; Geis and Joe Sanders are quoted in "PKD Otaku #3," https://efanzines.com/PKD/PKD-Otaku-03.pdf

43. Kovacs, "Literary Life, Part 2," 2:559–560; Kovacs, "Literary Life, Part 3," 3:512; ibid., 3:533, 538; Kovacs, "Literary Life, Part 4," 4:527, 530; ibid., 4:531.

44. Zelazny, *The Guns of Avalon*, in *The Great Book of Amber*, 250. All references in the text to this and all other books in the Amber series are to this all-in-one edition.

45. Zelazny, *The Hand of Oberon*, in *The Great Book of Amber*, 69. All references in the text to this and all other books in the Amber series are to this all-in-one edition.

46. Zelazny, *The Courts of Chaos*, in *The Great Book of Amber*, 576. All references in the text to this and all other books in the Amber series are to this all-in-one edition.

47. Brown, review of *The Courts of Chaos*, 12.

48. For example, Davidson, review of *The Guns of Avalon*, 36.

49. Panshin and Panshin, review of *Sign of the Unicorn*, 53.

50. Krulik, *Roger Zelazny*, 103–105.

51. Walton, *Among Others*, 203.

52. Zelazny, quoted in Kovacs, "Literary Life, Part 3," 3:538.

53. Zelazny, *Sign of the Unicorn*, in *The Great Book of Amber*, 337. All references in the text to this and all other books in the Amber series are to this all-in-one edition.

54. Lindskold, *Roger Zelazny*, 121.

55. Panshin and Panshin, review of *Sign of the Unicorn*, 53, 162.

56. Walton, *Among Others*, 202.

57. Wolfe, "Encounter with Fantasy," 75.

58. Zelazny, introduction to *Unearth*, III–112.

59. Zelazny, "Shadows," in *CS*, 2:527–528.

60. Krulik, *Roger Zelazny*, 112. In making this point, Krulik cites a somewhat different version of Zelazny's speech.

61. Kovacs, "Literary Life, Part 3," 3:523.

62. Zelazny, *Today We Choose Faces*, 40. All other citations in the text are to this edition.

63. Kovacs, "Literary Life, Part 3," 3:525; Thurston, "Introduction," vii.

64. Thurston, "Introduction," vii–xix.

65. Kovacs, "Literary Life, Part 3," 3:524; Lindskold, *Roger Zelazny*, 9.

66. Thurston, "Introduction," vii–xix; Monteleone, cited in J. Sanders, *Primary and Secondary Bibliography*, 79.

67. Geis, "Case of the Blown Clone," 43.

68. J. Sanders, *Primary and Secondary Bibliography*, 81; Smith, quoted in ibid., 82.

69. Kovacs, *Ides of Octember*, 72, 74.

70. Ironically, *To Die in Italbar*, which Zelazny considered far the lesser of his two 1973 novels, was ranked higher in the same *Locus* poll at number 8. See Kovacs, "Literary Life, Part 3," 3:526.

71. Zelazny, *Bridge of Ashes*, 78. All other citations in the text are to this edition.

72. Kovacs, "Literary Life, Part 3," 3:527–528.

73. Zelazny, "Guest of Honor Speech, Ozarkcon 2," *CS*, 2:517–518.

74. More subtly, Zelazny's aliens, who have arranged the affairs of humanity since time immemorial from their outposts beneath the sea, also evoke the Old Ones of H. P. Lovecraft's Cthulhu mythos.

75. Lindskold, *Roger Zelazny*, 18.

76. J. Sanders, *Primary and Secondary Bibliography*, 89.

77. Kovacs, "Literary Life, Part 4," 4:530.

78. Zelazny, quoted in ibid.

79. Blaschke, "Conversation with Samuel R. Delany," 95; Delany, "Zelazny!" 15.

80. Zelazny, *Doorways in the Sand*, 23. All citations in the text are to this edition.

81. See also Zelazny, "Doorways in the Sand Summary," *CS*, 3:563.

82. Zelazny thought enough of the poem, "Lobachevsky's Eyes," to include it in his 1981 poetry collection *To Spin Is Miracle Cat*.

83. Zelazny, *Illustrated Roger Zelazny*, 75.

84. See Krulik, *Roger Zelazny*, 66–67, and Lindskold, *RZ*, 89, 114, for additional discussion of Cassidy as a stage of evolution in the Zelazny protagonist.

85. Budrys, reivew of *Doorways in the Sand*, 107; Martin Last, quoted in J. Sanders, *Primary and Secondary Bibliography*, 91; Don D'Ammassa, quoted in ibid., 89; Wood, quoted in ibid., 96.

86. Kovacs, "Literary Life, Part 4," 4:532.

87. Zelazny, *My Name Is Legion*, 21. All other citations in the text are to this edition.

88. As noted by Spider Robinson in his review of *My Name Is Legion*, Zelazny never explains why the robot is known as the Hangman. See Robinson, "Galaxy Bookshelf," 146.

89. Brown, review of *My Name Is Legion*, 149.

90. Krulik, *Roger Zelazny*, 126–127; Lindskold, *Roger Zelazny*, 31.

91. Lindskold, *Roger Zelazny*, 4; Kovacs, "Literary Life, Part 4," 4:528–529.

92. Krulik further speculates that "RUMOKO," published the same year Zelazny quit the SSA, reflected "the unconscious satisfaction of creating a character who is totally free of mundane ties, a freedom that Zelazny was feeling himself." See Krulik, *Roger Zelazny*, 122.

93. See Yoke, *Roger Zelazny*, 74.

94. The same may be said of the female characters in *Bridge of Ashes*, who, when not acting as skilled professionals or political activists, are presented not as romantic goals for the male characters to pursue but as mothers or guardians. This evolution perhaps reflects Zelazny's experiences as the father of an expanding family.

95. Allyn B. Brodsky, cited in J. Sanders, *Primary and Secondary Bibliography*, 88; D'Ammassa, quoted in ibid., 90; Wood, cited in ibid., 97.

96. Yoke, *Roger Zelazny*, 76; Krulik, *Roger Zelazny*, 124.

97. Kovacs, "Literary Life, Part 4," 4:529.

98. Zelazny, *Roadmarks*, 45. All citations in the text are to this edition.

99. Kovacs, "Literary Life, Part 4," 4:545.

100. Ibid.

101. Ibid.

102. Krulik, *Roger Zelazny*, 141.

103. As does the *Leave of Grass* AI. For a more detailed discussion of Zelazny's presentations of "female" machines, see Lindskold, *Roger Zelazny*, 140–146.

104. Krulik, *Roger Zelazny*, 141.

105. Zelazny, quoted in Kovacs, "Literary Life, Part 4," 4:545; Lindskold, *Roger Zelazny*, 25.

106. Brown, quoted in J. Sanders, *Primary and Secondary Bibliography*, 104.

107. Zelazny, quoted in Kovacs, "Literary Life, Part 4," 4:545.

108. Zelazny, quoted in Walker, "Roger Zelazny," 83.

109. Kovacs, "Literary Life, Part 4," 4:531.

CHAPTER 5. NOTHING ON SPEC BUT STILL SOME JOY

1. Kovacs, "Literary Life, Part 4," 4:557.

2. Gaiman, "Of Meetings and Partings," 14.

3. Spinrad, "On Books," 168.

4. Zelazny, quoted in Kovacs, "Literary Life, Part 5," 5:498.

5. Ibid., 5:499–500.

6. Ibid., 5:511; Kovacs, "Literary Life, Part 6," 6:473.

7. Kovacs, "Literary Life, Part 4," 4:550; Kovacs, "Literary Life, Part 5," 5:510; Kovacs, "Literary Life, Part 6," 6:480.

8. Zelazny, Christmas card to Joseph L. Sanders, 1981, Joseph L. Sanders Correspondence, ZP Baltimore.

9. Kovacs, "Literary Life, Part 5," 5:481; Zelazny, quoted in ibid.

10. Hartwell, "On Roger Zelazny," 16. An advance in the low six figures in 1984 would have been the equivalent of almost half a million in 2020 dollars.

11. Zelazny, *Prince of Chaos*, in *The Great Book of Amber*, 1182. All references in the text to this and all other books in the Amber series are to this all-in-one edition.

12. Kovacs, "Literary Life, Part 5," 5:481.

13. Science Fiction Awards Database, "Roger Zelazny." http://www.sfadb.com/Roger_Zelazny.

14. Wooster, "Of Dune, Helliconia, and Other Worlds," n.p.; Feeley, "The Unknown Edges of the Universe," n.p.; Jonas, review of *Blood of Amber*, "Science Fiction," n.p.

15. Jonas, review of *Blood of Amber*, "Science Fiction," n.p.

16. Kovacs, "Literary Life, Part 5," 5:512.

17. Zelazny, *Trumps of Doom*, in *The Great Book of Amber*, 627. All references in the text to this and all other books in the Amber series are to this all-in-one edition.

18. Lindskold, *Roger Zelazny*, 132, 138–140; Khanna, "Chronicles of Amber Reread," n.p.

19. Although the ty'iga possesses both men and women, there are more of the latter than the former. For a more detailed discussion see Lindskold, *Roger Zelazny*, 138–140.

20. Khanna, "Chronicles of Amber Reread," n.p.

21. Kovacs, "Literary Life, Part 4," 4:556.

22. Ibid., 4:537–538, 556.

23. Ibid., 4:556.

24. Turzillo, quoted in ibid.

25. Kovacs, *Ides of Octember*, 254–259.

26. Kovacs, "Literary Life, Part 6," 6:469. After Zelazny's death, however, his estate sanctioned a series of Amber prequel novels written by John Betancourt. See ibid., 6:470.

27. Zelazny, *Eye of Cat*, 23. All additional citations in the text are to this edition.

28. Zelazny, "Constructing a Science Fiction Novel," *The Writer*, October 1984.

29. Ibid., 123.

30. For a fuller discussion of this aspect of the novel, see Lindskold, *Roger Zelazny*, 83–86.

31. Ibid., 84. Compare the chapter epigraphs in *Lord of Light*.

32. Zelazny, quoted in Lindskold, *Roger Zelazny*, 70.

33. Zelazny, "Constructing a Science Fiction Novel," 123.

34. Ibid., 122, 124.

35. Kovacs specifically links Singer to Godfrey Justin Holmes, the narrator of "This Moment of the Storm." See Kovacs, "Eye of Storm," n.p.

36. Zelazny, quoted in Kovacs, "Literary Life, Part 4," 4:555.

37. Spinrad, "On Books," 168–169; Jonas, "Other Worlds Than Earth," n.p.; "Kirkus Review: *Eye of Cat*," n.p.

38. Zelazny, "24 Views," *CS*, 5: 402. All additional references in the text are to this edition.

39. Kovacs, "Notes" following "24 Views," *CS*, 5:433.

40. Zelazny, postcard to Joseph L. Sanders, January 17, 1986, Joseph L. Sanders Correspondence, ZP Baltimore.

41. Lindskold, "About Donnerjack," n.p.; Pangburn, "How Roger Zelazny's Lord of Light Transformed into the CIA's Argo Covert Op," n.p.

42. Lindskold, *Roger Zelazny*, 102.

43. Ibid.

44. Ibid., 149.

45. Discussion of Gahan Wilson: ibid., 47, and Kovacs, "Literary Life, Part 4," 4:544; "put the idea aside": Lindskold, 47; date of draft: Kovacs, "Literary Life, Part 6," 6:475.

46. Zelazny, *A Night in the Lonesome October*, 1. All additional references in the text are to this edition.

47. Kovacs, "Fallen Books and Other Subtle Clues," n.p.

48. "Jack and Jill ran down the hill. Gray and I came after" (280).

49. As Zelazny's friends Jack Dann and Joe Haldeman testified: "Put a piece of string in Roger's hands, and he became a magician" (Dann); "he amused everybody with his

string games, the extra-complicated cat's cradle things" (Haldeman). Quoted in Kovacs, "Literary Life, Part 5," 5:483.

50. For a detailed discussion of the use of carnival in the dark fantastic, see Timothy Jones, *Gothic and the Carnivalesque.*

51. Lindskold, *Roger Zelazny,* 47.

52. Kirkus Review: *A Night in the Lonesome October,"* n.p.

53. Gaiman, "Of Meetings and Partings," 14; Martin, cover blurb for *A Night in the Lonesome October.*

54. Meghan Ball, "Best Halloween Book You've Never Heard Of," n.p.; Tadiana Jones, "A Night in the Lonesome October: An Annual Ritual for Fans, " n.p.

55. Gaiman, "Of Meetings and Partings," 14.

56. See Kovacs, "Literary Life of Roger Zelazny," Parts 4, 5, and 6; see also Joseph L. Sanders Correspondence, ZP Baltimore.

57. Kovacs, "Literary Life, Part 4," 4:565.

58. Zelazny, quoted in Lindskold, *Rober Zelazny,* 16.

59. Kovacs, "Literary Life, Part 5," 5:473, 491, 507.

60. Ibid., 5:490.

61. Lindskold, "Roger Zelazny," 15.

62. Kovacs, "Literary Life, Part 5," 5:490.

63. Lindskold, "Roger Zelazny," 15.

64. Ibid., 17.

65. Kovacs, "Literary Life, Part 6," 6:491.

66. Lindskold, "Roger Zelazny," 17.

67. Williams, "Singular Being," 15.

68. Zelazny, postcard to Joseph L. Sanders, May 10, 1995, Joseph L. Sanders Correspondence, ZP Baltimore.

69. Dann, quoted in Kovacs, "Literary Life, Part 6," 6:490.

70. Williams, "My Three Rogers," 41.

71. Kovacs, "Literary Life, Part 6," 6:503.

72. Ibid., 504.

AFTERWORD

1. On June 10, 2019, the book had an overall Amazon sales rank of 17,342; on March 13, 2020 it was 22,973—certainly the upper tier of a list containing literally millions of titles.

2. Max Gladstone, email to the author, March 11, 2019; Elizabeth Bear, email to the author, May 28, 2019; Laird Barron, email to author, June 13, 2019.

3. Delany, "Zelazny!" 25.

4. Kovacs, "Literary Life, Part 4," 4:546.

5. Pangburn, "How Roger Zelazny's Lord of Light Transformed into the CIA's Argo Covert Op." The unproduced screenplay, written by Barry Ira Geller, included visual designs by the legendary comic artist Jack Kirby. An announced documentary about grandiose plans connected with Geller's script—a "Science Fiction Land" theme park in Colorado—was cancelled in 2014 owing to "legal circumstances." See Erlich, "Thanking Everyone for Your Patience and Support."

6. Goldberg, "'Walking Dead' Creator Adapting 'Chronicles of Amber' for TV." Martin acknowledged Zelazny's influence by designating a House of Westeros "House Rogers of Amberly."

7. Otterson, "Hulu to Develop Shows Based on George R. R. Martin Book Series 'Wild Cards'"; Michael Cassutt, Facebook message to the author, March 11, 2019. In a blog entry dated June 23, 2020, Martin referred to an attempt to "relaunch" the Wild Cards project on Hulu. In February 2021, multiple outlets reported that *Roadmarks* would be adapted as an HBO television series, with Martin as executive producer. Martin, "Writing, Reading, Writing"; Templeton, "Roger Zelazny's *Roadmarks* is Coming to HBO."

8. Delany, "Zelazny!" 15.

9. Brown, "Editorial Matters," 63.

10. Silverberg, "Reflections: Roger and John," 8.

11. Williams, email to the author, August 7, 2018.

12. Shannon Zelazny, "Afterword," 235.

BOOKS, ARTICLES, AND REVIEWS

Aldiss, Brian. "Brian W. Aldiss" [afterword to "Still Trajectories"]. In *England Swings SF*, edited by Judith Merril, 278–282. New York: Ace, 1970.

———— [with David Wingrove]. *Trillion Year Spree: The History of Science Fiction*. London: Paladin, 1988.

Atheling, William, Jr. [Blish, James]. *More Issues at Hand*. Chicago: Advent, 1970.

Atteberry, Brian. *The Fantasy Tradition in American Literature: From Irving to Le Guin*. Bloomington: Indiana University Press, 1980.

Ball, Meghan. "The Best Halloween Book You've Never Heard Of: Celebrating the 25th Anniversary of *A Night in the Lonesome October*." io9, October 31, 2018, https://io9 .gizmodo.com/the-best-halloween-book-you-ve-never-heard-of-celebrat-1830068343

Blaschke, Jayme Lynn. "A Conversation with Samuel R. Delany." In *Conversations with Samuel Delany*, edited by Carl Freedman, 91–100. Jackson: University Press of Mississippi, 2009.

Blish, James. Review of *Jack of Shadows*, *Magazine of Fantasy & Science Fiction*, April 1972, 101–105.

————. Review of *Nine Princes in Amber*, *Magazine of Fantasy & Science Fiction*, May 1971, 38–44.

Bishop, Michael. "Roger Zelazny: An Appreciation." *Locus*, August 1995, 39.

Brown, Charles N. "Editorial Matters." *Locus*, July 1995, 63.

————. Review of *The Courts of Chaos*. *Isaac Asimov's Science Fiction Magazine*, May–June 1978, 12–15.

————. Review of *My Name Is Legion*. *Isaac Asimov's Science Fiction Magazine*, Spring 1977, 146–152.

Bryant, Edward. "Roger Zelazny: A Remembrance." *Locus*, August 1995, 43.

Budrys, Algis. Review of *Doorways in the Sand*. *Magazine of Fantasy & Science Fiction*, July 1977, 103–109.

————. Review of *This Immortal. Galaxy Magazine*, December 1966, 125–133.

Coleman, Sydney. Review of *To Die in Italbar*. *Magazine of Fantasy & Science Fiction*, August 1974, 51–58.

Cowper, Richard. "A Rose Is a Rose Is a Rose . . . in Search of Roger Zelazny." *Foundation*, March 1977, 142–147.

Crane, Hart. "A Letter to Harriet Monroe [1926]." In *Hart Crane: Complete Poems and*

Selected Letters, edited by Langdon Hammer, 165–169. New York: Library of America, 2006.

Davidson, Avram. Review of *The Guns of Avalon*. *Magazine of Fantasy & Science Fiction*, April 1973, 33–38.

Delany, Samuel R. "Faust and Archimedes: Thomas M. Disch and Roger Zelazny." In *The Jewel-Hinged Jaw: Notes on the Language of Science Fiction*, 43–58. Middletown, CT: Wesleyan University Press, 2011.

———. *In Search of Silence: The Journals of Samuel R. Delany*. Vol. 1, *1957–1969*. Middletown, CT: Wesleyan University Press, 2017.

———. "Sex, Race, and Science Fiction: The *Callaloo* Interview." In *Silent Interviews: On Language, Race, Sex, Science Fiction, and Some Comics*, 216–229. Hanover, NH: Wesleyan University Press, 1994.

———. "Zelazny!" In *The Magic (October 1961–October 1967). Ten Tales by Roger Zelazny*, 9–36. Floyd, VA: Positronic, 2018.

———. "Zelazny/Varley/Gibson—and Quality." In *Shorter Views: Queer Thoughts and the Politics of the Paraliterary*, 271–291. Hanover, NH: Wesleyan University Press, 1999.

Edwards, Malcom J., and John Clute. "Carr, Terry." *The Science Fiction Encyclopedia*. Accessed June 4, 2019. http://www.sf-encyclopedia.com/entry/carr_terry

Ellison, Harlan. "Introduction to Ozymandias." In *Again, Dangerous Visions: Forty-Six Original Stories*, 794–796. New York: Doubleday, 1972.

———. "Introduction: Thirty-Two Soothsayers." In *Dangerous Visions: Thirty-Three Original Stories*, xix–xxix. New York: Doubleday, 1967.

——. "Introduction: The Waves in Rio." In *The Beast That Shouted Love at the Heart of the World*, 1–7. New York: Avon/Science Fiction Book Club, 1969.

Erlich, Judd. "Thanking Everyone for Your Patience and Support." *Science Fiction Land*, October 3, 2014, https://www.kickstarter.com/projects/scifilandmovie/science-fiction -land-a-stranger-than-fiction-doc/posts/1006286.

Feeley, Gregory. "The Unknown Edges of the Universe." *Washington Post Book World*, November 23, 1986, https://www.washingtonpost.com/archive/entertainment/books /1986/11/23/the-unkown- edges-of-the-universe/593dca59-a29c-48d1-b4cb-2832f9260444 /?utm_term=.81954001747f.

Gaiman, Neil. "Of Meetings and Partings." In Grubbs, Kovacs, and Crimmins, *Collected Stories* 3:11–14.

Geis, Richard E. "The Case of the Blown Clone: A Review of *Today We Choose Faces*." *Alien Critic*, November 1973, 43.

Goldberg, Lesley. "'Walking Dead' Creator Adapting 'Chronicles of Amber' for TV." *Hollywood Reporter*, July 19, 2016, https://www.hollywoodreporter.com/live-feed/ walking-dead-creator-adapting-chronicles- 912132.

Greenland, Colin. *The Entropy Exhibition: Michael Moorcock and the British 'New Wave' in Science Fiction*. London: Routledge and Kegan Paul, 1983.

Grubbs, David G., Christopher S. Kovacs, and Ann Crimmins, eds. *The Collected Stories of Roger Zelazny*. 6 vols. Framingham, MA: NESFA Press, 2009.

Gustafson, Jon, Peter Nicholls, and David Langford. "Dillon, Diane and Leo." *The Science Fiction Encyclopedia*, accessed May 10, 2019. http://www.sf-encyclopedia.com/entry /dillon_diane_and_leo.

Hartwell, David. "On Roger Zelazny," in Grubbs, Kovacs, and Crimmins, *Collected Stories* 3:15–18.

Huntington, John. *Rationalizing Genius: Ideological Strategies in the Classic American Science Fiction Short Story*. New Brunswick, NJ: Rutgers University Press, 1989.

Jemisin, N. K. "The Appropriateness of Appropriation." The Angry Black Woman: Race, Politics, Gender, Sexuality, Anger. November 4, 2009, http://theangryblackwoman. com/2009/11/04/the-appropriateness-of-appropriation/.

Jonas, Gerald. Review of *Blood of Amber. New York Times Book Review*, November 23, 1986, https://archive.nytimes.com/www.nytimes.com/books/97/03/23/lifetimes/asi-r -foundationearth.html.

———. Review of *Eye of Cat*. "Other Worlds Than These." *New York Times Book Review*, December 19, 1982, https://www.nytimes.com/1982/12/19/books/other-worlds-than -earth.html.

Jones, Tadiana. "A Night in the Lonesome October: An Annual Ritual for Fans." *Fantasy Literature*, October 31, 2017, http://www.fantasyliterature.com/reviews/a-night-in-the -lonesome-october/.

Jones, Timothy. *The Gothic and the Carnivalesque in American Culture*. Gothic Literary Studies. Cardiff: University of Wales Press, 2015.

Khanna, Rajan. "The Chronicles of Amber Reread." Tor.com, 2013, https://www.tor.com /features/series/chronicles-of-amber-reread/.

———. "Revolutions in Fantasy: Four for the Fourth." Litreactor.com, July 3, 2012, https://litreactor.com/columns/revolution-in-fantasy-four-for-the-fourth.

———. "Taking from the World Tree: Mythology and Cultural Appropriation." Litreactor .com, August 28, 2012, https://litreactor.com/columns/taking-from-the-world-tree -mythology- and-cultural-appropriation.

Kirkus Review: *Blood of Amber*, September 25, 1986, https://www.kirkusreviews.com /book-reviews/roger-zelazny-7/trumps-of-doom/.

Kirkus Review: *Eye of Cat*, October 15, 1982, https://www.kirkusreviews.com/book -reviews/roger-zelazny-6/eye-of-cat/.

Kirkus Review: *Knight of Shadows*, November 27, 1989, https://www.kirkusreviews.com /book-reviews/roger-zelazny-8/knight-of-shadows/.

Kirkus Review: *A Night in the Lonesome October*, August 1, 1993, https://www.kirkus reviews.com/book-reviews/roger-zelazny/a-night-in-the-lonesome-october/.

Kirkus Review: *Prince of Chaos*, November 19, 1991, https://www.kirkusreviews.com /book-reviews/roger-zelazny/prince-of-chaos/.

Kirkus Review: *Trumps of Doom*, May 30, 1985, https://www.kirkusreviews.com/book -reviews/roger-zelazny-7/trumps-of-doom/.

Kovacs, Christopher S. ". . . And Call Me Roger: The Literary Life of Roger Zelazny, Part 1." In Grubbs, Kovacs, and Crimmins, *Collected Stories* 1:495–524.

———. "And Call Me Roger: The Literary Life of Roger Zelazny, Part 2." In Grubbs, Kovacs, and Crimmins, *Collected Stories* 2:531–570.

———. "And Call Me Roger: The Literary Life of Roger Zelazny, Part 3." In Grubbs, Kovacs, and Crimmins, *Collected Stories* 3:503–544.

———. "And Call Me Roger: The Literary Life of Roger Zelazny, Part 4." In Grubbs, Kovacs, and Crimmins, *Collected Stories* 4:523–570.

———. "And Call Me Roger: The Literary Life of Roger Zelazny, Part 5." In Grubbs, Kovacs, and Crimmins, *Collected Stories* 5:473–520.

———. "And Call Me Roger: The Literary Life of Roger Zelazny, Part 6." In Grubbs, Kovacs, and Crimmins, *Collected Stories* 6:469–520.

———. "Eye of Storm." *New York Review of Science Fiction*, June 2015, https://www.nyrsf .com/2015/06/christopher-s-kovacs-eye-of-storm.html.

———. "Fallen Books and Other Subtle Clues in Zelazny's 'A Night in the Lonesome October.'" *Lovecraft Ezine*, October 2012, https://lovecraftzine.com/magazine/issues /2012–2/issue- 18-october-2012/fallen-books-and-other-subtle-clues-in-zelaznys-a-night -in-the-lonesome- october-by-dr-christopher-s-kovacs/.

———. "The Raw Emotion Behind 'A Rose for Ecclesiastes.'" *New York Review of Science Fiction*, September 2014, 17–22.

———. "Suspended in Literature: Patterns and Allusions in *The Chronicles of Amber*." *New York Review of Science Fiction*, July 2012, https://www.nyrsf.com/2012/07/suspended-in -literature- patterns-and-allusions-in-the-chronicles-of-amber-by-christopher-s-kovacs -1.html.

Krulik, Theodore. *Roger Zelazny*. New York: Ungar, 1986.

Lindskold, Jane. "About Donnerjack." *Jane Lindskold's Official Website*, n.d. http:// janelindskold.com/wp/?page_id=284.

———. *Roger Zelazny*. Twayne's United States Authors. New York: Twayne, 1993.

———. "Roger Zelazny." In Grubbs, Kovacs, and Crimmins, *Collected Stories* 6:11–18.

Loeffelholz, Mary. "Introduction: American Literature, 1914–1945." In *The Norton Anthology of American Literature*, vol. D, *1914–1945*. 9th ed., 3–21. New York: Norton, 2017.

Martin, George R. R. "The Lord of Light." *Locus*, August 1995, 39–41.

———. "Writing, Reading, Writing." *Not a Blog*, June 23, 2020. https://georgerrmartin .com/notablog/2020/06/23/writing-reading-writing/.

Mebane, Banks. "Mebane's Magazine Mortuary: 1967 Autopsy Report." *WSFA Journal*, mid-December 1967, 3–4.

O'Connor, Flannery. "A Good Man Is Hard to Find." In *The Complete Stories*, 117–133. New York: Farrar, Straus and Giroux, 1971.

Otterson, Joe. "Hulu to Develop Shows Based on George R. R. Martin Book Series 'Wild Cards.'" *Variety*, November 13, 2018, https://variety.com/2018/tv/news/wild-cards -george-rr-martin-hulu-series-1203027787/.

Pangburn, D. J. "How Roger Zelazny's *Lord of Light* Transformed into the CIA's Argo Covert Op." *boingboing*, October 16, 2012, boingboing.net/2012/10/16/how-roger -zelaznys-lord-of-l.html.

Panshin, Alexei, and Cory Panshin. Review of *Sign of the Unicorn*. *Magazine of Fantasy & Science Fiction*, August 1975, 46–53, 162.

Pringle, David. "Obituary: Roger Zelazny." *Independent* (London), June 22, 1995, https:// www.independent.co.uk/news/people/obituary-roger-zelazny-1587694.html.

Robinson, Spider. Review of *My Name Is Legion*. *Galaxy*, May 1977, 138–146.

"Roger Zelazny, 1937–1995." *Locus*, July 1995, 7, 63.

Russ, Joanna. Review of *Lord of Light*. *Magazine of Fantasy & Science Fiction*, January 1968, 37–39.

Sanders, Joseph L. Introduction to *Roger Zelazny: A Primary and Secondary Bibliography*, ix– xxvii. Boston: G. K. Hall, 1980.

Sanders, William. Afterword to *Lord of the Fantastic: Stories in Honor of Roger Zelazny*, edited by Martin H. Greenberg, 252–253. New York: HarperCollins, 1998. Rpt. New York: Avon, 1999.

Schofield, Derek. "Hedy West." *Guardian* (UK), September 11, 2005. https://www.the guardian.com/news/2005/sep/12/guardianobituaries.artsobituaries1

Shawl, Nisi. "Appropriate Cultural Appropriation." In *Writing the Other: A Practical Approach*, edited by Nisi Shawl and Cynthia Ward, 85–98. Seattle: Aqueduct, 2005.

Silverberg, Robert. "Out of Nowhere." In Grubbs, Kovacs, and Crimmins, *Collected Stories* 1:11–15.

———. "Reflections: Roger and John." *Isaac Asimov's Science Fiction Magazine*, March 1996, 4–12.

———. "Zelazny Appreciation." *Locus*, August 1995, 42.

Skinner, Olivia. "Fantastic Convention: Science Fiction Addicts Rated Ozarkcon 2 Meeting Here as OOTW (Out of This World)." *St. Louis Post-Dispatch*, August 8, 1967. Roger Zelazny Papers, Special Collections Department, Syracuse University Libraries.

Smith, Patti. *M Train*. New York: Knopf, 2015.

Spinrad, Norman. [Appreciation.] *Locus*, August 1995, 39.

———. "On Books." *Isaac Asimov's Science Fiction Magazine*, July 1983, 164–172.

Stockwell, Peter. "Aesthetics." In *The Oxford Handbook of Science Fiction*, edited by Rob Latham, 35–46. New York: Oxford University Press, 2014.

Sturgeon, Theodore. Introduction to *Four for Tomorrow*, 7–12. New York: Ace, 1967.

Templeton, Molly. "Roger Zelazny's *Roadmarks* is Coming to HBO—With the Help of George R. R. Martin." Tor.com, February 19, 2021. https://www.tor.com/2021/02/19/roger-zelazny-roadmarks-hbo-adaptation/.

Thurston, Robert. Introduction to *Today We Choose Faces*, v–xix. Boston: Gregg Press/G. K. Hall, 1978.

Walker, Paul. "Roger Zelazny." In *Speaking of Science Fiction*, 79–84. Oradell, NJ: Luna, 1978.

Walton, Jo. *Among Others*. New York: Tor, 2012.

———. "Fantasy Disguised as Science Fiction Disguised as Fantasy: Roger Zelazny's *Lord of Light*." Tor.com, November 9, 2009, https://www.tor.com/2009/11/09/science-fiction-disguised-as-hindu-fantasy-roger-zelaznys-lemglord-of-lightlemg/.

Weil, Ellen, and Gary K. Wolfe. *Harlan Ellison: The Edge of Forever*. Columbus: Ohio State University Press, 2002.

Williams, Walter Jon. "My Three Rogers: An Appreciation." *Locus*, August 1995, 41.

———. "A Singular Being." In Grubbs, Kovacs, and Crimmins, *Collected Stories* 2:15–19.

Wolfe, Gary K. "The Encounter with Fantasy." In *Evaporating Genres: Essays on Fantastic Literature*, 68–82. Middletown, CT: Wesleyan University Press, 2011.

———. "Literary Movements." In *The Oxford Handbook of Science Fiction*, edited by Rob Latham, 59–70. New York: Oxford University Press, 2014.

Wooster, Martin Morse. "Of Dune, Heliconia, and Other Worlds." *Washington Post Book World*, May 26, 1985. [Review of *Trumps of Doom*], https://www.washingtonpost.com/archive/entertainment/books/1985/05/26/of-dune-heliconia-and-other-worlds/d2b408b2-d17c-4d34-8372-b233ad4721ea/?utm_term=.5faa60e774a6.

Yoke, Carl B. *Roger Zelazny*. Starmont Reader's Guide 2. West Linn, OR: Starmont House, 1979.

Zelazny, Shannon. Afterword to *In Shadows and Reflections: Stories from the Worlds of Roger Zelazny*, edited by Trent Zelazny and Warren Lapine, 231–235. Floyd, VA: Positronic, 2017.

BIBLIOGRAPHIES

Kovacs, Christopher S. *The Ides of Octember: A Pictorial Bibliography of Roger Zelazny*. Edited by David G. Grubbs, Christopher S. Kovacs, and Ann Crimmins. Framingham, MA: NESFA, 2010.
Levack, Daniel J. H. *Amber Dreams: A Roger Zelazny Bibliography*. Underwood-Miller, 1983.
Sanders, Joseph L. *Roger Zelazny: A Primary and Secondary Bibliography*. Boston: G. K. Hall, 1980.
Stephens, Christopher P. *A Checklist of Roger Zelazny*. Ultramarine, 1991.
Stephenson-Payne, Phil. *Roger Zelazny: Master of Amber; A Working Bibliography*. Galactic Central #38, 1991.

PAPERS

Collections of Zelazny's correspondence, manuscripts, and assorted papers may be found at the Syracuse University Libraries Special Collections Research Center and at the Albin O. Kuhn Library and Gallery, University of Maryland, Baltimore County. The latter separately collects Zelazny's correspondence with Joseph L. Sanders.

Fenn College (Cleveland State), 179n25

Ferman, Edward, 36

Finley Foster Poetry Prize, 13

Finnegans Wake (Joyce), 134

Flare (Zelazny and Thomas) 124

Flowers for Algernon (Keyes), 22, 50

Flowers of Evil (Baudelaire), 118

"For a Breath I Tarry" (Zelazny), 42–43, 51, 87, 139, 159; exclusion from *Doors of His Face . . .* collection, 185n9; textual variations, 181n52

"The Force That Through the Circuit Drives the Current" (Zelazny), 139

Forever After (ed. Zelazny), 147

Fort Bliss, Texas, 13

Fort Knox, Kentucky, 13

Foster, Stephen, 115

Foundation (journal), 5

Four for Tomorrow (Zelazny), 36–37, 49, 185n9

Frankenstein (Shelley), 45, 118

Frazer, James, 12

Freud, Sigmund, 12

Friend, Beverly, 18

Frost, Robert, 14

Fruits of the Earth (Gide), 65–66

Frye, Northrop, 50, 105

"The Furies" (Zelazny), 25–28, 35–36, 43, 88, 185n9

Future of the Future (McHale), 116

Gaiman, Neil, 124–25, 144, 146

Galaxy, 24, 27, 159, 183n12; publications of Zelazny's work, 41, 180n33; reviews of Zelazny's work, 37, 72

Game of Thrones, 150

Geis, Richard E., 91, 103, 153, 155–58

Geller, Barry Ira, 190n5

Gerrold, David, 87

Gibson, Walter, 115

Gibson, William, 3, 9, 138–39

Gide, Andre, 66

"Gilford Gafia," 85–86, 145

Gillespie, Bruce, 82

Gladstone, Max, 149

The Golden Bough (Frazer), 12

Goldsmith, Cele, 19, 21

"A Good Man Is Hard to Find" (O'Connor), 57–58

"The Graveyard Heart" (Zelazny), 24–27, 36

The Great Book of Amber (Zelazny), 147–48

The Great Steamboat Race (Brunner), 9

Greenwich Village, New York, 14–15

The Guns of Avalon (Zelazny), 86, 92–95, 97, 158

Haefele, Mark, 73

Haldeman, Joe, 85, 189–90n49

"Halfjack" (Zelazny), 139

"Hall of Mirrors" (Zelazny), 147

Hammer movie studio, 142

Hammett, Dashiell, 115

The Hand of Oberon (Zelazny), 86, 92–94, 96–97

Hard Case Crime, (publisher) 91

Hartwell, David G., 125, 147

Hausman, Gerald, 91, 124, 145

Heinlein, Robert A., 2, 3, 157

Hemingway, Ernest, 132

Herbert, Frank, 3, 37

"He Who Shapes" (Zelazny), 24, 30–37, 43, 66, 139, 185n9; allusiveness, 32, 138; car crash imagery, 31, 180n20; expansion into *The Dream Master*, 111, 180n29, 183n3; as literary tragedy, 30, 36; and *Lord of Light*, 51; Nebula winner, 3; and New Wave, 40; variant title, 149

Hillerman, Tony, 191n7

Hollywood Reporter, 150

"Home Is the Hangman" (Zelazny), 4, 112, 114–18, 151, 187n88

Homer 17, 35

Murray, John Middleton, Jr., 5. *See also* Cowper, Richard

My Name Is Legion (Zelazny), 86, 101, 115–18, 120, 139, 187n88; anonymity of narrator, 8, 35, 112, 136, 183n16; political violence in, 8, 113

mythology, 3, 5–7, 43, 68, 116, 148; in . . . *And Call Me Conrad*, 35, 37; in *Bridge of Ashes*, 105; in *Creatures*, 68, 71; critique of use in science fiction, 49–50; in *Eye of Cat*, 134–36; in "The Furies," 27; in "Horseman!," 20; in *Lord of Light*, 47–49, 53, 55; in "A Rose for Ecclesiastes," 17; in "This Mortal Mountain," 44; in "24 Views," 138; Zelazny's early interest in, 12, 49

Narrow Road to the Deep North, 138
National Book Award, 9
Nebula Award, 58, 72, 127, 137; Zelazny nominations, 46, 68, 111, 140, 144, 180n33; Zelazny wins, 3–4, 37–38, 46, 118
Nebula Award Stories Three (ed. Zelazny), 58–59
Neuromancer (Gibson) 9, 138
New England Science Fiction Association, 5, 147
New Scientist, 54
New Wave 3, 46, 54, 69, 124; application to science fiction, 38–40; *Creatures* as New Wave parody, 72; and cyberpunk, 138; origins of term, 38; Zelazny's attitudes towards, 40
New Worlds, 7, 38, 42
New York Review of Science Fiction, 148
New York Times, 128, 136
"Nightfall" (Asimov) 22
A Night in the Lonesome October (Zelazny), 17, 123, 140–44, 148, 149–51
Nine Princes in Amber (Zelazny), 3, 35, 61, 86, 180n20, 184n40; and other Amber novels, 92–95, 97, 129, 131; composition, 62, 158; critical response, 76, 184n41; and *Jack*

of Shadows, 80–82; literary influences, 75; narrative voice, 76–78; popularity, 4; publication history, 62, 73; as sword and sorcery, 6–7, 73, 75–76; synopsis, 73–75
"Nine Starships Waiting" (Zelazny), 21, 182n90
Niven, Larry, 115, 157
Noble Elementary School (Euclid), 11
Nova (Delany), 150

Omni, 138, 145
Ortega y Gasset, Jose, 138
Overkill (Schwartz), 116
Ozarkcon (St. Louis) 47, 50

Panshin, Alexei, 63, 98
Panshin, Cory, 98
"Passion Play" (Zelazny), 3, 19–21, 180n20
Peppard, George, 87
"Permafrost" (Zelazny), 132, 145
The Persistence of Memory (Dali), 132
Peter, Paul, and Mary, 14
Phantasmicom, 72, 153–61
Pink Floyd, 129
Planet Stories, 16
Poe, Edgar Allan, 142
Pohl, Frederik, 27–28, 38
political violence and terrorism, 6; in . . . *And Call Me Conrad*, 8, 34–35; in *Bridge of Ashes*, 8, 104, 106; in "The Furies," 27; in "The Keys to December," 8; in *Lord of Light*, 8; in *My Name Is Legion*, 8, 113, 116; in *To Die in Italbar*, 8, 89
Prince of Chaos (Zelazny), 126, 131
Pringle, David, 4
Purgatorio (Dante), 44
Psycho (Bloch), 59

Redfern, Paul, 54
Renaissance, 72
Reynolds, Mack, 84, 86
Roadmarks (Zelazny), 7, 86, 92, 101, 118–22

F. BRETT COX is Charles A. Dana Professor of English at Norwich University. He is the author of *The End of All Our Exploring: Stories* and coeditor of *Crossroads: Tales of the Southern Literary Fantastic*.

MODERN MASTERS OF SCIENCE FICTION

THE UNIVERSITY OF ILLINOIS PRESS

is a founding member of the

Association of University Presses.

———————————————————————

Composed in 10.75/14.5 Dante

with Univers display

by Kirsten Dennison

at the University of Illinois Press

University of Illinois Press

1325 South Oak Street

Champaign, IL 61820-6903

www.press.uillinois.edu